Managing Job Stress

Managing Job Stress

Arthur P. Brief
New York University

Randall S. Schuler
University of Maryland

Mary Van Sell
Michigan State University

Little, Brown and Company
Boston   Toronto

Library of Congress Catalog No. 80-83293

ISBN 0-316-107999

9 8 7 6 5 4 3 2 1

ALP

Published simultaneously in Canada by Little, Brown & Company (Canada) Limited

Printed in the United States of America

Acknowledgements

Chapter 3

Pages 33-35: Reprinted by permission of the *Harvard Business Review*. Excerpt from "What Killed Bob Lyons?" by Harry Levinson (January-February 1963). Copyright © 1963 by the President and Fellows of Harvard College: all rights reserved. *Table 3.1:* From J.P. Campbell, *Research into the Nature of Organizational Effectiveness: An Endangered Species?* Unpublished manuscript, University of Minnesota, 1973. Reprinted by permission of author.   *Table 3.2:* Adapted from "Problems in the Measurement of Organizational Effectiveness" by R.M. Steers published in *Administrative Science Quarterly*, Vol. 20, 1975 by permission of *The Administrative Science Quarterly*. Copyright © 1975, Cornell University.   *Pages 42-43:* From *Organizational Effectiveness: A Behavioral View* by Richard M. Steers. Copyright © 1977 by Goodyear Publishing Co. Reprinted by permission.   *Figure 3.2:* From James Gibson, John Ivancevich, and James Donnelly, *Organizations: Behavior, Structure, Processes*, 3rd ed. (Dallas, Texas: Business Publications, Inc., 1979), p.30. © 1979 by Business Publications, Inc. Reprinted by permission.   *Table 3.3:* From S. Seashore, "Job Satisfaction as an Indicator of the Quality of Employment," *Social Indicators Research*, Vol. I, 1974, pp. 135-168. Reprinted by permission of D. Reidel Publishing Company. *Page 46:* From D. Katz and R.L. Kahn, *The Social Psychology of Organizations* (New York: John Wiley & Sons, 1978). Reprinted by permission.

(Acknowledgements continued on page 234.)

TO OUR MENTORS

Alan, Andre, and Larry—Bob, Henry, John, and Stu—Art, Ethel, Jerry, and Ray.

Preface

Job stress is one of those so-called hot topics. It is of interest to almost everyone who works, and it has received considerable attention in the popular press, as well as in professional writings for management, medicine, psychology, and sociology. As management educators, we found ourselves seeking a concise source for students of management which would provide an overview of the literature on the topic and would incorporate both personal and organizational strategies for coping with job stress. We found none.

Most of the books we encountered either ignored the available scientific literature or treated it in a flippant manner. Many were too technical in nature for a nonacademic audience. Others were exclusively concerned with individuals and not their organizations, or vice versa. Thus, we decided to undertake writing a short book which we hoped would provide the source and focus needed, while overcoming the common problems we had found in the available literature.

To this end, the reader will find that this book draws upon the research findings of physicians, psychologists, sociologists, and other professionals concerned with the study of human stress. We have referenced this research throughout the text. In addition, a topical bibliography is included to aid access to additional information about the numerous topics introduced in the text.

Although the content of the book is reflective of current research, it is written in a manner easily understood by the reader with no background in the behavioral, medical or social sciences. To facilitate further understanding, applied examples are provided in every chapter. The book addresses two types of readers: the individual already in, or about to enter, the labor force; and managers, current or future. For the first group, the antecedents and consequences of job stress are vividly described, and a guide to self-help techniques for coping with the strains of work is provided. For the second group, an organizational perspective on job stress is offered which focuses on how various organizational conditions contribute to the prevalence of job stress, what the impact of job stress is on organizational effectiveness, and which managerial strategies can help organizational members cope with the stresses of their jobs. Importantly, an entire chapter is devoted to the unique stresses women are likely to experience as members of the labor force and a number of specific coping strategies are offered for the female reader.

In sum, we hope we have written a scientifically accurate, yet highly readable, book for those preparing to enter a work organization and for those already on the job. We believe that this book is a timely supplement for courses in management, organizational behavior, and personnel administration and wish that it proves to be a valuable development aid for practicing managers in formal training programs or in independent study. You the reader will be the final judge of whether we have accomplished our objectives.

The book, while exclusively our responsibility, was influenced by several other persons. Milton Johnson of Little, Brown and Company provided needed support in many ways. Sharon Carmody-Holmes, Marty Gannon, Tim Hall, Robert Holmes, Don Houtakker, Janina Latack, Lou Pondy, Arnon Reichers, Ben Schneider, Ethel Smith, Patricia Van Sell, and Cynthia Wolfe added helpful comments on the text. The secretarial staffs of the University of Iowa, Michigan State University, and Ohio State University contributed valuable assistance. And finally, numerous friends and family members gave the warmth and social support which made the writing of this book considerably less stressful than it might otherwise have been.

Arthur Brief
New York, New York

Randy Schuler
College Park, Maryland

Mary Van Sell
East Lansing, Michigan

Contents

Managing Job Stress

Chapter 1

Introduction

THE PREVALENCE OF STRESS

"Complete freedom from stress is death," according to Hans Selye, one of the great pioneers of medicine and probably the most noted authority on stress (Selye 1974, p. 20). His words clearly imply that stress cannot be avoided. In the same work Selye states that because stress may be associated with pleasant or unpleasant experiences, it should be viewed as an inevitable human condition which, if mismanaged, can result in distress. Even though stress has been widely experienced and talked about, it is poorly understood and we have yet to develop effective mechanisms for avoiding the distresses of stress. The purpose of this book, therefore, is to help the reader gain the necessary level of understanding to find such mechanisms.

This book does not offer a comprehensive treatment of the innumerable stresses people experience in the various domains of their lives; rather, it focuses almost exclusively on the stresses related to the work domain. There, too, stress is inevitable. The production line worker in an automobile manufacturing plant, the carpenter on a home construction site, the staff nurse in a community hospital, the vice-president of a large conglomerate, and all other workers at one time or another experience the dysfunctional consequences of job stress, which may include job dissatisfaction, a general feeling of unhappiness in life, and various physical and mental illnesses. Obviously, these consequences are of concern to the affected individuals as well as to the managers of employees under stress because of the possible detrimental effects on an organization. Job stress among individual employees may have spillover effects that influence the ability of the organization to attain its goals. Employees under excessive stress may be expected to psychologically or physically withdraw from their jobs and, thereby, to reduce their contributions to the organization. This book addresses the concerns of such individuals as well as those of managers charged with the responsibilities of attaining organizational goals.

Definition of Job Stress

Before considering the structure of the book, we should examine the concept of "job stress." *Job stress* is a condition arising from the interaction of people and their jobs and is characterized by changes within people that force them to deviate from their normal functioning (Beehr and Newman, 1978). This definition is best understood by considering that the body and mind of a person are in a state of equilibrium at the outset of a job experience, but that as a result of an occurrence related to work, the person's equilibrium is disrupted. In attempting to recover from this disturbance or imbalance, the person functions differently.

This book identifies types of person-job interactions that result in imbalances, describes the consequences of employees' reactions to these imbalances, and provides personal and organizational strategies for the effective management of job stress. The importance of this last idea, that job stress can be managed, needs to be emphasized. In extreme cases, job stress can lead to serious consequences, and therefore it demands the attention of both labor and management.

One extreme case of stress reported by Senator Edward M. Kennedy (1972) before a congressional subcommittee hearing involves a worker who went berserk in the Eldonaxte plant in Detroit and shot three foremen. His defense was insanity brought about by working in the noise, filth, and danger of that plant. The judge and jury visited the plant and their verdict was unanimous. It was a verdict for acquittal. Although this appears to be an extreme case of the dysfunctional consequences of job stress, we believe that such incidents are brought about by the mismanagement of job stress. It is therefore the responsibility of every individual to learn how to cope effectively with the stresses of work. Furthermore, it is the economic and social responsibility of management to guard against such occurrences.

THE STRUCTURE OF THIS BOOK

The relationship of person-job interactions to job stress is depicted in Figure 1.1. This model is the framework on which this book is built, and the reader should consider it to be a tool for organizing and digesting the information that follows.

According to the model, the sources of job stress to which people are exposed are a function of two factors: their own behaviors and psychological and physiological states, and the processes and outcomes of their employing organization. Thus, employees are not viewed as passive agents; rather, they are seen as active agents who can influence their own destinies through the selection of the stressors to which they expose themselves, and through control of their reactions to stress. Similarly, employers are active agents in terms of both creating stressful working conditions and, if they choose, acting to alleviate those conditions.

The model indicates that employee behaviors and their psychological and physiological states result from the job stressors they are exposed to as well as from other conditions of their employment that act directly on the employee (e.g., compensation and promotional policies). Finally, the model suggests that organizational processes and outcomes are a result of employee behaviors and the job stressors per se. In other words, the conditions that characterize a stressful event influence organizations not only indirectly through their impact on employees, but also directly through a detrimental impact on the organization. Thus, management's mishandling of stress can be said to reflect generally poor managerial practices.

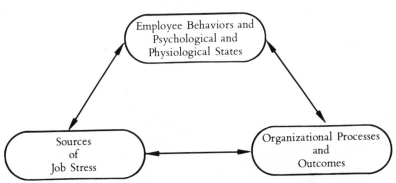

Figure 1.1
A Model for Understanding Job Stress.

Our model for understanding job stress is complex in that all components of the model simultaneously influence one another. Such complexity cannot be avoided because it is reflective of the "real world." Thus, it should be recognized that personal and organizational strategies for coping with job stress influence not only the prevalence of stressors in the work environment, but they also influence one another.

Following is a brief description of the remaining chapters. Each one treats some aspect of the relationships depicted in Figure 1.1.

Chapter 2, entitled "Job Stress and the Quality of Life," focuses on the personal consequences of job stress. It discusses the interrelationships between the quality of working life and the overall satisfaction of workers with life. Job stress is also discussed in broad terms as a determinant of the quality of working life. Finally, specific relationships between job stress and life satisfaction are proposed. Throughout the chapter, physiological, behavioral, and psychological consequences of job stress are identified. "Organizational Effectiveness and Employee Stress," Chapter 3, shifts attention to the organizational consequences of employee stress. The concept of *organizational effectiveness* is first defined and then discussed in terms of the potential impact of employee stress reactions on organizational success. Particular emphasis is placed on employee health as a result of job stress and as an antecedent of organizational effectiveness.

Chapter 4, "Sources of Job Stress," examines in detail the sources of job stress. It begins by identifying certain characteristics and processes of organizations that are thought to be major causes of stress at work. Next, it examines the sources of stress inherent in particular job demands, working conditions and interpersonal work relationships. The chapter closes by reviewing individual characteristics and needs that may increase job stress.

Building on the foundation of the preceding chapters, the next two chapters consider remedies for job stress. Chapter 5, entitled "Personal Mechanisms for Coping with Job Stress," describes a number of ways in which individual employees respond to stress. This chapter first tells how individuals differ in responding to stressful conditions at work. Secondly, it demonstrates that social support may be an essential ingredient to effective coping processes. Finally, the chapter addresses the question, "Which coping strategies appear to be most personally productive?" Chapter 6, "Organizational Stress Management Strategies," complements the preceding one by describing a number of organizational stress management strategies that can improve the organization's effectiveness. Decentralization of decision making, role clarification exercises, goal setting and feedback, the development of cohesive work groups, and several other approaches are offered as potential means of achieving higher levels of organizational success through controlling employee stress. Together, Chapters 5 and 6 provide both employees and their managers with a guide to the resources available for combating the dysfunctional consequences of job stress.

The book concludes in Chapter 7, "Working Women and Stress," with a detailed discussion of the unique problems confronted by one particular group of employees, working women. The three principal topics of this section are traditional sex role expectations for women, the sex typing of occupations and the sources of stress for women in traditional and nontraditional jobs, and conflicts between women's work and home roles. Suggestions for alleviating or coping with the stresses identified are offered throughout the chapter.

As you read each of the following chapters, you will note that a wealth of information is available on the subject of job stress. No one source can provide a totally comprehensive treatment of the subject matter, but we hope to provide at least a detailed, articulate review of the literature on job stress in a fashion that will be useful to both individuals and organizations. Supplementing the material provided in each chapter, a topic-by-topic bibliography appears at the end of the book. This bibliography provides an abundance of alternative sources for the reader seeking additional information on any of the topics reviewed elsewhere in the book.

In sum, we sincerely hope you find this book to be a valuable resource. If the book merely serves to open for readers new options for gaining a better quality of life or for improving their effectiveness as managers, then we as authors have succeeded.

REFERENCES

Beehr, T.A., and Newman, J.E. 1978. Job stress, employee health, and organizational effectiveness: A facet analysis, model, and literature review. *Personnel Psychology* 31: 665-99.

Kennedy, E.M. 1972. *Worker alienation.* Subcommittee on Employment, Manpower, and Poverty of the United States Senate. Washington, D.C.: U.S. Government Printing Office.

Selye, H. 1974. *Stress without distress.* New York: Lippincott.

Chapter 2

Job Stress and the Quality of Life

Mary, a recent Wharton MBA, spent a sleepless night contemplating her first presentation before the executive committee of her new employer. She had spent much of the last six months preparing the report for her presentation and felt it was the first real test of her managerial potential. Mary's presentation lasted five minutes and was followed by about ten minutes of questions from committee members. Mary was thanked for making a fine presentation and dismissed from the meeting by the firm's president. She quickly went to the nearest women's lounge and in a release of tension shook uncontrollably.

Jane is becoming increasingly worried about her husband, Bob. Several months ago Bob was passed over for a promotion to plant supervisor which he felt he deserved through his fifteen years of loyal service to the company. Bob used to come home from work tired but cheery and spend an hour or so playing with their two boys. Lately, however, Bob walks into the house, grabs a can of beer, and plops down in front of the TV. Except for dinner, he spends his evenings watching television and drinking beer. He has little to do or say to either Jane or the kids. Jane is at wits' end. She has begged Bob to go to the doctor; but, he just says, "Hell, nothing is wrong with me. It's your imagination."

Ray, a successful advertising account executive, was finishing his typical "two martini" lunch with a potential client, but Ray's mind wasn't on business as usual. He was thinking about the pain in his stomach and the diagnosis his doctor had given him yesterday. Ray's doctor had told him that he had a spastic colon induced by his lifestyle. Ray, a recent divorcee, knows his gin consumption, smoking habit, and twelve-hour workdays aren't good for him, but his job is now the most important thing in his life and the advertising business just happens to be stressful as hell. Ray doesn't know what to do and resolves not to worry about his health and to concentrate on selling his luncheon partner one fantastic contract.

The above incidents depict relationships that can exist between job-induced stress and the quality of life we experience. As individual workers, we obviously care about the impact of our working lives on our total well-being and on the welfare of our families. As will be shown, even government has taken an interest in the negative consequences associated with job stress. The reason for such widespread interest is the aggregate impact of the quality of working life on society and its institutions. Many prominent persons have speculated that a deterioration in the quality of working life is linked to social ills such as political alienation, drug and alcohol abuse, and the inability to parent appropriately (Kennedy 1972). Regrettably, much of this type of speculation has been accepted as fact. The purpose of this chapter, therefore, is to separate fact from fiction so that we might understand the true relationships between job stress and the quality of life. The first step is to review the pertinent medical, psychological, and sociological literature concerned with job stress. In particular, we are concerned in this chapter with defining "quality of life" and its relationship to work, with particular physical and mental health consequences of job stress, and with the personal costs incurred in occupying a stressful job.

THE QUALITY OF LIFE

Quality of life may be defined as the individual's sense of psychological well-being or avowed happiness (Bradburn 1969). Overall happiness in life (i.e., life satisfaction or positive orientation toward life) is commonly measured in research surveys by the response to a single question, "Taking all things together, how would you say things are these days—would you say that you're very happy, pretty happy, or not too happy these days?" This type of subjective measure reflects to what extent persons are happy with the various domains of their lives. Reseachers have identified the following life domains as generally being most important to overall happiness: family, health, community, work, and spare-time activities (Andrews and Withey 1973; Bharadwaj and Wilkening 1977; Campbell et al. 1976). The relative importance of these domains varies among individuals as well as within them. Some people who are dissatisfied with the natural environment and national government domains of their lives may still report a high level of overall happiness because they are satisfied with the quality of life in their preferred domains, which may be work and spare-time activities. A list of life domains that are important to many people is shown in Figure 2.1.

Individual Differences in the Importance of Work

The relative importance that people place on the various aspects of their lives varies according to the interests, needs, and concerns of those persons. The family domain is said to be more important to life satisfaction for women than it is for men; spare-time activities are more important to persons sixty-five years of age and older than they are to persons under thirty; and work is more important to persons with incomes of less than $4,000 than it is to persons with incomes of $16,000 and over (Brahadwaj and Wilkening 1977).

Our understanding of such differences can be enhanced if we examine certain concepts related to the work domain and its influence on life satisfaction; in particular "career salience," "central life interests," "job involvement," "organizational commitment," "Protestant Work Ethic," and "Type A behavior pattern" are of interest here. Throughout the remainder of the book more will be said about each of these concepts and their relationships to stress, but for now the concepts will be merely defined and their proposed associations with the relative importance of the work domain will be briefly discussed.

Career salience is the importance of work and a career to one's total life. Career salience can be described in terms of three factors: (1) the relative priority of a career compared with other sources of life satisfaction, (2) the degree to which work is viewed with a positive attitude and anticipation, and (3) the degree of emphasis on career advancement and planning for a career.

Central life interests are the focal area of individual preferences for behaving, given a choice of behavioral settings. Central life interests commonly are dichotomized as falling into either the work or nonwork areas.

Job involvement is the degree to which people identify with their work, or the importance of work to their total self-image.

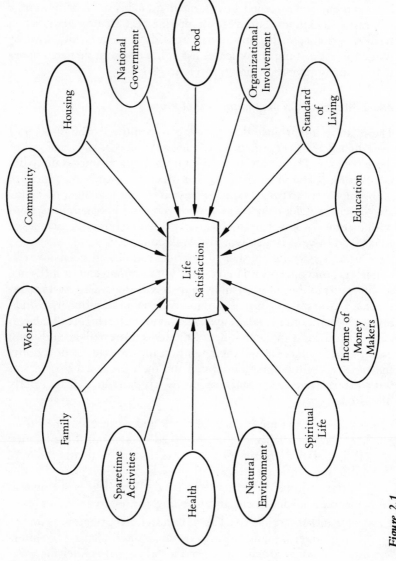

Figure 2.1
Life Domains and Life Satisfaction.

Organizational commitment is the relative strength of an individual's identification with and involvement in a particular organization. Organizational commitment involves a strong belief in and acceptance of the organization's goals and values, a willingness to exert considerable effort on behalf of the organization, and a strong desire to maintain membership in the organization.

Protestant work ethic ideals reflect the degree to which work in general is viewed as good, important, and central to one's life.

Type A behavior pattern is exhibited by individuals who engage in a relatively chronic struggle to obtain an unlimited number of poorly defined things from their environment in the shortest possible period of time and, if necessary, against the opposing effects of other forces or persons in this same environment. The characteristics of Type A behavior include competitive achievement striving, exaggerated sense of time urgency, and aggressiveness and hostility.

These definitions indicate some overlap in meaning and indeed may reflect the relative importance of the work domain to overall life satisfaction. It is useful to examine each concept, however, as a method of evaluating the types and characteristics of people who place a heavy emphasis on the work domain of their lives. As shown in Figure 2.2, many persons highly involved in their jobs are thought to view the work domain as an important source of life's satisfactions, and compared to nonjob-involved persons, job-involved persons are known to be older, occupy stimulating jobs, participate in decisions that affect them, and have histories of success (Rabinowitz and Hall 1977).

One should not be led by the above example to conclude that people placing a heavier emphasis on the work domain are necessarily "better off" in life. For instance, it is expected that persons exhibiting a Type A behavior pattern also view the work domain as an important source of life's satisfactions. But after conducting interviews with a large number of such men, researchers (Friedman and Rosenman 1974, Jenkins 1975) concluded that Type A men:

1. Work long hard hours under constant deadline pressures and conditions of overload.

2. Often carry work home on evenings and weekends and are unable to relax.

3. Constantly compete with themselves, setting high standards of productivity they seem driven to maintain.

4. Tend to become frustrated by the work situation, irritated with the work efforts of their subordinates, and misunderstood by superiors.

Further evidence linking Type A behavior with stress and with dysfunctional personal outcomes is presented in Chapter 4, "Sources of Job Stress." It appears then that people differ in terms of the relative importance they place on the work domain; clues exist to identify persons who place a heavy emphasis on the work domain; and, placing a heavy emphasis on the work domain may or may not be associated with experiencing a high quality of life.

Facets of the Quality of Working Life

A central theme of this chapter is that for persons who see the work domain as relatively important, their quality of life will be enhanced to the degree that they experience satisfaction in work and, a major

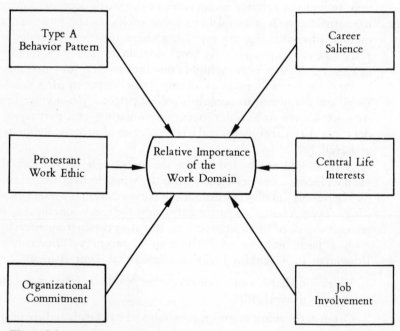

Figure 2.2
Some Determinants of the Relative Importance of the Work Domain to Life Satisfaction.

determinant of the "quality of working life" is job stress. *Quality of working life* is defined as the individual's psychological well-being at work or avowed happiness with work. Richard E. Walton (1973) has suggested that eight salient features of work taken together determine the quality of working life, or contribute to avowed satisfaction with work:

1. *Adequate and fair compensation.* The income earned from the person's work meets socially determined standards of sufficiency and bears an appropriate relationship to the pay received for other types of work.

2. *Safe and healthy working conditions.* The person is not exposed to physical conditions or hourly arrangements that are unduly hazardous or detrimental to health.

3. *Immediate opportunity to use and develop human capacities.* Work enables the individual to develop skills and abilities, to become involved, to enhance his or her self-esteem, and to perceive a challenge.

4. *Opportunity for continued growth and security.* Work contributes to maintaining and expanding the person's capabilities rather than to obsolescence; it is expected that the person's skills and abilities will be expanded or further utilized; advancement opportunities are evident; and, the person's employment or income is secure.

5. *Social integration in the work organization.* The person is not treated in a prejudicial manner; egalitarianism prevails; upward mobility exists; the person is supported by primary groups and feels a sense of community; and, relationships between people are characterized as open.

6. *Constitutionalism in work organizations.* The person's right to privacy is respected; free speech is advocated; equitable treatment is evident; and due process are observed.

7. *Balanced work role.* Work schedules, career demands, travel requirements, and required transfers on a regular basis do not have negative effects on the person's leisure and family time.

8. *Social responsibility of the work organization.* The person perceives his or her employer to behave in a responsible manner to society.

Here, too, people differ in terms of the relative importance they place on each of the above eight features of the quality of working life. For instance, pay, job security, and fringe benefits have been found to be more important to "blue-collar" workers than to "white-collar" workers (Quinn, Staines, and McCullough 1974).

Differences have also been reported in the levels of life satisfaction. In general, persons who are young, healthy, well educated, well paid, extroverted, optimistic, worry-free, religious, married with high self-esteem, high job morale, and modest aspirations appear to be happy (Wilson 1967). Further, there appears to be a general trend in avowed happiness in the United States. Happiness rose from the late 1940s to the late 1950s, declined until the early 1970s, and then, possibly after some rebound, remained stable from the early 1970s to the present (Smith 1979). Various patterns and trends also are evident in studies of job satisfaction. White, older, professional and managerial workers appear to be the ones most satisfied with their jobs (Hamner and Organ 1978), and in general job satisfaction appears to have increased from the late 1940s until the early 1960s, followed by some decline through the subsequent decade (Organ 1977).

High job morale was identified above as a descriptor of the happy person. This again indicates that satisfaction with the work domain of life is one determinant of the quality of life. The heavier the emphasis on the work domain, the stronger the association between job satisfaction and life satisfaction. These relationships are depicted in Figure 2.3. Further, the eight previously defined features of the quality of working life are potential sources of job satisfaction. The greater the importance of a particular feature, the stronger the relationship between satisfaction with that feature and overall job satisfaction. Thus, people who place heavy emphasis on the domain of work, and see "adequate and fair compensation" as particularly central to their quality of working life, will find their satisfaction in life greatly influenced by their reactions to the pay they receive.

The relationship between reactions to the work domain and the quality of life has been demonstrated in studies exploring the associations between life changes and health status. Recent research in epidemiology—a branch of the medical sciences that deals with the incidence, distribution, and control of disease in a population—focuses on the theme that the magnitude of change occurring in an individual's life is predictive of that person's susceptibility to the onset of physical and mental illness. Life change has been found to be related to tuberculosis, acute glaucoma, inguinal hernia, rheumatoid arthritis, leukemia, myocardial infarction, sudden cardiac death, schizophrenia, depression, and attempted suicide.[1]

One explanation for these findings is that life change situations which require adaptive behavior also cause significant alterations in

---

[1]The medical terms used will be defined elsewhere in this chapter whenever necessary.

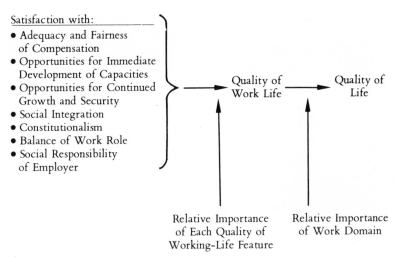

Figure 2.3
Relationships between Quality of Work-Life Features and Quality of Life.

the psychophysiological system of the person, and these alterations lower resistance to illness (Rahe et al. 1964). A "life change" is any event that requires a modification in the individual's accustomed way of life (Holmes and Mosuda 1974; Rahe 1974). These events may be either positive or negative and may occur in any life domain, including the work domain. The Social Readjustment Rating Scale (Holmes and Rahe 1967) is an instrument commonly used to measure the amount of change required by life events. The events contained in the scale (see Table 2.1) include the following work-related events:

1. Fired from work
2. Retirement
3. Business readjustment
4. Change in responsibilities at work
5. Change to a different line of work
6. Outstanding personal achievement
7. Change in work hours or conditions
8. Trouble with boss.

It can readily be seen that changes in the work domain are related to changes in the quality of life, at least with respect to health status.

A study by Stanislav Kasl and Sidney Cobb (1970) provides a particularly interesting example of the link between work domain

Table 2.1
Life Events from the Social Readjustment Rating Scale

Death of spouse
Divorce
Marital separation
Death of a close family member
Sex difficulties
Major personal injury or illness
Fired from work
Jail term
Marriage
Marital reconciliation
Retirement
Death of a close friend
Pregnancy
Change in financial state
Business readjustment
Major change in health of family member
Gain of a new family member
Mortgage or loan over $10,000
Change in number of arguments with spouse
Change in responsibilities at work
Change to a different line of work
Trouble with in-laws
Foreclosure of mortgage or loan
Change in living conditions
Son or daughter leaving home
Begin or end school
Wife begins or stops work
Outstanding personal achievement
Change in work hours or conditions
Change in residence
Mortgage or loan less than $10,000
Change in social activities
Trouble with boss
Change in schools
Revision of personal habits
Change in recreation
Change in number of family get-togethers
Change in church activities
Vacation
Change in eating habits
Change in sleeping habits
Christmas
Minor violations of the law

Source: Ruch and Holmes (1971).

changes and health status. For two years they studied the blood pressure changes in married, stably-employed men who lost their jobs because of a permanent plant shutdown. Kasl and Cobb found that blood pressure levels during anticipation of job loss and unemployment (or probationary reemployment) were clearly higher than after subsequent stabilization on new jobs; and that men whose blood pressure levels remained high longer had more severe unemployment, reported longer-lasting subjective stress, and failed to show much improvement in reported well-being. These findings clearly demonstrate the interrelationships among work domain changes, stress, and psychological well-being (in other words, the quality of life). In addition to blood pressure, other symptoms of occupational ill health have been linked to sources of stress at work. These symptoms include cholesterol level, heart rate, smoking, depressive mood, escapist drinking, job dissatisfaction, and reduced aspiration (Cooper and Marshall 1976).

In general, the above examples indicate that job stress can play a central role in establishing a person's quality of life. The remainder of this chapter considers particular physical and mental health consequences of job stress. It will not attempt to isolate particular sources of job stress but will focus on the personal consequences of job stress without fully addressing the antecedents of such stress which are treated comprehensively in Chapter 4, "The Sources of Job Stress."

PERSONAL CONSEQUENCES OF JOB STRESS

Responses to perceived job stress may be physiological, psychological, or behavioral in nature. As will be shown, these response categories can be viewed in terms of their negative consequences for the individual. Since Chapter 3, "Job Stress and Organizational Effectiveness," is concerned with the impact of responses to job stress on organizational processes and outcomes, the following discussion focuses largely on the employee's nonwork domains of life. Of course, a hard and fast boundary between work and nonwork domains cannot be established.

Physiological Responses

A long list could be compiled of the possible physical health consequences of job stress. Cardiovascular disease, gastrointestinal disorders, respiratory problems, cancer, arthritis, headaches, bodily injuries, skin disorders, physical strain or fatigue, and death have been purported to be responses to job stress (Beehr and Newman 1978). This section will concentrate on cardiovascular disorders as an illustrative example.[2] First, however, we should consider the general linkages between job stress and physical health.

In a fifteen-year study of aging, satisfaction with work was found to be the most reliable predictor of longevity (Palmore 1969). Most other investigations of job stress phenomenon and physical health, have not yielded such striking results. In general, researchers have found large differences in morbidity, mortality, and accident rates among occupational grouping of workers. These gross differences tell us little about the relationships between specific job stressors and health status.[3] Recently, Daniel Katz and Robert Kahn (1978) concluded from their review of recent work and health literature that the following stress-health linkages have been determined:

1. Four occupational categories can be ordered with respect to the job characteristics of participation in decisions, social support, certainty about the future, complexity, and freedom from quantitative overload and unwanted overtime. The categories ordered form least to most are: blue-collar unskilled, blue-collar skilled, white-collar nonprofessional, and white-collar professional.

2. Absence of the above job characteristics is seen to be stressful. Thus, the occupational ordering can be taken to reflect relative stress levels.

3. Stressful working conditions are associated with boredom and dissatisfaction with work role, which in turn are related to feelings of depression, irritation, and anxiety.[4]

4. Finally, the negative feelings noted are associated with somatic symptoms and the expected health patterns.

Katz and Kahn's conclusions suggest that certain working conditions (or job stressors) lead to dysfunctional psychological states and that these negative states ultimately are detrimental to physical health. Further, higher levels of job stressors are associated with lower status occupations. Thus, the notion that executives experience

[2]Cardiovascular disorders involve the heart and blood vessels.

[3]Cross-sectional studies of occupational status and worker health also ignore the "chicken and egg" dilemma. It may be the case that persons likely to experience certain health disorders select particular occupations rather than selection of the occupation leading to the disorder.

[4]These psychological outcomes are discussed later in this chapter.

unduly high levels of stress relative to other categories of workers in general is a commonly held misconception. Some evidence, however, is supportive of this managerial stress syndrome. The nature of managerial work dictates that managers at all organizational levels are held responsible for the actions of others; this responsibility for other people has been tied to the incidence of peptic ulcers. One problem with the research standing behind this finding is that foremen and other lower-level managers rather than top managers (or executives) typically have been the target of investigation. Thus, managerial work per se should not be singled out as a particularly stressful source of ill health.

Of parallel interest are the research findings concerning status incongruity and health. *Status incongruity* occurs when different characteristics of a person simultaneously place that individual at different levels of the social hierarchy. A classical example of such incongruity is the successful corporate manager having a grade-school education. In this case, job status is incongruent with educational status. Because numerous investigators have found higher levels of status incongruity to be associated with stress and ill health, it may be that although executive working conditions are not unduly stressful, executives (owing to the high status of their jobs) are more prone to experiencing status incongruity and its negative consequences. Of course, the same can be said of persons relatively underemployed.

In general, then, various links exist between sources of stress at work and symptoms of occupational ill health and health status, and various psychological states help to determine job stress-health status relationships. In addition, it should be noted that an array of individual characteristics, which will be discussed in later chapters, also determine the worker's responses to job stressors. The general relationships established here are summarized in Figure 2.4.

In the following discussion of the relationship between job stress and cardiovascular disorders,[5] particular attention will be focused on coronary heart disease (CHD). Two major manifestations of CHD are angina pectoris and myocardial infarction. *Angina pectoris* is a disorder involving a type of chest pain caused when the heart muscle receives an insufficient level of oxygen, owing to an inadequate blood supply occasioned by the obstruction of one or more coronary arteries (Friedberg 1966). Angina is usually preceded by physical exertion or psychological stress and is relieved by rest or drugs. Anginal episodes rarely involve permanent and substantial damage to heart

[5]The framework for this disscussion is drawn in part from Glass (1977).

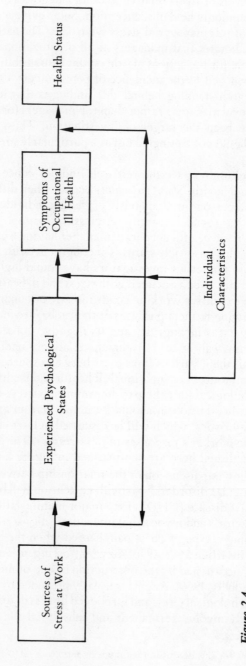

Figure 2.4
A Model of Job Stress–Health Status Relationships.

tissue. *Acute myocardial infarction* is the disorder commonly called a heart attack and involves death of heart tissue caused by an insufficient oxygen supply over a relatively long period of time (Brest and Moyer 1967; Friedberg 1966). Chest pain is evident but is of greater severity and duration than that associated with angina. Sudden death may follow acute myocardial infarction.

Despite the impressive quantity of research on various job-stress phenomena in association with CHD and related risk factors, many of the findings are in conflict and controversial in nature (Kasl 1978). Nonetheless three generalizations arising from this research, appear to be warranted. These generalizations are listed below, together with an example of the relevant research for each.

1. Job problems and dissatisfaction are associated with CHD and related risk factors. Example: James House (1972), in a sample of 288 men representing a full range of occupations in one community, found job dissatisfaction to be related to a number of risk factors including smoking, obesity, cholesterol, blood pressure, and blood sugar.

2. Job pressures (such as heavy workload) are associated with CHD and related risk factors. Example: Friedman, Rosenman, and Carroll (1958) found marked increases in cholesterol levels in tax accountants as the deadline for filing federal income tax returns approached.

3. Type A behavior pattern is associated with CHD and related risk factors. Properties of the Type A behavior pattern include hard-driving attitudes, emphasizing competitiveness, effort, and responsibility; job involvement,[6] dealing with the challenges arising from everyday life and the habit of keeping very busy and active; and speed and impatience, reflecting a style of life marked by haste and impulsiveness (Zyzanski and Jenkins 1970). (Type A behavior pattern was previously defined and discussed as a determinant of the relative importance placed on the work domain of life.) Example: Howard, Cunningham, and Rechnitzer (1976) investigated the health patterns associated with Type A behavior among a sample of 236 managers drawn from twelve Canadian companies. They found Type A managers to have high blood pressure and cholesterol levels, more likely to be cigarette smokers, and less interested in exercise.

[6]The job involvement property referred to here is conceptually distinct from the "job involvement" concept previously hypothesized as a determinant of the relative importance placed on the work domain of life.

In sum, it is clear that job stressors in numerous instances have been shown to be related to physical health status. Although it is evident that stressful working conditions can be hazardous to health, one must not lose sight of the fact that a host of individual characteristics determine a person's response to stressful conditions. Thus, not all people respond similarly to the same configuration of stressors.

Psychological Responses

As in the case of possible physical health consequences of job stress, the list of potential psychological outcomes is lengthy: anxiety, tension, depression, dissatisfaction, boredom, somatic complaints, psychological fatigue, feelings of futility, inadequacy, and low self-esteem, alienation, psychoses, anger, repression, and loss of concentration (Beehr and Newman 1978). These potential consequences are not only important in themselves, but many of them are also predictors of physical health status.

Throughout each of the prior sections of this chapter, job satisfaction has been discussed from a variety of perspectives. Thus, it is not surprising to note that job satisfaction is the most well-established psychological consequence of job stress. As stress levels increase, job satisfaction decreases.

Anxiety is another well-established outcome of job stress. The anxious person feels upset, nervous, jittery, "high strung," overly excited, "rattled," and fidgety. Anxiety in and of itself is a painful reaction to stress; however, when the pressures of anxiety are excessive and cannot be relieved by practical problem-solving methods, people sometimes turn to defense mechanism.[7] Defense mechanisms deny, falsify or distort reality. Various defense mechanisms include:[8]

1. *Repression.* The exclusion of unacceptable conscious impulses from consciousness.

2. *Projection.* The unconscious attribution of one's own thoughts and feelings to other people.

3. *Reaction formation.* The development of behavior patterns that are the opposite of those that might create tension and anxiety.

4. *Displacement.* The redirection of urges toward a substitute object.

[7]Defense mechanisms are a type of personal strategy for coping with job stress. Other strategies are discussed in detail in Chapter 7, "Personal Mechanisms for Coping with Job Stress."

[8]The framework for the discussion to follow in part is drawn from McNeil and Rubin (1977).

5. *Rationalizations.* The attempt to substitute "good" reasons for the "real" reasons.

6. *Intellectualizations.* The intellectual analysis of emotional issues and their subsequent conversion to theory rather than action.

In the face of high levels of anxiety these mechanisms are occasionally employed by almost everyone; however, after frequent use they become habitual and, indeed, may lead to a psychological disorder known as neurosis.[9]

The previous discussion illustrates how job stress may lead to a poor state of mental health. Depression is another mental health problem that in some instances may be traced to job stress. *Depression* is characterized by feelings of worthlessness, hopelessness, lethargy, and helplessness and has been referred to as the "common cold" of mental illness; however, depression can range from a neurotic (mild) to psychotic (severe) condition.[10] In the more severe cases, the depressed person may remain motionless for hours on end, lose their appetite, have a great deal of difficulty in sleeping, and experience uncontrollable outbursts of crying. Further, states of depression can be classified as either exogenous (reactive) or endogenous. Endogenous cases of depression have no apparent external causes; thus, the type of depression associated with job stress is said to be exogenous.

A recent study by Caplan, Cobb, and French (1975) at the Institute of Social Research at the University of Michigan assessed depression and anxiety as consequences of various forms of job stress in a sample of almost 400 persons drawn from 8 occupational groupings. These psychological responses again were found to be related to a number of job stressors. Caplan, Cobb, and French examined two additional psychological consequences, irritation and somatic complaints. Table 2.2 presents the items used to measure anxiety, depression, irritation, and somatic complaints. As expected, irritation and somatic complaints also were shown to be related to job stress. Interestingly, the impact of job stress on psychological disorders was not direct; rather, evidence indicated that job stressors directly influence work load dissatisfaction and boredom, which in turn lead to ill mental health.

[9]*Neuroses* are relatively mild psychological disorders characterized by anxiety, inability to cope effectively with challenges, and difficulty in interpersonal relationships. The neurotic individual remains in touch with reality and has some insight into the disorder.

[10]*Psychoses* are major psychological disorders characterized by loss of contact with reality and loss of control over feelings and reactions, with such symptoms as delusions and hallucinations.

Table 2.2
Measures of Psychological Disorders

SOMATIC COMPLAINTS
"Did you experience either one of the following during the past month?"
Your hands trembled enough to bother you.
You were bothered by shortness of breath when you were not working hard or exercising.
You were bothered by your heart beating hard.
Your hands sweated so that you felt damp and clammy.
You had spells of dizziness.
You were bothered by having an upset stomach or stomach ache.
You were bothered by your heart beating faster than usual.
You were in ill health which affected your work.
You had a loss of appetite.
You had trouble sleeping at night.

DEPRESSION, ANXIETY, AND IRRITATION
"Here are some items about how people may feel. When you think about yourself and your job nowadays, how much of the time do you feel this way?"

Depression

I feel sad.
I feel unhappy.
I feel good. (reverse)
I feel depressed.
I feel blue.
I feel cheerful. (reverse)

Anxiety

I feel nervous.
I feel jittery.
I feel calm. (reverse)
I feel fidgety.

Irritation

I get angry.
I get aggravated.
I get irritated or annoyed.

From Caplan, Cobb, and French (1975).

In addition to the direct individual psychological costs incurred by job stress, there is a limited amount of evidence concerning spillover effects on the person's family. For instance, Burke, Weir, and

DuWors (1979) investigated the satisfaction and well-being of women married to men exhibiting various levels of Type A behavior. Higher Type A levels of behavior in husbands were associated with wives reporting less material satisfaction, fewer friends and less frequent contact with those friends, greater levels of depression, worthlessness, tension, anxiety, guilt, and isolation.

Sufficient evidence has been presented to conclude that job stress is associated with a number of negative psychological consequences; and, it should be recalled that these psychological outcomes are frequently related to health status. Finally, as depicted in Figure 2.4, various characteristics of the individual exposed to job stress determine the nature and severity of the person's response to that stress. For example, genetic characteristics (heredity) have been closely tied to the onset of psychotic depression (Shields 1976).

Behavioral Responses

Research on physiological and psychological responses to job stress has discussed behavioral responses as well. Potential behavioral outcomes include dispensary visits, drug use and abuse (including alcohol, caffeine, and nicotine), over- or under-eating, nervous gesturing, pacing, risky behavior (e.g., reckless driving and gambling), aggression, vandalism, stealing, poor interpersonal relations, and suicide or attempted suicide (Beehr and Newman 1978).

The following interview with a steelworker provides a vivid example of two behavioral responses to job stress, aggression, and escapist drinking:

> I worked on a truck dock once and I was single. The foreman came over and he grabbed my shoulder, kind of gave me a shove. I punched him and knocked him off the dock. I said "Leave me alone. I'm doing my work, just stay away from me, just don't give me with-the-hands business."
>
> Hell, if you whip a damn mule he might kick you. Stay out of my way, that's all. Working is bad enough, don't bug me. I would rather work my ass off for eight hours a day with nobody watching me than five minutes with a guy watching me. Who you gonna sock? You can't sock General Motors, you can't sock anybody in Washington, you can't sock a system.
>
> After work I usually stop off at a tavern. Cold beer. Cold beer right away. When I was single, I used to go into hillbilly bars, get in a lot of brawls. Just to explode. I got a thing on my arm here. I got slapped with a bicycle chain. Oh wow! Mmm. I'm getting older. I don't explode as much. You might say I'm broken in. No, I'll never be broken in.

When you get a little older, you exchange the words. When you're younger, you exchange the blows.

When I get home, I argue with my wife a little bit. Turn on TV, get mad at the news.

From Terkle, *Working (1973), pp. 2-3, 6.*

Little is known about the relationships between job stress and aggressive behavior; but, the general causes of aggression understandably have received considerable attention. This growing body of literature may provide some clues to understanding job stress-aggression relationships. *Aggression* commonly refers to behavior that is intended to harm or injure someone, either physically or otherwise. *Frustration,* the blocking of one's efforts to obtain a goal, is a form or symptom of stress. Aggressive behavior sometimes but not always follows frustration. Frustration tends not to lead to aggression in situations where inhibitions to aggression are strong or when the individual has learned nonaggressive responses to frustration. It would be expected, therefore, that aggression in response to stress would appear on the job in relatively few instances. Rather, persons are more likely to make gestures of appeasement, to submit, or to express anger without attacking; however, blame may be shifted from the real object of frustration or threat, job stress, to some scapegoat. This process is known as *displacement.* Thus, as in the case of the steelworker, an unknown bystander or a member of one's family may end up being the target of aggression generated in job stress.

Knowledge of the job stress-alcohol consumption relationships is also limited, but, indirect evidence permits speculation. First, the stereotype of the derelict does not correspond with the alcoholic.[11] According to the National Council on Alcoholism, forty-five percent of alcoholics in America occupy professional or managerial positions; and, it has been estimated that five million workers are alcoholics (Follman 1976). Only ten percent of all Americans who drink are alcoholics. Those that are tend to share several characteristics: (1) inability to handle tension in a mature manner, (2) deep dependency on other people, (3) severe, unexpressed hostility to close friends, and (4) egocentricity (or self-centerdness). In addition, heavily drinking parents tend to raise heavily drinking children, and children from nondrinking families are very unlikely to become alcoholics. On the basis of these findings, one would anticipate only a weak relationship between job stress and alcoholism. For instance, it

[11]The framework for the following discussion in part is drawn from McNeil and Rubin (1977).

may be that the tensions an alcoholic is unable to cope with emanate from on-the-job stresses.

As for smoking behavior, job stress again has not been consistently identified as a principal predictor; however, the stressful Type A behavior pattern has been shown to influence ability to quit. When Caplan, Cobb, and French (1975) investigated Type A behavior and cessation of smoking among 200 male administrators, engineers, and scientists, they found that employees least likely to quit smoking exhibited a Type A behavior pattern. One explanation for this finding is that smoking probably is a means of coping with stress (Ikard and Tomkins 1973; Nesbitt 1973), and Type A behavior is stressful. Thus, quitting for person's exhibiting a Type A pattern is particularly stress inducing.

In general, the above discussion demonstrates that less is known about such behavioral consequences of job stress as aggression, alcohol consumption, and smoking than is known about physiological and psychological outcomes. From this statement, we cannot conclude that job stress is not associated with dysfunctional behavioral consequences; rather, regardless of commonly held beliefs it apears that little attention has been paid by researchers to the behavioral consequences of job stress which may impact the individual.

In sum, ample medical, psychological, and sociological evidence indicates that the employee experiencing job stress in fact does incur a number of costs. These costs are manifested in lowered levels of physical and mental well-being. As will be demonstrated in the next chapter, the consequences of at least moderate levels of job stress are not entirely harmful. Nevertheless, job stress should not be dismissed lightly. It can be hazardous and, at the minimum, can induce feelings of discomfort. Chapter 6 presents various personal mechanisms for coping with job stress. In addition, it specifies many of the individual characteristics associated with perceiving and responding to job stress that largely were ignored in the previous discussions.

AN OVERVIEW

Degree of psychological well-being can be viewed as the quality of life experienced. Life satisfaction is derived from numerous domains of life, including the work domain. People differ in terms of how much importance they place on the work domain as a source of life satisfaction. Placing a heavy emphasis on the work domain does not

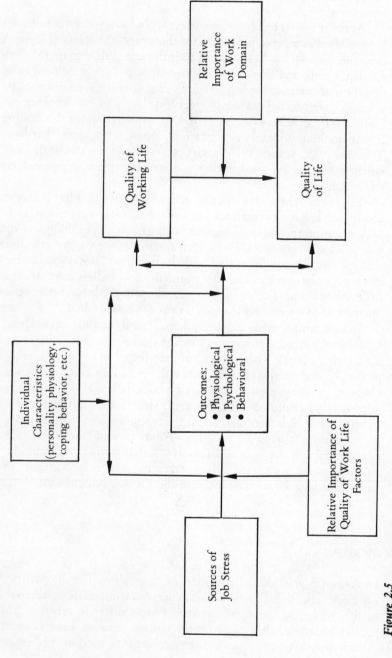

Figure 2.5
A Model of Job Stress–Quality of Life Relationships.

necessarily mean that the quality of working life experienced will be high.

Job stress is a major determinant of quality of working life, which is composed of several factors. People also differ in terms of the importance they place on each of these factors.

The personal consequences of job stress can be classified as physiological, psychological, and behavioral. For all categories of outcomes, it was shown that job stress is associated with personally dysfunctional experiences. Further, it was noted but not elaborated upon that various individual characteristics and coping strategies can reduce the negative impact of high levels of job stress.

In summary, the quality of working life was linked to quality of life, job stress was shown to be a determinant of quality of working life, and specific job stress-quality of life relationships were established. These relationships are depicted in Figure 2.5. Organizationally relevant outcomes of job stress, specific job stressors, and personal and organizational strategies for coping with job stress are discussed in the following chapters.

REFERENCES

Andrews, F.M., and Whithey, S.B. 1973. Developing measures of perceived life quality: Results from several national surveys. Paper presented at the meetings of the American Sociological Association, New York City, August 1973.

Beehr, T.A., and Newman, J.E. 1978. Job stress, employee health, and organizational effectiveness: A facet analysis, model, and literature review. *Personnel Psychology* 31:665-99.

Bharadwaj, J., and Wilkening, E.A. 1977. The prediction of perceived well-being. *Social Indicators Research* 4:421-39.

Bradburn, N.M. 1969. *The structure of psychological well-being.* Chicago: Aldine Publishing Company.

Brest, H.N., and Moyer, J.H. 1967. *Atherosclerotic vascular disease.* New York: Appleton-Century-Crofts.

Burke, R.J., Weir, T., and DuWors, R.E., Jr. 1979. Type A Behavior of administrators' and wives' reports of marital satisfaction and well-being. *Journal of Applied Psychology* 64:57-65.

Campbell, A., Converse, P.E., and Rodgers, W.I. 1976. *The quality of American life: Perceptions, evaluations, and satisfactions.* New York: Russell Sage Foundation.

Caplan, R.D., Cobb, S., and French, J.R. 1975. Relationships of cessation of smoking with job stress, personality, and social support. *Journal of Applied Psychology* 60:211-19.

Cooper, C.L., and Marshall, J. 1976. Occupational sources of stress: A review of the literature relating to coronary heart disease and mental ill health. *Journal of Occupational Psychology* 49:11-28.

Follman, J. 1976. *Alcoholism and business.* New York: AMACOM.

Friedberg, C.K. 1966. *Diseases of the heart.* 3rd. ed. Philadelphia: Saunders.

Friedman, M., and Rosenman, R.H. 1974. *Type A Behavior and your heart.* New York: Alfred A. Knopf.

Friedman, M., Rosenman, R.H., and Carrol, V. 1958. Changes in serum cholesterol and bloodclotting time in men subjected to cyclic variation of occupational stress. *Circulation* 17:852-61.

Glass, D.C. 1977. *Behavior patterns, stress, and coronary disease.* Hillsdale, N.J.: John Wiley.

Hamner, W.C., and Organ, D.W. 1978. *Organizational behavior: An applied psychological approach.* Dallas: Business Publications, Inc.

Holmes, T.H., and Masuda, M. 1974. Life change and illness susceptibility. In *Stressful life events: Their nature and effects,* B.S. Dohrenwend, and B.P. Dohrenwend, eds. pp. 45-72. New York: Wiley.

Holmes, T.H., and Rahe, R.H. 1967. The social readjustment rating scale. *Journal of Psychosomatic Research* 11:213-18.

House, J.S. 1972. *The relationship of intrinsic and extrinsic work motivations to occupational stress and coronary heart disease risk.* Ph.D. dissertation, University of Michigan.

Howard, J., Cunningham, D.A., and Rechnitzer, P.A. 1976. Health patterns associated with Type A behavior: A managerial population. *Journal of Human Stress* 2:24-31.

Ikard, F.F., and Tomkins, S. 1973. The experience of affect as a determinant of smoking behavior. *Journal of Abnormal Psychology* 81:172-81.

Jenkins, C.D. 1975. The coronary-prone personality. In *Psychological aspects of myocardial infarction and coronary care,* W.D. Gentry and R.B. Williams, Jr., eds. pp. 5-30. Saint Louis: Mosley.

Kasl, S.V. 1978. Epidemiological contributions to the study of work stress. In *Stress at work,* C.L. Cooper and R. Payne, eds. New York: John Wiley and Sons.

Kasl, S.V., and Cobb, S. 1970. Blood pressure changes in men undergoing job loss: A preliminary report. *Psychosomatic Medicine* 32:19-38.

Katz, D., and Kahn, R.L. 1978. *The social psychology of organizations.* 2nd ed. New York: John Wiley and Sons.

Kennedy, E.M. 1972. *Worker alienation,* 1972. Subcommittee on Employment, Manpower, and Poverty of the United States Senate. Washington, D.C.: U.S. Government Printing Office.

McNeil, E.B., and Rubin, Z. 1977. *The psychology of being human.* San Francisco: Canfield Press.

Nesbitt, P.D. 1973. Smoking, physiological arousal, and emotional response. *Journal of Personality and Social Psychology* 25:137-44.

Organ, D.W. 1977. Inferences about trends in labor force satisfaction: A causal-correlation analysis. *Academy of Management Journal* 20:510-19.

Palmore, E.B. 1969. Physical, mental and social factors in predicting longevity. *Gerontologist* 9:103-108.

Quinn, R.P., Staines, G.L., and McCullough, M.R. 1974. *Job satisfaction: Is there a trend?* Washington, D.C.: U.S. Printing Office.

Rabinowitz, S., and Hall, D.T. 1977. Organizational research on job involvement. *Psychological Bulletin* 84:265-88.

Rahe, R.H. 1974. The pathway between subject's recent life changes and their new future illness reports: Representative results and methodological issues. In

Stressful life events: Their nature and effects, B.S. Dohrenwend and B.P. Dohrenwend, eds. pp. 73-86. New York: Wiley.

Rahe, R.H., Meyer, M., Smith, M., Kjaer, G., and Holmes, T.H. 1964. Social stress and illness onset. *Journal of Psychosomatic Research* 8:35-44.

Ruch, R.O., and Holmes, T.H. 1971. Scaling of life change: Comparison of direct and indirect methods. *Journal of Psychosomatic Research* 15:224.

Shields, J. 1976. Heredity and environment. In *A textbook of human psychology,* H.J. Eysenck and G.D. Wilson, eds. Baltimore: University Park Press.

Smith, T.W. 1979. Happiness: Time trends, seasonal variations, inter-survey differences, and other mysteries. *Social Psychology Quarterly* 42:18-30.

Terkel, S. 1972. *Working: People talk about what they do all day and how they feel about what they do.* New York: Pantheon.

Walton, R.E. 1973. Quality of working life: What is it? *Sloan Management Review* Fall:11-21.

Wilson, W. 1967. Correlates of avowed happiness. *Psychological Bulletin* 67:294-306.

Zyzanski, S.J., and Jenkins, C.D. 1970. Basic dimensions within the coronary-prone behavior pattern. *Journal of Chronic Diseases* 22:781-95.

Chapter 3

Organizational Effectiveness and Employee Stress

Those who knew Bob Lyons thought extremely well of him. He was a highly successful executive who held an important position in a large company. As his superiors saw him, he was aggressive, with a knack for getting things done through other people. He worked hard and set a vigorous pace. He drove himself relentlessly. In less than ten years with this company, he had moved through several positions of responsibility.

Lyons had always been a good athlete. He was proud of his skill in swimming, hunting, golf, and tennis. In his college days he had lettered in football and baseball. On weekends he preferred to undertake rebuilding and repairing projects around the house, or to hunt, interspersing other sports for a change of pace. He was usually engaged, it seemed, in hard, physical work.

His life was not all work, however. He was active in his church and in the Boy Scouts. His wife delighted in entertaining and in being with other people, so their social life was a round of parties and social activities. They shared much of their life with their three children.

Early in the spring of his ninth year with the company, Bob Lyons spoke with the vice president to whom he reported. "Things are a little quiet around here," he said. "Most of the big projects are over. The new building is finished, and we have a lot of things on the ball which four years ago were all fouled up. I don't like this idea of just riding a desk and looking out the window. I like action."

About a month later, Lyons was assigned additional responsibilities. He rushed into them with his usual vigor. Once again he seemed to be buoyant and cheerful. After six months on the assignment, Lyons had the project rolling smoothly. Again he spoke to his vice president, reporting that he was out of projects. The vice president, pleased with Lyons' performance, told him that he had earned the right to do a little dreaming and planning; and, furthermore, dreaming and planning were a necessary part of the position he now held, toward which he had aspired for so long. Bob Lyons listened as his boss spoke, but it was plain to the vice president that the answer did not satisfy him.

About three months after this meeting, the vice president began to notice that replies to memos and inquiries were not coming back from Lyons with their usual rapidity. He noticed also that Lyons was developing a tendency to put things off, a most unusual behavior pattern for him. He observed that Lyons became easily angered and disturbed over minor difficulties which previously had not irritated him at all.

Bob Lyons then became involved in a conflict with two other executives over a policy issue. Such conflicts were not unusual in the organization since, inevitably, there were varying points of view on many issues. The conflict was not a personal one, but it did require intervention from higher management before a solution could be reached. In the process of resolving the conflict, Lyons' point of view prevailed on some questions, but not on others.

A few weeks after this conflict had been resolved, Lyons went to the vice president's office. He wanted to have a long private talk, he said. His first words were, "I'm losing my grip. The old steam is gone. I've had diarrhea for four weeks and several times in the past three weeks I've lost my breakfast. I'm worried and yet I don't know what about. I feel that some people have lost confidence in me."

He talked with his boss for an hour and a half. The vice president recounted his achievements in the company to reassure him. He then asked if Lyons thought he should see a doctor. Lyons agreed that he should and, in the presence of the vice president, called his family doctor for an appointment. By this time the vice president was very much concerned. He called Mrs. Lyons and arranged to meet her for lunch the next day. She reported that, in addition to his other symptoms her husband had difficulty sleeping. She was relieved that the vice president had called her because she was beginning to become worried and had herself planned to call the vice president. Both were now alarmed. They decided that they should get Lyons into a hospital rather than wait for the doctor's appointment which was still a week off.

The next day Lyons was taken to the hospital. Meanwhile, with Mrs. Lyons' permission, the vice president reported to the family doctor Lyons' recent job behavior and the nature of their conversations. When the vice president had finished, the doctor concluded, "All he needs is a good rest. We don't want to tell him that it may be mental or nervous." The vice president replied that he didn't know what the cause was, but knew Bob Lyons needed help quickly.

During five days in the hospital, Lyons was subjected to extensive laboratory tests. The vice president visited him daily. Lyons seemed to welcome the rest and the sedation at night. He said he was eating and sleeping much better. He talked about company problems, though he did not speak spontaneously without encouragement. While Lyons was out of the room, the other executive who shared his hospital room confided to the vice president that he was worried about Lyons. "He seems to be so morose and depressed that I'm afraid he's losing his mind," the executive said.

By this time the president of the company, who had been kept informed, was also becoming concerned. He had talked to a psychiatrist and planned to talk to Lyons about psychiatric treatment if his doctor did not suggest it. Meanwhile, Lyons was discharged from the hospital as being without physical illness, and his doctor recommended a vacation. Lyons then remained at home for several days where he was again visited by the vice president. He and his wife took a trip to visit friends. He was then ready to come back to work, but the president suggested that he take another week off. The president also suggested that they visit together when Lyons returned.

A few days later, the president telephoned Lyons' home. Mrs. Lyons could not find him to answer the telephone. After 15 minutes she still had not found him and called the vice president about her concern. By the time the vice president arrived at the Lyons' home, the police were already there. Bob Lyons had committed suicide.

From Levinson, Harvard Business Review (1963).

The illustration of what happened to Bob Lyons is relevant to the discussion of stress and organizational effectiveness. What happened to Bob is really both a sympton and a consequence of stress in organizations, but it is only one of many possible indicators of organizational stress. In viewing the issue we must ask whether or not what happened to Bob was related to the effectiveness of his organization. That is, should an overall evaluation of the effectiveness of Bob's organization take into account what happened to him? Is it possible that other employees continue to experience similar stresses and are lessening organizational effectiveness as a result? If the evaluation does not include Bob's suicide as an indicator of the effectiveness of the organization, then on what basis or with what standards (i.e., criteria) should the organization be evaluated? Furthermore, from whose standpoint should this evaluation be made, the employees' or the organization's?

Answers to these questions should be of concern to anyone studying or working in organizations, and particularly to managers or aspiring managers. The answers are not easy, however. In order to derive solutions, an understanding of organizational effectiveness, employee stress, and their interrelationships is necessary. It will become obvious that answers must be found which take into account employee stress in general and employee health in particular.

ORGANIZATIONAL EFFECTIVENESS

The term "organizational effectiveness" is difficult to define because it is an abstract concept, the meaning of which may vary from one organization to another. According to R.M. Steers (1977), *organizational effectiveness* is a construct (i.e., a mental image) against which to develop measures or criteria by which an organization is evaluated. Because organizational effectiveness is an abstraction, the standards that should be used to measure it are difficult to agree upon. Therefore, what frequently happens is that the definition of effectiveness remains vague and is not explicitly stated. Rather, the standards habitually used are assumed to be related to effectiveness.

Whatever standards are selected, if a single standard or criterion is used, it is referred to as a "univariate effectiveness measure;" while if a set of such criteria is used, it is referred to as a "multivariate effectiveness measure." Both approaches to the measurement of effectiveness will be explained in detail in this chapter. Examples of univariate and multivariate measures that have been used to evaluate organizations are shown in Tables 3.1 and 3.2.

Table 3.1
Univariate Measures of Organizational Effectiveness

OVERALL EFFECTIVENESS
The degree to which the organization is accomplishing all its major tasks or achieving all its objectives. A general evaluation that takes in as many single criteria as possible and results in a general judgment about the effectiveness of the organization.

QUALITY
The quality of the primary service or product provided by the organization. This may take many operational forms, primarily determined by the kind of product or service provided by the organization.

Table 3.1 Continued
Univariate Measures of Organizational Effectiveness

PRODUCTIVITY
The quantity of, or volume of, the major product or service that the organization provides. Can be measured at three levels: individual, group, and total organization. This is not a measure of efficiency; no cost/output ratio is computed.

READINESS
An overall judgment concerning the probability that the organization could successfully perform some specified task if asked to do so.

EFFICIENCY
A ratio that reflects a comparison of some aspect of unit performance to the costs incurred for that performance. Examples: dollars per single unit of production, amount of down time, degree to which schedules, standards of performance, or other milestones are met. On occasion, just the total amount of costs (money, material, etc.) a unit has incurred over some period can be used.

PROFIT OR RETURN
The return on the owner's investment in the organization. The amount of resources left after all costs and obligations are met, sometimes expressed as a percentage.

GROWTH
An increase in such things as manpower, plant facilities, assets, sales, market share, and innovations. A comparison of an organization's present state with its own past state.

UTILIZATION OF ENVIRONMENT
The extent to which the organization successfully interacts with its environment, acquiring scarce, valued resources necessary to its effective operation. This is viewed in a long-term, optimizing framework and not in a short-term, maximizing framework. For example, the degree to which it acquires a steady supply of manpower and financial resources.

STABILITY
The maintenance of structure, function, and resources through time, and more particularly through periods of stress.

TURNOVER OR RETENTION
Frequency or amount of voluntary terminations.

ABSENTEEISM
The frequency of occasions of personnel being absent from the job.

Adapted from Campell (1973). Used by permission of the publisher.

The decision to evaluate an organization by a univariate measure or by a multivariate measure means that a fundamental distinction in the concept of the organization has been made. The use of a univariate measure implies that one standard can be used to measure the success or failure of the organization, whereas a multivariate measure implies that many factors may affect organizational effectiveness, and thus more than one standard must be used to measure organizational success or failure. This distinction is important when trying to answer the questions posed at the beginning of this chapter.

Univariate and Multivariate Measure Approaches

Univariate measure. A great deal of the early work on organizational effectiveness was based on the notion that it was possible to establish an ultimate criterion by which to evaluate all organizations (Campbell, 1973). It was thought that one standard alone was sufficient to evaluate the effectiveness of all organizations, regardless of their differences, but because of the lack of agreement on which standard should be used, each univariate measure in Table 3.1 was regarded by different researchers as the ultimate criterion. The most widely used univariate measures were (1) overall performance, (2) productivity, (3) employee job satisfaction, (4) profit or rate of return on investment, and (5) employee withdrawal (Steers 1977).

Although the use of a univariate measure simplifies the evaluation of organizational effectiveness, a few problems accompany its use. First, one standard, or a one-dimensional assumption, may fail to reflect the goal of effectiveness evaluation, which is to determine the degree of an organization's success. For example, just because an

Table 3.2
Studies Using a Set of Multivariate Measures for Organizational Effectiveness

STUDY	SET OF MULTIVARIATE CRITERIA
Georgopoluos and Tannenbaum (1957)	Productivity, Flexibility, Absence of Organizational Strain
Bennis (1962)	Adaptability, Sense of Identity, Capacity to Test Reality
Blake and Mouton (1964)	Simultaneous Achievement of High Production-Centered and High People-Centered Enterprise

Table 3.2 Continued
Studies Using a Set of Multivariate Measures for Organizational Effectiveness

STUDY	SET OF MULTIVARIATE CRITERIA
Caplow (1964)	Stability, Integration, Volunteerism Achievement
Katz and Kahn (1966)	Growth, Storage, Survival, Control over Environment
Lawrence and Lorsch (1967)	Interpersonal Relations, Optimal Balance of Integration and Differentiation
Seashore (1967)	Successful Acquisition of Scarce and Valued Resources, Control over Environment
Friedlander and Pickle (1968)	Profitability, Employee Satisfaction, Societal Value
Schein (1970)	Open Communication, Flexibility, Creativity, Psychological Commitment
Mott (1972)	Productivity, Flexibility, Adaptability
Duncan (1973)	Short-run: Production, Efficiency, Satisfaction
	Intermediate: Adaptiveness, Development
	Long-run: Survival
Negandhi and Reimann (1973)	Behavioral Index: Manpower Acquisition, Employee Satisfaction, Manpower Retention, Interdepartmental Relations, Manpower Utilization,
	Economic Index: Growth in Sales, Net Profit
Child (1974-1975)	Profitability, Growth
Webb (1974)	Cohesion, Efficiency, Adaptability, Support
Price (1968)	Productivity, Conformity, Morale, Adaptiveness, Institutional

Adapted from Steers (1975). Used by permission of the publisher.

organization has a high turnover rate does not mean that the organization is unsuccessful. However, it does seem logical that high turnover might contribute to decreased effectiveness. Secondly, studies which used a univariate measure of effectiveness did not explain or interpret the relationship between the measure and the idea of effectiveness. It was assumed that the measure itself was a valid or appropriate indicator of organizational effectiveness. Thus, the univariate measure often provided little useful information for the manager in terms of how to increase the success of the organization.

Multivariate measures. The univariate approach was based on, or at least reflected, a closed system view of organizations. As managers and researchers discovered that many factors could contribute to organizational effectiveness, a completely different conceptualization of organizations emerged and organizational evaluation shifted from a univariate to a multivariate approach. The multivariate approach reflected an open systems view. The important components of an organization as seen from the open system view are shown in Figure 3.1.

This illustration of the open systems view indicates that four main components should be considered in a study of organizations, particularly in determining their degree of success. These four components represent a model of organizations in which success depends upon obtaining inputs (human and natural resources), taking the product to market, and then changing and adapting as necessary to the market and the rest of the environment. It assumes that each component is dynamic and subject to continuous change and adaptation. Since each component is considered to contribute to organiza-

ORGANIZATIONAL BOUNDARY

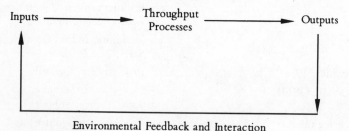

Environmental Feedback and Interaction

Figure 3.1
Components of an Open Systems View of Organizations.

tional success, they comprise a multivariate measure for evaluating organizational effectiveness. The closed system view is primarily concerned with the throughput, or production, component of the same model and assumes that the other components are static and given; thus, the measure is single and therefore univariate.

As described by Katz and Kahn (1978), the organization viewed as an open system may be said to consist of these five interdependent subsystems:

Productive subsystem. Conducts the major functions or work of the system (for example, a department or group of departments that manufacture a product or provide a service.)

Supportive subsystem. Secures needed inputs for the productive subsystem and distributes the system's outputs (for example, the purchasing, marketing, and public relations departments of a company).

Maintenance subsystem. Focuses on maintaining and protecting the organization's structural integrity and character (for example, training functions, compensation plans, company newspapers).

Adaptive subsystem. Concentrates on the survival and adaptation of the organization in a changing environment (for example, research and development department, long-range planning functions).

Managerial subsystem. Focuses on coordinating, controlling, and directing the other subsystems so that maximum effort can be directed toward desired ends.

Evaluating organizational effectiveness within the open systems view should be more comprehensive than within the closed system view, since criteria for organizational effectiveness will be related not to one subsystem, but to five, and to their interrelationships.

According to Porter, Lawler, and Hackman (1975), the view of organizations as an open system is complementary with the characterization of organizations as having:

1. Social composition: the levels, or groups, within the organizational structure or the people component.

2. Goal orientation: the desired organizational outcome, such as production, sales, or profit.

3. Differentiated functions: the various roles people in the organization have in producing the end product.

4. Intended rational coordination: coordination of organizational activities to efficiently meet the goals.

5. Continuity through time: the ability of the organization to survive and produce regardless of changes which may occur.

Individuals are viewed as working together for common goals. They assume unique parts, or roles, in the organization which combine to produce the intended product goals. The effectiveness of the organization is then evaluated in terms of the achievement of those product goals.

There may also be some nongoal activities related to the success of the organization. In fact, the open systems view assumes that "some means must be devoted to such nongoal functions as service and custodial activities, including means employed for the maintenance of the organization itself" (Etzioni 1971). According to Steers (1977, pp. 14-15) an organization's requirements for maintenance, stability, and survival which also allow it to attain its stated goals, include the following:

Resource acquisition. Organizations must be able to compete successfully for scarce and valued resources to serve as inputs for organizational work activities.

Efficiency. Organizations must strive to secure the most advantageous ratio of inputs to outputs in the transformation process.

Production/output. It is necessary that organizational systems be capable of steady and predictable delivery of the goods or services it intends to provide.

Rational coordination. The activities of the organization must be integrated and coordinated in a logical, predictable fashion that is consistent with the ultimate goals of the entity.

Organizational renewal and adaptation. In most organizations, it is necessary that some resources be set aside and invested in activities that will enhance the net worth of the organization in the future. Without such renewal efforts, organizational survival is easily threatened by short-term shifts in market demands, resources, and so on.

Conformity. Because of the close interrelationship between an organization and its external environment, it is often necessary that organizations follow the prevalent dictates and norms of the environment. Wide deviation from social norms, laws, regulations, and moral prescriptions can result in a variety of sanctions being levied against the organization that serve to reduce its sources of legitimacy and threaten its survival.

Constituency satisfaction. Organizations are composed of a variety of constituencies, including employees, investors, consumers, and so forth. It is important for system effectiveness that organizations strive to satisfy the various—and divergent—needs of these constituents if they are to continue receiving necessary support and cooperation. Given the often conflicting demands made by the various constituents (for example, employees want more money, while investors want increased profits and consumers want lower prices), a major function of modern management is to somehow achieve a workable synthesis that at least marginally satisfies all parties.

But Steers argues there is a difference between meeting the requirements for maintenance, stability, and survival and an organization's effectiveness.

The real question insofar as effectiveness is concerned is whether or not an organization meets its intended goals and, unless survival is its only objective, an organization must do far more than simply meet these requirements in order to be truly successful.

We can conclude that to be successful, an organization must meet its requirements at a minimum, and it must be effective (that is, attain its goals). The requirements of an organization appear to be relatively similar and consistent across diverse strata; but many factors influence the fulfilling of these requirements, such as technologies, work climate, structures, tasks, size, physical characteristics and leader characteristics. Additionally, the goals of these organizations are likely to be unique.

As this discussion indicates, organizational requirements such as maintenance, stability, and survival, as well as organizational effectiveness, or goal attainment, are required for organizational success; and they are highly interdependent. In fact, organizational requirements are often stated in terms of goals to be attained, and as such they can be used as measures of organizational effectiveness; therefore, the lines of distinction between requirements and effectiveness are less than sharp and are perhaps even arbitrary. Gibson, Ivancevich, and Donnelly (1979), for example, took the requirements of organizations that Steers described and used them as criteria for effectiveness over time, as shown in Figure 3.2.

Organizational effectiveness is difficult to evaluate because of factors such as the diversity of organizational goals, the lack of consistent distinctions between organizational requirements and goals,

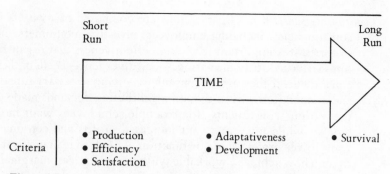

Figure 3.2
Criteria of Organizational Effectiveness. (Adapted from Gibson, Ivancevich, and Donnelly 1979)

and the differences in effectiveness criteria as a function of time (Steers 1977). Furthermore, how to specify and measure goals, organizational requirements, and effectiveness criteria are commonly debated issues, so that a complete definition of organizational effectiveness continues to elude researchers. With all of these difficulties and disagreements regarding organizational effectiveness, managers would appear to be justified in ignoring the issue.

But at a practical level, managers are engaged in organizational effectiveness issues every day through their association with individual and group effectiveness. Using the effectiveness criteria as an example, Gibson, Ivancevich, and Donnelly (1979) suggest that managers are continually interacting with, and influencing, individuals and groups who are in some degree efficient, productive, satisfied, developed and adaptive. Thus they relate individual and group effectiveness to organizational effectiveness. Although it would appear that this specification would help reduce some of the difficulties in evaluating organizational effectiveness, such is not the case. In using only those five criteria, there is a problem with weighing the importance of each. Seashore (1974) suggests that the differences in importance of these criteria depend upon the perspective from which they are viewed: the manager's or organization's, the employee's or society's. Table 3.3 illustrates these perspectives and associated criteria.

Of the five criteria listed in Figure 3.2, it appears that the manager's perspective places most importance on efficiency, productivity, and adaptability, while the employee's perspective values satis-

Table 3.3
Indicators of Work Role Effectiveness as Viewed from Three Perspectives.

FROM THE PERSPECTIVE OF A WORKER
Job satisfaction assessed both generally and with regard to specific aspects of job and job environment
Job-related feelings of excessive strain or tension
Self-esteem
Affective states, such as anxiety, depression, resentment, hopelessness, etc.
Physiological states, such as fatigue, work-related illness or injuries, coronary heart disease risk symptoms, drug dependency if work-related, etc.
Satisfaction with work-role potential for personal development adaptability, career-long value realization, etc.

FROM THE PERSPECTIVE OF AN EMPLOYER
Productivity, including quantity and quality of output, innovative behavior, initiation of new techniques or procedures that increase productivity, etc.
Adaptability to changing work procedures, skill acquisition
Turnover, absenteeism, lateness
Counterproductive behaviors, such as theft, sabotage, work stoppage, etc.
Alienation from work
Identification with work organization

FROM THE PERSPECTIVE OF SOCIETY
Gross national product
Increasing value of manpower pool
Cost of welfare protection for workers and their dependents
Political behaviors and attitudes
Consumer behaviors and attitudes
Societal adaptability
Life satisfaction rates in society
Alienation
Quality of life with regard to nonwork roles and situations

From Seashore (1974). Used by permission of the author and publisher.

faction and development. Thus the goals of the organization (represented by the manager) and of the employee appear to be in conflict. Katz and Kahn (1978) describe this conflict in slightly different terms. They argue that all five goals are equally important. Katz and Kahn depict employees as individual systems, and organizations as organizational systems. The organizational system has roles, or parts, to play and the individual systems enact those roles. The behavioral enactment of the roles represents the intersection (overlapping cycles) of the two systems. Katz and Kahn then argue:

> We are accustomed to studying the extent to which these shared or overlapping cycles contribute to efficiency, productivity, growth and other criteria of organizational effectiveness. Has the individual performed his or her role with the energy, skill, regularity, and judgment that are sufficient for the continuing success of the organization? *It is equally appropriate, however, to ask the complementary questions:* Does the enactment of the organizational role enhance or reduce the well-being of the individual? Does it enlarge or diminish the person's valued skills and abilities? Does it increase or restrict the person's opportunity and capacity for other valued role enactments?
>
> *Katz and Kahn, The Social Psychology of Organizations (1978).*

It is equally appropriate and important to address these questions not only for the concern of the employee, but also for the concern of the organization and society. These multiple perspectives are consistent with the open systems view of organizations where the parts of the organization are viewed as highly interdependent with each other and the environment. That is, ineffective employees, those whose needs and values are not being fulfilled, can reduce the effectiveness of organizations. And, viewed from the perspective of society at large, if an employee's needs and values are not attended to by the organization, society may not only have less effective organizations but also more alienated, dissatisfied, and less productive employees.

The Definition of Organizational Effectiveness

Thus the attention to employee needs and values (really attention to the answers to those questions in the preceding quote) is important for managers and organizations because they are related to the effectiveness of the individual, the organization and society. *Organizational effectiveness is, therefore, defined here to encompass the requirements of organizations (as listed above) and the goal attainment of organizations within an open systems perspective. Thus the concerns of the organization, the employee, and the society are part of organizational effectiveness and success.*

Using this definition of effectiveness, Steers and Gibson, Ivancevich, and Donnelly also suggest that managers can influence organizational effectiveness most practically through these four factors which have been found to be associated with effectiveness:

1. Organizational characteristics
2. Environmental characteristics

3. Employee characteristics

4. Managerial policies and practices

But these are the same factors, in combination with employee needs and values, that are associated with employee stress! Therefore, concern for employee stress is really concern, in part, for organizational effectiveness, as it most directly relates to employee effectiveness. Since criteria that have been related to employee effectiveness have also been related to the symptoms of employee stress, attention to employee stress will have both direct and indirect effects on organizational effectiveness.

In order to support such a view, we need to cite research that has been conducted on the symptoms of stress as associated with organizational and environmental conditions, employee characteristics, and managerial policies and procedures. Previous chapters have already outlined the definition of stress and its impact on the quality of life of the individual. Therefore, this discussion focuses on organizational processes and outcomes resulting from functioning of the individual on the job.

EMPLOYEE STRESS

Although employee health, physical and mental, is an important output of organizations, organizational researchers and managers alike have paid relatively little attention to the topic. This has been the case because employee health is an unintended output, and it is relatively low on the list of organizational priorities. Therefore, organizations seldom measure, count, or become aware of their effect on the health of their employees. There are exceptions, but they are related to specific ill effects, such as the black lung disease of coal miners. Even when organizations become more concerned about employee health, there are occasions when the employee's health is less influenced by the work role than some nonwork role:

> For example, an interviewer talked with Joe Brown, who complained about conditions in the shop, the draft, smoke, and fumes.... Then he talked about his brother, who had recently died of pneumonia... the complaints were really an indication of his preoccupations about his health.
>
> Another employee complained that his piece rates were too low. As he continued to talk, he related that his wife was in the hospital, and that he was worried about his doctor bills. In effect the complaint about piece rate is an expression of his concern about his ability to pay bills.

Another employee complained of his boss being a bully....As the talk turned to his past experiences, he talked to his father, an overbearing, domineering man whose authority could not be questioned. Gradually the interviewer could see that the employee's dissatisfaction was rooted somewhere in his attitude towards authority, developed during early childhood.

Cass and Zimmer, Man and Work in Society (1975).

Thus investigation and concern for general employee health in organizations are fraught with difficulties and reasons for relative neglect. Nevertheless, some research is being done regarding employee health in organizations within the area of employee stress.

Although it has not received a great deal of attention, stress in organizations is becoming increasingly important in both academic research and organizational practices. Unfortunately, a great deal is still unknown (Beehr and Newman 1978). Most of what we know about stress has been derived from the research done in the medical and health sciences, although several important studies in management have applied and extended the work. However, as the discussion in the preceding chapter suggests, what is known about stress indicates that the importance now being given it is warranted, and perhaps overdue.

Chapter 2 discussed *physiological, psychological* and *behavioral symptoms of stress* as they related to an individual's quality of life. They are reviewed here in the context of organizational effectiveness because all of them are associated with employee effectiveness. By identifying the specific stress conditions associated with these symptoms, we may be able to find remedies, and thus improve employee effectiveness. Therefore, by extension, we should be able to increase organizational effectiveness at will.

Symptoms or Consequences of Stress in Organizations.

The definition of stress given in Chapter 1 can be expanded by examining situations where an individual is:

1. Confronted with an opportunity for being/having/doing what is desired *and/or*

2. Confronted with a constraint on being/having/doing what is desired *and/or*

3. Confronted with a demand for being/having/doing what is desired but for which the resolution is perceived to be uncertain, and will lead to important outcomes.

These situations illustrate several important aspects of the previous stress definitions and are drawn from stress research in both the medical and health sciences and organizational behavior and industrial psychology. It is useful to examine each of these and relate them to the previous work.

Needs vs. Values. The adage, "One person's poison is another's meat," provides the essence of the term "desires." The *desires* of an individual reflect the needs and values (physiological, psychological or behavioral) of that individual. "The concept of need arises from the fact that the existence of living organisms is conditional; life depends upon a specific course of goal-directed action. The concept of need refers to those conditions which are required to sustain the life and well-being of a living organism" (Locke 1976). Locke distinguishes two categories of needs for survival: the *physical* (physiological) need requirements of the body, such as food and water, and the *psychological* need requirements of a healthy consciousness, such as sensory stimulation, self-esteem, and self-actualization. To relate needs to organizational effectiveness, one may consider that physiological needs of the individual will be met when the individual is compensated for services provided to the organization. If the employee contributes to organizational effectiveness, the employee will in turn have the means to satisfy physiological need requirements. More important, the psychological need requirements may also be met. As the goal-directed actions of individuals contribute to organizational success, they may also be able to meet psychological needs such as sensory stimulation, self-esteem, and self-actualization.

A distinction between needs as objective requirements of the organism and values as subjective requirements is necessary. Needs exist whether the individual is aware of them or not. Values only exist to the extent that an individual is consciously or subconsciously desiring, wanting, or seeking to attain something. Values are learned, while needs are innate. Not all authorities distinguish between needs and values, but rather use them interchangeably or define needs as if they were values. For example, Salancik and Pfeffer (1978) define a need as an outcome produced by a person, rather than an inherent property.

For the definition of stress presented here, both the concepts of needs and values will be maintained and distinguished as Locke suggested. While needs generally refer to physiological and psychological requirements, values generally reflect behavioral requirements.

In combination, needs and values may represent what an individual desires to be, to have, and to do, with *being* and *having* more closely associated with needs and *doing* more closely associated with value.

Given this definition, the needs of an individual may be met by producing certain outcomes, such as a promotion, or pay increase, or by contributing to the effectiveness or success of one's organization. The way in which these needs are met will probably reflect an individual's values as reflected by behavior within the organization. The Protestant Work Ethic discussed in Chapter 2 is an example of behavior based on individual values. This aspect of the definition of stress allows us to integrate the physiological approach to stress (traditionally represented mainly by the medical and health sciences area) and the psychological and behavioral approaches to stress (traditionally represented mainly by the organizational behavior and industrial psychology area). Therefore, it is important to realize that we must begin to approach stress research from a multidisciplinary perspective (Cooper and Marshall, 1976)

Opportunities, Constraints, and Demands

Defining stress partly in terms of needs and values not only paves the way for a multidisciplinary approach to stress research, but it also allows us to define stress in terms of an opportunity, constraint, or demand. An *opportunity* is a dynamic condition in which an individual may be, have, or do whatever that individual desires; this is a situation of potential gain. A *constraint* on the other hand, is a dynamic condition in which an individual may be prevented form being, having, or doing what that individual desires; this creates a potentially static situation. A *demand* is a dynamic condition in which the desired objective to be, have, or do may be diminished or removed, and it is therefore a situation of potential loss. Stress may be associated with any one of these situations. Many individuals experience all three situations and the attendent stress simultaneously. Thus, in an organizational setting the individual may experience positive stress symptoms when the opportunity for advancement or reward becomes available. A person might also experience positive stress simply from a challenging job, project, or task. However, if that person is prevented from meeting certain goals because of factors that cannot be controlled, such as lack of information or cooperation, that person may suffer negative stress symptoms.

An example of all three factors acting simultaneously as stressors would be the case in which opportunity arises only after the demands are met; that is, a positive outcome or attainment of goals, as well as constraints, are present and hamper the individual's performance. In this situation, a negative outcome could be demotion, dismissal, or lack of further opportunities. As Selye (1956, 1973, 1975, 1976) has suggested, stress is an additive concept, so that the more dynamic the conditions of opportunity, constraint, or demand, the greater the potential stress. The potential stress becomes actual or real stress only under two other conditions: resolution uncertainty and important outcomes.

McGrath (1976) aptly demonstrated the relation of uncertainty to stress, but his definition of stress differs from that presented here. McGrath has shown that although an individual may be in dynamic conditions of opportunity, constraint, or demand vis-a-vis desired objectives, it is only when the individual is uncertain that the opportunity will be seized, the constraint removed or the demand conquered (the loss avoided) that stress arises. McGrath reported that stress was highest for those individuals who perceived that they were uncertain about whether they would win or lose and lowest for those individuals who thought that winning or losing was a certainty.

Implicit in McGrath's example of winning and losing is the influence of important outcomes, for even if the winning or losing was uncertain, it is assumed here that, if winning or losing was an unimportant outcome, there would be no stress (Sells, 1970). The nature of an important outcome is determined by an individual's needs and values, their relative importance, and the degree of correspondence between the outcome and the needs and values. What is an important outcome for one individual may, therefore, not be important for another. Because an individual may have several needs and values of varying importance, and because situations of opportunity, constraint, and demand may be associated with one or several of them, the resolution will vary; therefore, outcomes of varying importance will be produced. Additionally, the relative importance of an individual's needs and values may change, so that what is an important outcome today may not have the same potential importance as it will tomorrow. Thus stress becomes a dynamic condition.

Stress then is associated with several conditions which may be positive as well as negative, but most of the literature regarding stress focuses on the negative conditions symptoms.

This expanded definition of stress is important to our understanding of employee and organizational effectiveness. It indicates that some types of stress improve effectiveness; for example, an employee may regard a promotion as an opportunity and because of the uncertainty about doing well on the new job may experience stress. This stress, however, may be associated with high performance and satisfaction (positive symptoms related to effectiveness). An employee working on a highly repetitive task, however, may experience stress from the constraint of not being able really to do what is desired and not being sure of how to get out of that situation. In this case, the symptoms of stress may be low satisfaction and performance so stress is negatively related to organizational effectiveness.

As Chapter 2 noted, the effects of stress can be observed in three major areas: (1) physiological (2) psychological and (3) behavioral. Looking at the role of these effects and relating them to organizational effectiveness, we see that the effects of stress on physiology are negative for both the individual and the organization. The current data on stress and physiological symptoms suggest the relationship depicted in Figure 3.3 that:

> Opportunity, constraint and demand stresses are all positively related to the probability of the incidence of physiological symptoms.

Since the limited nonorganizational stress research suggests that certain physiological symptoms may not always occur with stress, it is believed that types of stresses cannot be directly correlated with specific physiological symptoms. However, it is suggested that the

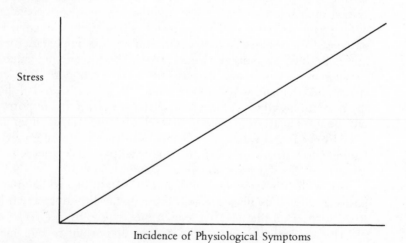

Figure 3.3
The Association between Stress of All Kinds and Physiological Symptoms.

appearance of physiological symptoms due to all types of stress will have a negative impact on organizational effectiveness. Even a person who suffers minor physical symptoms, such as tension headaches, is not going to be able to concentrate fully on the task at hand—and that means less organizational effectiveness.

Role and task characteristics. It is important to note that much of the research on stress in the areas of organizational behavior and industrial psychology has investigated the association between psychological symptoms and stress. The variables most frequently used to represent psychological symptoms are satisfaction, job involvement, self-esteem, tension, anxiety, depression, boredom, and psychological fatigue. The stressors generally related to these symptoms are the organizational qualities, such as role and task characteristics. For example, the role the individual plays within an organization may prove to be a source of conflict, ambiguity, or overload. When this occurs, research indicates the result is generally individual tension, anxiety, depression, low self-esteem, and dissatisfaction. It should be noted that wherever role underload has been measured, patterns of symptoms were found to be analogous to those reported for role overload. Thus, the individual who has either too little or too much to do is a likely candidate for increased stress within the organization. Furthermore, in a limited number of studies of role characteristics, those psychological symptoms were also related to physiological symptoms. Data from Russek and Zohman (1958) even suggests that psychological symptoms precede physiological symptoms. This finding is consistent with the depiction of the stress-stress symptom relationship provided by Margolis, Kroes, and Quinn (1974), who suggested that stress leads to five types of strain (symptoms): short-term subjective conditions, such as anxiety; long-term and more chronic psychological responses, such as depression and alienation; transient physiological changes, such as changes in blood pressure and catecholoamine levels; physical illnesses, such as heart attacks and ulcers; and changes in work performance.

The stress patterns found in role characteristics-stress research are similar to those found in task characteristics research, where the task is defined as the nature of the job itself. It has been found that the less control the individual has over the pace of work, the worse the individual's physical and mental health becomes. As seen in task characteristics research (although not in the stress research), individuals experience increasing satisfaction and job involvement when task characteristics referred to as variety, significance, autonomy, feedback and identity are present. This suggests that the more these characteristics exist, the less the stress and the more the satisfaction and involvement. Levi's (1972) model of the stimulation-stress relationship (Figure 3.4), suggests that stress should be high under highly stimulating task conditions, as well as under task conditions with low levels of stimulation. It has been discussed that conditions either of role underload or role overload are stressful, and that outcome is indicated in this model as well. From recent research we can assume that the relationships shown in Figure 3.5 exist between stress and psychological symptoms. Figures 3.4 and 3.5 indicate that opportunity stress is positively related to affective psychological outcomes, such as satisfaction and job involvement, and that constraint and demand stress are negatively related to affective psychological outcomes. Therefore, the opportunity to gain valued outcomes (such as promotion) and to fulfill one's needs and values should be associated with satisfaction and job involvement, with the positive effect of stress on the individual being increased organizational effectiveness. On the other hand, Figure 3.5 indicates that:

> Demand stress, constraint stress and opportunity stress are positively related to cognitive psychological outcomes, such as tendency to misjudge others.

These stress effects suggest that organizational effectiveness cannot be increased unless opportunity stress is increased and constraint and demand stress are decreased. However, some contrary evidence

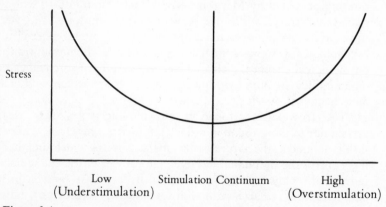

Stress

Low   Stimulation Continuum   High
(Understimulation)   (Overstimulation)

Figure 3.4
Relationships between Levels of Stimulation and Stress. (Levi 1972)

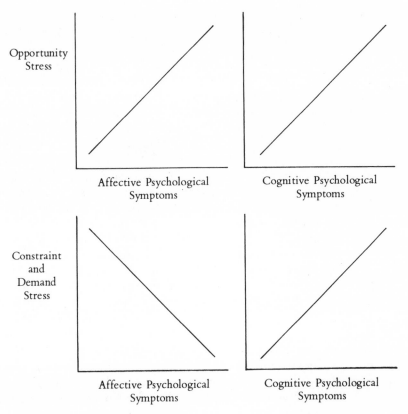

Figure 3.5
The Relationships between the Types of Stress and Types of Psychological Symptoms.

indicates that cognitive psychological outcomes such as perceptual distortion, tunnel vision, and tendency to misjudge others increase with any type of stress. As a result, positive effects of increased opportunity stress may be somewhat offset by negative responses. It is clear that more research must be done on the positive effects of stress and their relationship to organizational effectiveness.

As Chapter 2 mentioned, the three major types of responses to stress are physiological, psychological, and behavioral in nature. The first two have been discussed as they relate to the individual and to organizational effectiveness. The third stress symptom, behavioral response, will now be discussed with the results of research that relate behavior to organizational effectiveness.

Behavioral symptoms. Stress research using behavioral symptoms such as absenteeism and turnover indicates that the higher the stress (as measured, for example, by role conflict and ambiguity) the greater the absenteeism and turnover. The results using performance appear to be more complex. Sales (1969) found that individuals increased their performance with increased work load (stress). However, that was only when quantity was the performance measure. When quality (as measured by error rate) was the performance measure, performance declined with increased load. McGrath reported that "If one takes account of task difficulty, then performance increases monotonically with increasing demand and with increasing arousal." Whereas Sales accounted for differences in performance measures but not task characteristics, McGrath accounted for differences in task characteristics but not performance measures. These results suggest that an individual's performance increases as stress increases, but only on simple tasks and where quantity is the measure of performance. This finding, however, is inconsistent with activation theory, which suggests that performance will eventually decline because of increased stimulation (Scott 1966). If the task is difficult, as stress increases, performance (quality or quantity) increases up to a point and then declines. This response may be related to the psychological response already discussed in which the presence of any stressor, even opportunity stress, may have some positive as well as negative effect on organizational effectiveness and on the individual.

Other behavioral measures that have been used include smoking, quitting smoking, and escapist drinking. These symptoms are associated with stressors in such a way that quitting smoking is negatively related to some stressors, and escapist drinking and smoking are positively related to some stressors (Caplan, Cobb, and French 1975). Smoking may not be highly related to employee and organizational effectiveness, but drinking appears to be an ever-increasing problem for effectiveness, as reflected in data on the relationships between drinking and lost time, accidents, productivity, and turnover. Employees who drink as a behavioral response to stress are likely to show increased absenteeism, accidents, and turnover, and their productivity is likely to decrease. The obvious outcome of these behaviors is decreased organizational effectiveness.

In general the relationships among stress and the behavioral symptoms vary greatly depending upon the stress and the symptoms, as shown in Figure 3.6, and it is concluded that:

Opportunity stress is negatively related to some behavioral symptoms such as absenteeism and turnover.

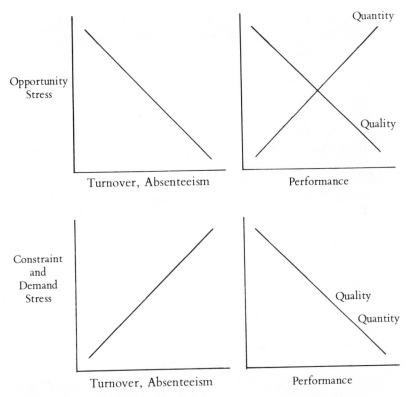

Figure 3.6
The Relationships between the Types of Stress and Selected Behavorial Symptoms.

Under opportunity stress the individual has the potential to gain more of what is desired. The potential, however, can be experienced and realized only when the individual engages in the behavior, that is, stays with the organization in which the opportunity stress is experienced. Thus increasing opportunity stress should be associated with greater organizational effectiveness, but:

> Opportunity stress increases the quantity of work but may cause a decline in the quality.

As was pointed out, this is true for simple tasks which were measured by McGrath. Activation theory, however, indicates that on more difficult tasks, performance quality increases under stress up to a point, and then declines. The key here in increasing organizational effectiveness lies in determining when a positive stressor is simply too much stress! The final part of Figure 3.6 indicates that:

> Constraint and demand stress results in a decrease in both quantity and quality of performance, and an increase in turnover and absenteeism.

We can conclude that demand and constraint stress should be minimized in order to maximize organizational effectiveness.

Although researchers have begun examining the effects of stress on organizational effectiveness, it is evident that much more research is needed to establish not only the relationship between stress and stress symptoms (or responses), but also the interrelationships among the symptoms. It is necessary to understand the interaction of physiological and psychological states with behavior in order to elicit the highest possible levels of both individual and organizational effectiveness. Investigation of these relationships may be effectively carried out by gaining an understanding of the individual qualities associated with these relationships.

STRESS AND EFFECTIVENESS

Several important conclusions can be drawn from the discussions of organizational effectiveness and stress. The following observations made by Sales, although based on a single study of role overload and role underload, reveal something about the relationship between stress and effectiveness:

> The data thus suggests (sic) that extremely high objective work loads may have strong, diverse, and pervasive effects upon individuals exposed to them, and that some of these effects may be observed in biochemical and physiological variables known to be related to health. The data imply that increased work loads may improve system performance on some levels—such as productivity—but that these same increased work loads may also exert deleterious influences both upon system performance (e.g., with respect to errors) and upon individuals involved (e.g., with respect to their self-esteem and their experienced tension and anger). Seen from another perspective the present findings suggest that avoidance of work overload will lead to a variety of beneficial consequences, although these consequences may be accompanied by a reduction in overall productivity. The present data thus allow one to determine some of the gains—and losses—which accompany various levels of work load in ongoing organizations. Presumably, such infor-

mation would allow an organizational administrator knowledgeably to decide whether the gains which might accompany an increase in work load would justify the associated costs.

From Sales, Organizational Behavior and Human Performance (1970).

Sales's observations clearly imply that organizational effectiveness encompasses individual, and perhaps societal, as well as organizational perspectives such as those shown in Table 3.3, and that organizational effectiveness from the individual perspective must be concerned with physiological, psychological, and behavioral symptoms related to individual effectiveness. These perspectives are entirely consistent with the open systems view of organizations and thus support the need for multivariate criteria in determining organizational effectiveness. The observations, however, also illustrate the multiple criteria problem discussed by Steers (1977):

> For example, consider the two criteria of work productivity and employee satisfaction. Productivity can often be increased in the short run by pressuring workers to increase their effort, potentially resulting in decreased job satisfaction. Satisfaction, on the other hand, could possibly be increased by reducing work pressures and strain or by allowing workers more leisure time, potentially having an adverse effect on productivity.

Steers concludes his discussion with an observation of extreme importance for the relationship between stress and effectiveness:

> The important point here is that, if we accept such criteria for effectiveness, organizations by definition cannot be effective; they cannot maximize both dimensions.

Perhaps organizations cannot be effective using stress and effectiveness as criteria when defining effectiveness as maximizing each criterion in a set of criteria. But even if one were to use only productivity as the criterion of effectiveness, it could not be maximized over the long term. This would be true for any criterion for organizational effectiveness over the long term, except perhaps for survival itself. This conclusion might not have been accurate at the turn of the century or for turn-of-the-century thinkers, because the open systems view and the interrelationships of the organization with the environment and with the subsystems of the organization would not have been recognized or valued.

The extensive work in organizational theory and design presents some documentation for showing the importance of the organization-environment relationships. The work in stress demonstrates the interrelationships among subsystems in organizations, especially (though not exclusively) between the maintenance and productive subsystems. The current stress research is far from conclusive, however, on the exact relationship among the symptoms or criteria related to organizational effectiveness. Nonetheless, stress is known to be both positively and negatively related to organizational effectiveness. Although more work needs to be done on the positive relationships, evidence regarding the negative relationships suggests that stress should be managed so that benefits accrue to individual and, therefore, add to organizational effectiveness. We now need to examine the ways in which an organization can help manage stress, but in order to do that, we must first examine the causes of stress.

REFERENCES

Beehr, T., and Newman, J.E. 1978. Job stress, employee health, and organizational effectiveness: A facet analysis, model and literature review, *Personnel Psychology (Winter)*.

Campbell, J.P. 1973. *Research into the nature of organizational effectiveness: An enlarged species?* Unpublished manuscript, University of Minnesota.

Caplan, R.D., Cobb, S., and French, J.R.P. 1975. Relationships of cessation of smoking with job stress, personality and social support. *Journal of Applied Psychology* 60:211-19.

Cass, E.L., and Zimmer, F.G. 1975. *Man and work in society.* New York: Van Nostrand Reinhold.

Cooper, C.L., and Marshall, J. 1976. Occupational sources of stress: A review of the literature relating to coronary heart disease and mental ill health. *Journal of Occupational Psychology* 49:11-28.

Etzioni, A. 1971. Two approaches to organizational analysis: A critique and a suggestion. In *Assessment of organizational effectiveness,* Faisingh Ghorpade, ed. Pacific Palisades, Calif.: Goodyear Publishing Co.

Gibson, J. L., Ivancevich, J. M., and Donnelly, J. H. 1979. *Organizations: behavior, structure, processes.* 3rd ed. Dallas: Business Publications, Inc.

Katz, D., and Kahn, R. L. 1978. *The social psychology of organizations.* New York: John Wiley and Sons.

Levi, L. 1972. *Stress and distress in response to psychosocial stimuli:* Elmsford, N.Y.: Pergamon Press.

Levinson, Harry. 1963. "What Killed Bob Lyons?" *Harvard Business Review* July-August.

Locke, E.A. 1976. The nature and causes of job satisfaction. 1976. In *Handbook of industrial and organizational psychology.* M.D. Dunnette, ed. Chicago: Rand McNally College Publishing Company.

Margolis, G.L., Kroes, W.H., and Quinn, R.P. 1974. Job stress: An unlisted occupational hazard. *Journal of Occupational Medicine* 16:659-61.

McGrath, J.E. 1976. Stress and behavior in organizations. In *Handbook of industrial and organizational psychology,* M.D. Dunnette, ed. Chicago: Rand McNally College Publishing Co.

Porter, L.W., Lawler, E.E., III, and Hackman, J.R. 1975. *Behavior in organizations.* New York: McGraw-Hill Book Company.

Russek, H.I., and Zohman, B.L. 1958. Relative significance of hereditary diet, and occupational stress in CHD of young adults. *American Journal of Medical Science.* 235:266-75.

Salancik, G.R., and Pfeffer, J. 1978. A social information processing approach to job attitudes and task design. *Administrative Science Quarterly* 23:224-53.

Sales, S.M. 1969. Organizational roles as a risk factor in coronary heart disease. *Administrative Science Quarterly* 14:325-36.

Sales, S.M. 1970. Some effects of role overload and role underload. *Organizational Behavior and Human Performance* 5:592-608.

Scott, W.E. 1966. Activation theory and task design. *Organizational Behavior and Human Performance* 1:3-30.

Seashore, S.E. 1974. Job satisfaction as an indicator of the quality of employment. *Social Indicators Research* 1:135-168.

Sells, S.B. 1970. On the nature of stress. In *Social and psychological factors in stress,* J.E. McGrath, ed. New York: Holt, Reinhart & Winston.

Selye, H. 1956. *The stress of life.* New York: McGraw-Hill Book Co.

_____. 1973. The evolution of stress concept. *American Scientist* 61:692-99.

_____. 1975. Confusion and controversy in the stress field. *Journal of Human Stress* 1:37-44.

_____. 1976. *The stress of life.* rev. ed. New York: McGraw-Hill Book Co.

Steers, R.M. 1975. Problems in the measurement of organizational effectiveness. *Administrative Science Quarterly* 20:4.

_____. 1977. *Organizational effectivness: A behavioral view.* Santa Monica, Calif.: Goodyear Publishing Company, Inc.

Chapter 4

Sources of Job Stress

Pat Halverson is a young, single registered nurse who works in the emergency room at General Hospital. Capable and conscientious, Pat is enthusiastic about his work because it also gives him the opportunity to, as he puts it, "do something that matters. You help people when they really need help." Pat's coworkers value his skill and unflappable temperament in the frequently tense atmosphere of the emergency room where the work is, of necessity, often rushed and the workload heavy.

Recently though Pat has decided to change jobs and is thinking of leaving hospital nursing altogether. The problem for Pat is his rotating work schedule. At General Hospital Pat works from 7 a.m. to 3 p.m. for eight days, has two days off, works eight evenings from 3 p.m. to 11 p.m., has two days off, then works eight nights from 11 p.m. to 7 a.m. "I love my work," Pat says, "but it wrecks the rest of my life. I can't take a class at the university. I can't attend all the meetings of the Sailing Club or the University Choir rehearsals. Forget about being in a karate tournament. I can't go anywhere on most weekends."

"The worst of it is that I'm tired so much of the time. For the first three or four days after my schedule rotates I just can't force myself to sleep when I have time to sleep. When I get used to working nights, sleeping days, and having free time in the evenings, I need to be wide awake for a 7 a.m. shift and sleepy at night. So I stumble around at work. I'm afraid that one of these days I'm going to hurt somebody. I don't see how nurses with families survive."

"I'm going to find a job with a better schedule. This is no way to live!"

Jim Gardner, an aggressive and successful attorney, was feeling frightened and angry as he drove home through the heavy rush hour traffic. The doctor's report that afternoon had scared Jim: either he slowed down, stopped smoking, lost weight, drank less, got more exercise and—above all—stopped driving himself so hard, or the chest pain would turn into a heart attack before he was 40.

The traffic light turned green, and Jim's car charged into the intersection, narrowly missing a blue sedan. "Idiot!" Jim exploded at the driver. "How can I slow down? I've got four new cases coming to trial next month. Relax! How can I relax when I'm responsible for those briefs? What am I supposed to do, retire at age 36?"

Soberly Jim recalled the doctor's final words: "Jim, right now you have a choice. But if you keep pushing yourself and neglecting your health, you won't live to see your kids grow up."

"Damn it all!" The light changed. "Hey, you!" Jim yelled at the driver of the car ahead. "Get moving! I don't have time to waste!"

Dr. Olivia Shipla, professor of finance, looked up angrily from the budget report she was trying to read before the committee meeting just twenty minutes away. "Come in!" she said, and Ms. Anne Stevens, the department secretary, edged nervously into the room. "Excuse me, Dr. Shipla," she began. Her voice was interrupted by the phone's jangling. Dr. Shipla grabbed it. "No, Mr. Carlson, I have not graded your capital budgeting paper yet. Check back on Monday." She replaced the phone receiver and raised an eyebrow at the waiting secretary. "What is it?"

"Dr. Shipla, perhaps I had trouble reading the note you left with this book on my desk." Ms. Stevens held a thick, faded green book in her hand. "Did you want fifteen copies of one of the chapters by tomorrow morning?"

"Ms. Stevens, can't you read?" Dr. Shipla inquired sarcastically. I quite clearly asked for fifteen copies of the book. The whole book!"

Anne Steven's jaw jutted forward almost imperceptibly. "I'm sorry, Dr. Shipla, but that's not possible. As you know, the new cost cutting directives, which I *did* read, require that a job of this size have at least five days' notice so that we can send it through the Central Printing Service. It's cheaper. I'm afraid I have to obey those rules."

Ms. Stevens opened the office door, then turned before closing the door deliberately to say, "I will send it out this afternoon, but I'm afraid it will be at least a week."

Back in her own office, Anne Stevens set the book on her desk and took several deep breaths to calm her anger, then sat down to resume

her typing chores. Seeing that Olivia Shipla's "rush job" man
was on the top of her stack of typing, she paused a moment, then ⟩
under the stack and smiled as she began typing a letter.

MAJOR SOURCES OF STRESS

The above examples illustrate some common sources of job stress.
Because stress can have so many destructive consequences for an individual and an organization, the objective of this chapter is to identify the major sources of job stress. Although job stress has been
linked to literally dozens of experiences and conditions (Table 4.1),
this chapter focuses on three major groups of stress sources: characteristics and processes of organizations; particular job demands,
working conditions, and interpersonal relationships; and characteristics and needs of individuals. The chapter concludes with a brief
summary.

Before addressing these topics, a brief word of caution is in
order. The following discussions of the organizational, task, interpersonal, and personal sources of job stress make almost no reference
to nonwork sources of stress. The point has been made elsewhere that
we are living in a crowded, fast-paced society which is changing so
quickly that the rate of change itself has become another source of
stress. Similarly, the contribution to stress of changes in the family,
other interpersonal relationships, the media, and religious and civic
institutions—to cite just a few nonwork sources of stress in our
lives—has been detailed elsewhere and will not be discussed here. It
should be recalled, however, that stress is cumulative and that the
levels of stress experienced at work are added to the stress from these
other parts of our lives.

Organizational Characteristics and Processes

Organizations can be defined as "social units (or human groupings)
deliberately constructed and reconstructed to seek specific goals"
(Etzioni 1964, p. 3). The goals of work organizations include productivity, cost efficiency, employee satisfaction and retention, and
adaptiveness (Hage 1965). According to this view, executives design
and change their organizations over time, so that the organization
rationally invests capital and directs employees' energies and talents
as a means toward organizational goals. For example, executives are

ARACTERISTICS AND PROCESSES

LICIES
...adequate performance evaluations
...rties
...mbiguous or arbitrary policies
Rotating work shifts
Frequent relocation
Idealistic job descriptions before hiring

ORGANIZATIONAL STRUCTURE
Centralization; low participation in decision making
Low opportunity for advancement or growth
Size
Excessive formalization
Excessive specialization and division of labor
Interdependence of organizational units

ORGANIZATIONAL PROCESSES
Poor communication
Poor or inadequate feedback on performance
Ambiguous or conflicting goals
Ineffective delegation
Training programs

JOB DEMANDS AND ROLE CHARACTERISTICS

WORKING CONDITIONS
Crowding
Lack of privacy; poor spatial arrangements
Noise
Excessive heat or cold
Lights: inadequate, glaring, or flickering
Presence of toxic chemicals
Safety hazards
Air pollution, including radiation

INTERPERSONAL RELATIONSHIPS
Inconsiderate or inequitable supervisors
Lack of recognition or acceptance
Lack of trust
Competition
Difficulty in delegating responsibilities
Conflict within and between groups

Table 4.1 Continued
Sources of Job Stress

JOB DEMANDS AND ROLE CHARACTERISTICS

JOB DEMANDS
Repetitive work
Time pressures and deadlines
Low skill requirements
Responsibility for people
Underemployment; overemployment

ROLE CHARACTERISTICS
Role conflict
Role ambiguity
Role underload/overload
Role-status incongruency

INDIVIDUAL CHARACTERISTICS AND EXPECTATIONS

CAREER CONCERNS
Under/overpromotion
Midcareer crises
Obsolescence
Unmet expectations and goals
Job insecurity

INDIVIDUAL CHARACTERISTICS
Type A behavior pattern
Anxiety
Intolerance of ambiguity
Flexibility/rigidity
Introversion/extroversion

---

said to set up the organization's hierarchy of authority so that decisions are made and resources allocated by those persons most qualified to do so. The organization is then a rational link between well-defined ends and limited means.

Several facts, however, cast doubt on this rational model of organizations. First, members of organizations do not always act in pursuit of their organization's goals but may at times use their positions in organizations to pursue primarily their own goals and to satisfy their own needs. Some organizational theorists believe that it is inaccurate to suggest that *organizations* have goals since, in fact, the goals pursued in organizations are those of individuals and groups of individuals. It can be said, however, that the members of any organization are in pursuit of multiple goals, some of which conflict with each other and with the goals of other organizational members. This goal conflict can be a source of stress for organizational members.

Secondly, human beings are not perfectly logical. There are also limits to the amount of information that people can assimilate and use, even with computer assistance; and individuals are limited in their ability to locate and to understand relevant information. Furthermore, much of the information on which organizational decisions are based can be interpreted in more than one way, so its use is necessarily affected by the subjective perspectives of the human beings who utilize the information. Both informational overload and differences in interpreting information contribute to the stress associated with positions in organizations.

Thirdly, and most important for the present discussion, the environments in which organizations operate, and from which they obtain the resources they need to survive and prosper, can be successfully adapted to only after they are first accurately perceived, and this perception is shared among organizational members who need it. For the most part, the environments surrounding contemporary work organizations (depicted in Figure 4.1) are complex and dynamic. Each part of an organization's environment presents the organization with a potential source of uncertainty that forces it to select and use information so that limited organizational resources can be rationally—or satisfactorily—employed.

Thus, our approach to understanding organizations as sources of individual stress takes work organizations to be social systems:

1. Whose members (working individually and in groups) pursue multiple, often conflicting, goals;

2. Where decisions are made on the basis of subjective interpretations of large amounts of equivocal, but relevant information; and

3. Which survive and prosper by perceiving accurately, and adapting successfully to, the environment.

Goal conflict, informational overload and uncertainty, and the complexity and rate of change in the organization's environment are stressful. The set of relatively enduring organizational properties and characteristics through which organizations gather relevant information and share it among organizational members, compensate for human cognitive limitations and subjective biases, and ensure that organizational resources are used in pursuit of common—rather

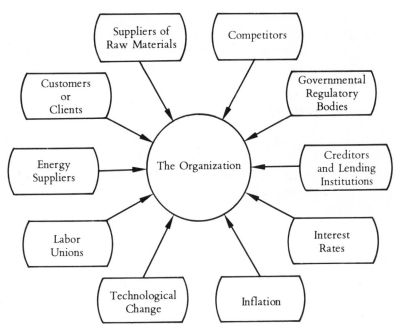

Figure 4.1
Environmental Sources of Uncertainty for Organizations.

than individual or subgroup—goals is termed organizational structure.

From the list of dimensions of organizational structure that affect job stress shown in Table 4.1, we will examine three in particular: "organizational size," "technology," and "organicism/mechanism." Each characteristic is elaborated and its relationship to employee stress is addressed below.

Organizational Size

Organizational size is the scale and scope of an organization's activities and is generally measured by counting the number of employees. Organizations grow and decline over time in response to environmental conditions and management decisions. As size increases, problems of coordination and communication multiply. In a growing organization, new, more specialized positions emerge to give it direction, the number of levels of management increases—with the consequence that lower-level employees and their problems are further removed from the executives who make decisions—and formalized, bureaucratic rules may be adopted as the organization becomes even more complex.

For the individual employee, working in a large department or organization can mean that it is harder to get to know one's co-workers. Close, satisfying work groups may be less likely to form, so that the social support that helps people to cope with stress may be absent. As the size of work groups increase, supervisors take over more of the decisions, which in smaller departments are made by subordinates. The usual consequences for the individual worker include lower job satisfaction, greater absenteeism, increased turn-over, more accidents and labor disputes, and greater stress.

Technology

In addition to the stressful conditions resulting from organizational size, the technology used by an organization to produce the goods or services it provides can also be a significant source of job stress. *Technology* is defined as "the types and patterns of activity, equipment and material, and knowledge or experience used to perform tasks" in organizations (Gillespie and Mileti 1977, p. 8). *Technology, in other words, is the process used to produce goods and services.

Task variability. While technologies can be analyzed in several ways, two descriptions in particular can contribute to our understanding of the links between technology and job stress. One of these, provided by Perrow (1970), views technology primarily as the expertise available to solve the problems posed by production or service goals. He classifies technologies according to two factors: (1) the number of exceptional cases encountered in the work (or the degree to which problems are perceived as either similar or vari-able, and (2) the nature of the problem-solving process employed upon the discovery of exceptional cases (or the degree to which ex-ceptions are understood and the expertise exists to analyze excep-tional cases). Combining the two dimensions produces the matrix displayed in Table 4.2.

In cell 1 the production process has few exceptions, but the expertise does not exist to analyze these exceptions adequately. In-stead, problem solving must rely on intuition, chance, inspiration, guesswork, and other nonstandardized, and often risky, procedures. Such technologies are found in craft industries, for example, that of specialty glass. In cell 3, engineering technology, there are many exceptions, but procedures for dealing with them are well under-stood. Cells 2 and 4 are either nonroutine or routine in both respects.

Table 4.2
Types of Technologies

NUMBER OF EXCEPTIONS (PROBLEM VARIABILITY)	PROBLEM-SOLVING PROCESS	
	EXCEPTIONS WELL UNDERSTOOD	EXCEPTIONS NOT WELL UNDERSTOOD
FEW EXCEPTIONS	Routine (steel mills) 4	Craft industries (specialty glass) 1
MANY EXCEPTIONS	3 Engineering (heavy machinery)	2 Nonroutine (aerospace)

Source: Perrow (1970).

This view of technologies implies that the content of particular jobs, especially the extent to which the job is made routine, depends on the extent to which production processes are well understood and can be standardized. As the discussion of task dimensions later in this chapter will show, jobs which become either overly routine so that they offer little variety, or which are extremely complex and uncertain, are sources of job stress.

Production complexity. Another description of technologies, provided by Woodward (1965), focuses not on task variability and uncertainty, but on the technical complexity of the production process. *Unit and small-batch* production technologies are characterized in Woodward's typology by self-contained units which make products tailered to customer specifications. For example, custom-tailored suits and prototype equipment are produced in unit or small-batch technologies. *Large-batch and mass production* technologies use moving assembly lines to produce large batches of relatively standardized products. Examples of this type of process include automobile assembly lines and high-volume bakeries. The most advanced state of technical complexity—*continuous processing technology*—is used by firms such as oil refineries, which produce a standardized product on a continuous basis.

In her study of 100 British industrial firms, Woodward (1965) found technology to be related to several characteristics of organizational structure and relationships. These findings (see Table 4.3) show that firms with mass production technologies tend to have the type of structure referred to in a later section of this chapter as mechanistic, because it strongly emphasizes formal rules and hierarchical relationships. Low-skilled production workers are supervised in very large groups by first-line supervisors; interpersonal relationships are poor; and considerable conflict occurs between the managers and the advisory staff throughout the organization. Conversely, as will be seen, the firms having small-batch and process technologies tend toward the organic system, which deemphasizes formal rules and promotes interpersonal relationships and employee participation in organizational decisions. The consequences for stress of mechanistic and organic structural systems are discussed later in this chapter.

Table 4.3 suggests that technology affects structure through its effect on techniques for controlling behavior in the organization. Routine, automated, analyzable tasks like those on an assembly line make the individual worker much more easily replaceable and therefore less valued. Consequently, individuals have less power in the organization (although outside organizations such as unions formed by such workers may exert significant power over the work organization). Workers find themselves subject to close control through rules, as well as through the machine-paced workflow. It is important to note that production technology used by firms is to some extent a choice made by top management, rather than a necessary consequence of the existing state of expertise. For example, while most automobiles are produced on assembly lines, some firms continue to build cars by hand and others (e.g., Volvo) have changed from assembly lines to team (small-batch) production methods.

The use of continuous, or rotating, shifts is another example of a technology-linked cause of stress which can be avoided in some cases. The continuity requirements of many technological processes as well as the high cost of capital equipment and demands of world markets have encouraged or forced many industries and public services to operate in three shifts, over twenty-four-hour schedules. For example, utilities, steel, petroleum, and paper products require a continuous production process. Likewise, the services of police officers, fire fighters, medical, and military personnel must be avail-

Table 4.3
Relationships between Technology and Organizational Characteristics

TECHNOLOGY	ORGANIZATIONAL CHARACTERISTICS
UNIT AND SMALL-BATCH	Good interpersonal relationships Personnel: skilled workers and experienced managers Flexibility in job interrelationships Regular use of small groups who participate in decision making Average number of employees reporting to the first-line supervisor: 21-30
LARGE-BATCH AND MASS PRODUCTION	Generally bad interpersonal relationships Personnel: low-skilled production workers and foremen Considerable line-staff conflict Clear delineation of duties through the chain of command Average number of employees reporting to the first-line supervisor: 41-50
PROCESS	Good interpersonal relationships Personnel: skilled maintenance workers and young, technically competent managers Use of top management committees rather than single chief executive officer to make decisons Average number of employees reporting to the first-line supervisor: 11-20

Summarized from Woodward (1965).

able twenty-four hours a day. It is estimated that *shift work,* defined here as afternoon, evening, or rotating work schedules rather than steady daytime work hours, is a way of life for approximately one-fifth of the U.S. workforce (Winget, Hughes, and LaDou 1978).

Individuals on shift schedules live in an abnormal time frame, because they work when most of the world is asleep; yet they must adapt their times of sleep and leisure to those of the community if they wish to maintain a social life. Attempting to cope with the dissatisfactions caused by an afternoon or evening work schedule, management has tended more and more to favor rotational shift working, in which an individual works a certain part of the time on a normal day shift, part of the time on an evening shift, and part of the time on a night shift. But, as illustrated in nurse Halverson's story at the beginning of this chapter, this type of shift scheduling carries with it physiological and social stresses for the individual that can be debilitating. Table 4.4 summarizes the stress symptoms associated with shift work.

The physiological problems that occur, particularly with rotational shifts, arise because the human body functions approximately according to a twenty-four hour pattern called "circadian rhythms" (Haus 1976). Body temperature, bladder activity, and the endocrine, cardiovascular, respiratory, and autonomic nervous systems all exhibit these rhythmic patterns. Circadian rhythms are synchronized with each other and with the individual's environment by periodic factors in the environment called *zeitgebers* (from German words meaning "time givers"). The alternation of light and dark

Table 4.4
Stress Symptoms Associated with Shift Work

PHYSIOLOGICAL SYMPTOMS
Inability to obtain enough sleep
Fatigue
Disturbances in appetite, digestion, and elimination
Upper gastrointestinal disorders
Respiratory problems

DISTURBANCES IN FAMILY AND INTERPERSONAL RELATIONSHIPS
Parenting role difficulties
Higher divorce rate
Higher incidence of sexual problems
Unfavorable family reactions
Increase in solitary leisure activities
Lower participation in social, religious, and civic organizations
Fewer contacts with friends

WORK PRODUCTIVITY
More mistakes
More accidents
Lower productivity

PSYCHOLOGICAL REACTIONS
Impaired mental health
Fewer needs fulfilled at work
Lower commitment to the organization

---

and, to a lesser extent, changes in environmental temperature are important zeitgebers for human beings. When the phase of a zeitgeber is shifted, the circadian rhythms either shift with the zeitgebers or become unsynchronized both with the external environment and with each other. An example of this is when the light–dark cycle is shifted by rotational work schedules. The reason rotational shifts are so stressful for the individual, even apart from the havoc this may play with the person's life off the job, is that the zeitgebers are shifted so frequently that the circadian rhythms never have an adequate opportunity to become synchronized again on the new schedule.

Organizational Structure

An organization's *structure* is defined as the arrangement of, and systematic relationships of, divisions and positions within the organization. Thus, dimensions of structure describe the social system within which organizational employees interact. Each of the dimensions of structure controls the flow of work and communication and the attempts at coping with the sources of irrationality identified earlier in this chapter; and each dimension has an effect on employee attitudes and behaviors, including stress. In a classic study of innovation in the electronics industry, Burns and Stalker (1966) coined the terms "organismic" and "mechanistic" to describe the structures of two opposite types of work organizations.

Mechanistic organizations. This type of organization is adapted to relatively certain and stable environments, where tasks are broken down into isolated specialties. The technical methods, duties, and authority attached to each position are precisely defined, often in writing. Interactions are impersonal and communication follows hierarchical lines of authority. The management system is usually visualized as the familiar bureaucratic organizational chart and operates as a single, orderly control system. Information flows upward to a final authority, and decisions and instructions flow downward.

Organismic systems. These systems, in contrast, are adapted to uncertain, unstable environments where unfamiliar problems which cannot be broken down and assigned to specialized roles continually arise. In this system, jobs lose much of their precise, formal definition; instead, each individual participates in common tasks to solve common problems. Interactions run horizontally across departments, as often as vertically along lines of formal authority. Individuals do their jobs knowing the overall situation of the company; the boss at the top has no more information than any subordinate employee.

The experience of working in these organizations is quite different for lower-level employees, as well as for professional and managerial workers. Mechanistic systems tell an employee to what and how to pay attention and also make clear what is not expected. Characteristic sources of stress in mechanistic systems are likely to be overly-routine jobs or rigid rules. In an organismic system, individuals cannot exercise just their specialized competence but must be knowledgeable about, and committed to, the success of the company's undertakings as a whole. The complexity of this system is probably its most characteristic source of work stress.

One structural difference between organismic and mechanistic systems relative to job stress is the extent to which decision making is centralized. *Centralization* of decision making and authority means that the power of making decisions is limited to a small proportion of employees, specifically those at the highest levels of the organization. Centralization is efficient when an organizational environment is stable and the organization is small. In this case relatively few people are needed to gather information and to coordinate the efforts of employees. Centralized organizations respond to changes slowly since all decisions must be made by the same few people. Therefore, when the organization's environment is more complicated and dynamic and the uncertainty is high, organizations tend to decentralize. That is, decision-making authority is given to middle- and lower-level managers, because they are closer to necessary information than top managers. The separate, self-contained units of decentralized organizations, however, usually present top management with coordination problems. A lower-level manager may be extremely capable of reacting to local changes but may be unaware of the situations created in other departments by those decisions.

While decentralization has been linked to role conflict and role ambiguity (two types of job stress discussed later in this chapter), centralized organizations, or departments, can be even more stressful for the lower-level employees who are left out of the decision making. This lack of participation in decision making has been linked to job stress. For example, among a national sample of over 1400 U.S. workers, lack of participation in decision making was the most significant and consistent predictor of job stress and of a series of concomitant health risk factors (Cooper and Marshall 1978). Another major study among Canadian employees also concluded that the employees' lack of power in organizations is a significant cause of job stress (Zaleznik, Ket de Vries, and Howard 1977).

In general, employees at lower levels excluded from decision making have no legitimate (that is, role-prescribed) power in the organization. Lack of power in influencing the outcomes experienced at work causes many employees to feel alienated, powerless, meaningless, and isolated both from themselves and from their work and organizations. These employees "turn off" to their low-power positions in the organization, and at the same time they cut themselves off from other people, their work, and their own feelings. While one active response to jobs with low power is to unionize, individuals often "fight back" against their lack of legitimate power in ways that can provoke stress for themselves, their coworkers, and their supervisors. Employees at lower levels can, by capitalizing on the resources they do have, come to exert considerable influence on the work or outcomes for other persons. Sources of power for lower-level employees include:

1. Personal attractiveness

2. Control of access to information, or to persons

3. Expertise, especially when there would be difficulty replacing the person in question

4. Strict adherence to highly formalized rules.

Like Anne Stevens, the secretary described at the beginning of this chapter, employees who have little formal power may affect the work and increase the stress of other organizational members.

In summary, three aspects of organizational structure have been discussed: size, technology, and organicism/mechanism. Each of these organizational dimensions was linked to the occurence of job stress. Thus, it has been demonstrated that work organizations *per se* and their characteristics can unavoidably present sources of stress to the employee. It is important to note that the structural dimensions reviewed are only a few examples of those aspects of work organizations that are stress inducing.

THE JOB AS A SOURCE OF WORK STRESS

Recent research on stress has determined that some jobs are much more stressful than others for the individuals who hold them. For example, physicians, welfare workers, air traffic controllers, psychiatrists, dentists, health technicians, waiters and waitresses, nurses, paramedics, and sea pilots have particularly stressful jobs. Instead of focusing on the antecedents of stress inherent in these or other specific jobs, we will examine three general sources of job stress. These are the quality of role relationships, job demands, and working conditions.

Role-related Stress

Within an organizational context, the term *role* refers to the set of expectations applied to the incumbent of a particular organizational position by the individual and by others, both within and beyond the organization's boundaries. Figure 4.2 depicts the individual as the

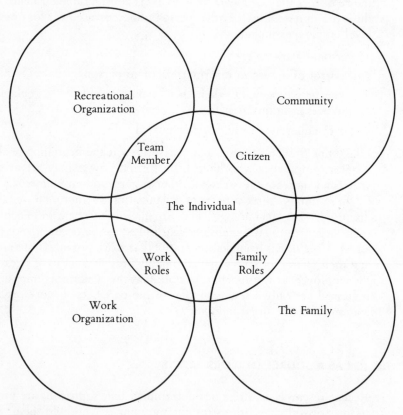

Figure 4.2
The Individual as the Incumbent of Roles in Several Social Systems.

enactor of roles in several social systems, including the work organization. Each role typically includes some freedom in role performance, so that different individuals can fill the same role without experiencing stress.

Each role carries with it expectations about the behaviors, attitudes, sometimes even the appearance of the individual role incumbent. Frequently, individuals are confronted with roles in which they are expected to behave in ways which conflict with their value systems, or to play two or more roles that conflict with each other. In addition, one or more of the roles that individuals occupy may not be clearly defined in terms of the behaviors or performance levels required. The first situation is known as "role conflict" and the latter as "role ambiguity"; both are significant sources of job stress. Table 4.5 lists typical items used to gauge role conflict and role ambiguity. *Role conflict* is defined as the incongruity of expectations associated with a role. Several types of role conflict have been identified:

1. Intrasender role conflict: incompatible expectations from a single role sender. For example, a supervisor may want a report carefully prepared, while at the same time cutting in half the time allotted to prepare it.

2. Intersender role conflict: expectations from one role sender that are incompatible with those from another role sender. Pressure from customers to speed up orders while suppliers are unable to deliver parts on time is an example of intersender role conflict.

Table 4.5
Sample Items Used to Gauge Role Conflict and Role Ambiguity

ROLE CONFLICT ITEMS
I receive incompatible requests from two or more people.
I work on unnecessary things.
I work with two or more groups who operate quite differently.
I have to buck a rule or policy in order to carry out an assignment.

ROLE AMBIGUITY ITEMS
I know that I have divided my time properly.
I know exactly what is expected of me.
I feel certain about how much authority I have on this job.
I have clear, planned goals and objectives for my job.

From the fourteen-question scale developed by Rizzo, House, and Lirtzman (1970). See Schuler, Aldag, and Brief (1977) for further data in support of the reliability and validity of this instrument.

3. Person-role conflict: incompatibility between the expectations held by the role incumbent and the expectations otherwise associated with his or her position. For example, job duties may conflict with an individual's personal preference, as for a supervisor who must fire several good workers because of a budget cutback.

4. Interrole conflict: role pressures arising from one position are incompatible with the role demands stemming from a different position. Conflicts between work and family demands on one's time are examples of this type of role conflict.

5. Role overload: expecting the role incumbent to engage in several role behaviors, all of which may be mutually compatible in the abstract, but which are expected within too short a realistic time period.

6. Role underload: expecting the role incumbent to engage in a limited variety or quantity of behaviors. Repetitive jobs of limited scope, such as an assembly-line job, evidence role underload.

This discussion focuses on two sources of role conflict: the occupancy of a boundary-spanning role, and the supervisory responsibility for other persons.

Boundary-spanning roles (BSRs), as the name implies, are organizational roles that require employees to transfer information back and forth between the organization and some part of the organization's environment. Examples of these roles are sales representatives, purchasing agents, and research and development scientists. The dependence of organizations on gathering and processing information from the environment has been previously discussed. Information comes into an organization through boundary roles. BSR occupants represent the organization and attempt to influence, as well as understand, the environment.

Boundary-spanning roles are the best documented antecedents of role conflict. As Adams (1976) explains, the occupant of such a position is subject to behavioral expectations which arise from role senders located in separate social systems, the employing organization and some organization in the environment. For example, conflict may arise over scarce resources or over divergent norms between organizations. The sheer diversity of role senders adds to the sources of conflicting expectations, so that persons in boundary-spanning roles are subjected to constant role conflict.

Another source of role conflict repeatedly identified in organizational investigations is *supervisory responsibility for other persons.* Responsibility for persons frequently means spending more time interacting with others, attending meetings, working independently rather than with peers, and in trying to meet deadlines and schedules. People whose role include these demands display significantly higher levels of stress.

Role ambiguity is the degree to which clear information is lacking regarding the expectations associated with a role, methods for fulfilling known role expectations, or the consequences of role performance. In other words, role ambiguity is the discrepancy between the amount of information people have and the amount they need in order to perform their roles adequately. Role ambiguity is stressful because it prevents individuals from completing important tasks and contributes to a sense of insecurity and uncertainty. A common example is the lack of adequate information about the bases for merit pay raises.

Possible causes of role ambiguity documented by research in organizations include a significant negative relationship between role ambiguity and:

1. Degree of work formalization
2. Amount of feedback
3. Closeness of supervision
4. Allowed participation in goal-setting
5. Tenure in the organization
6. The task-structuring behavior of the supervisor.

Kerr (1977) argues that hierarchical leadership in organizations is sometimes not needed because certain individual, task, and organizational characteristics act as substitutes for leadership. These hypothesized substitutes for leadership are presented in Table 4.6. Role ambiguity results from inadequate information; supervisors are but one source of that information. Since the role incumbent has several potential and possibly redundant sources of information, the "substitutes for leadership" hypothesis implies that role ambiguity will occur when leaders do not provide task-relevant information and, in addition, no other substitutes for task-focused leadership are present in the role incumbent's coworkers or self, the task, or the organization. Table 4.6 obviously offers a list of potential cures for role ambiguity.

To summarize, two types of role-related stress, and antecedents of each, have been discussed. Role conflict, which has been linked to boundary-spanning roles and to responsibility for persons, occurs when the job incumbent is subjected to conflicting expectations.

Table 4.6
Potential Substitutes for Hierarchical Leadership

SUBORDINATE	TASK	ORGANIZATION
Ability	Repetitiveness and unambiguity	Formalization
Experience		Inflexibility
Training	Methodological invariance	Highly-specified active advisory and staff functions
Knowledge	Intrinsic satisfaction	Closely knit cohesive work groups
"Professional" orientation	Task with feedback concerning accomplishment	
Need for independence		Rewards not within the leader's control
Indifference toward organizational rewards		Spatial distance between leader and subordinates

Reprinted from Kerr (1977).

Role ambiguity, the lack of information necessary to perform one's job, can occur when information is not provided by the leader, work group members, formal organizational procedures, the task, or the training of the jobholder. Both types of role stress result in tension, dissatisfaction, and other dysfunctional outcomes.

Job Demands

Jobs that demand either too much or too little of employees cause stress. In an earlier section of this chapter it was shown that production technologies differ by the extent to which they are routine or machine-paced. It was also shown that the inability to participate in decisions affecting one's own work because of centralization is a significant source of job stress. Thus, the stress associated with low decision latitude can result from the production technology or the degree of centralization, or both. Current research in organizations indicates that the worst possible job producing the highest levels of stress is one in which low decision latitude is combined with great amounts of pressure and routine, unchallenging tasks. For example, in a recent study of job characteristics and mental strain among U.S. and Swedish working men, Karasek (1979) found that exhaustion and depression were highest among workers whose jobs involved both low authority to make decisions and high job pressures.

Jobs that are repetitive, lacking in challenge, and require only low levels of skill are boring to many people. In addition, such work may be experienced as meaningless or insignificant. For those individuals who value challenge or personal growth on the job, repetitive, low-skilled tasks may produce alienation and job stress.

Job stress can also result, as previously discussed, from supervisory responsibility for other people. Job stress can also be caused by complexity and by qualitative or quantitative overload, where the individual is required to perform tasks which are too demanding or too numerous to complete in the available time. In this type of job individuals are pushed past the limits of their physical, intellectual, or emotional abilities.

Recent work on the properties of motivating jobs, which apart from pay and other extrinsic rewards sustain the effort of jobholders, provides some strategies that organizations can use to redesign "underdemanding" stressful jobs. These strategies are reviewed in Chapter 5. We have hardly begun to study ways to reduce the stresses of "overdemanding" jobs, but the consequences of stress from these (or any) jobs can be reduced by following the personal coping strategies outlined in Chapter 6.

Working Conditions

Working conditions refer to the dimensions of the physical surroundings in which an individual works. Potentially stressful workplace conditions include:

1. Air pollution, such as that resulting from radiation, or the presence of toxic chemicals in the workplace
2. Excessive heat or cold
3. Noise
4. Uncomfortable spatial arrangements
5. Crowding
6. Glaring, flickering, or inadequate lighting
7. Other safety hazards.

Noise, a pervasive phenomenon in many work organizations, has been selected as a representative example for this discussion.

Noise is defined here, simply, as unwanted sound. Figure 4.3 represents the consequences of noise. Noise loud enough to cause deafness is approximately as loud as the sounds of a busy street. Individuals who work without protection close to mechanical hammers, jet planes, and pounding machinery eventually lose their hearing, either totally or in part. As shown in Figure 4.3, some immediate results of noise are lower performance and accidents, since noise interferes with speech and thinking, masks auditory feedback, and distracts individuals from the task at hand. Finally, the increased arousal produced by noice results in tension.

WORK STRESS AND INDIVIDUAL CHARACTERISTICS

In addition to the sources of job stress that surround the employees at work, the needs, expectations, and characteristics of individuals can be sources of stress. Many of these factors are considered in Chapter 6, since they also influence the extent to which people are able to cope with stress. In this chapter, the discussion will focus primarily on the Type A behavior pattern, since extensive research indicates that it is a significant cause of job stress.

First, however, it should be noted that an endless array of factors can cause stress. The idea that stress results from a lack of fit between the person and the job is one finding of the considerable research on role conflict, and is supported by a large body of work done by vocational counselors. For example, the strength of an individual's need for autonomy, a need to be self-directing and independent, and for occupational achievement have been linked to stress when the job or the organization provides little latitude for self-determination.

It was previously noted that incompatible expectations associated with a position can be a source of stress. A special and important case of stress caused by incompatible expectations occurs when the employee enters an organization with an unrealistic, perhaps idealistic, idea of the job he or she will hold. For example, in a recent investigation of role conflict and role ambiguity among a sample of registered nurses, it was found that the degree of professional training a nurse had received prior to employment in the hospital was significantly positively related to both role conflict and role ambiguity. Furthermore, tenure on the job did not reduce either type of role

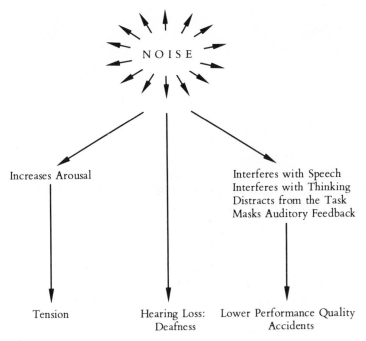

Figure 4.3
Some Stress-Provoking Consequences of Noise.

stress (Brief et al. 1979). Thus, it appears that if the expectations about the job formed before employment (in this case the expectation that hospital nursing would include a variety of professional role demands) are unmet, the resulting stress can last throughout one's career.

Type A Behavior Pattern

In Chapter 2, the Type A behavior pattern was briefly discussed as one characteristic that increases the importance of the work domain in relation to other sources of life satisfaction. Some harmful consequences of the Type A behavior pattern were also noted. In fact, an impressive body of scientific evidence suggests that the Type A pattern is a significant predictor of coronary heart disease and a major contributor to job stress.

The Type A pattern is a style of living that consists of both a pattern of actions and supporting emotions. The lifestyle of the Type A individual, illustrated by the story of Jim Gardner at the beginning of this chapter, is characterized by extreme competitiveness and aggressive, constant striving for achievement. These traits are accompanied by a sense of time-urgency, impatience and irritation, hyperalertness, perfectionism, and feelings of being under the challenge of responsibility. In contrast to the Type A individual is the Type B individual, who has a significantly lower risk of coronary heart disease and who is generally free of the stressful Type A behavior pattern. A scale to measure your Type A or Type B pattern is shown in Table 4.7.

While most research to date on the Type A individual has been concerned with establishing the links between Type A behavior and coronary heart disease, we do know something about the demographic characteristics of Type A individuals, their typical reactions, and the environmental variables to which they react. Taken together, this information provides some insight into the meaning of the stressful Type A behavior pattern.

The Type A individual is more likely to be male than female, although significant numbers of women, particularly women employed outside the home after age 30, are classified as Type A. Slightly more than 50 percent of random samples of urban American men show signs of the Type A behavior pattern. The proportion of Type As among male managers is higher, from 61–76 percent. The highest incidence of Type A behavior is found among employed men and women between the ages of 26–35. Small but statistically significant positive relationships have been isolated among individuals with the Type A pattern and education, occupational status, and income for men, and Type A and socioeconomic status for men and women. Type A individuals are more likely to have been raised in middle-class than in working-class homes. Type A men are more likely to have had Type A than Type B fathers.

Compared with Type B individuals, Type As are significantly more likely to suppress their feelings of fatigue and to ignore physical symptoms in order to persist at a task, to prefer to work alone, and to respond with hostility and increased heart rate and blood pressure to a frustrating or pressing task, or to an increase in work load. Type As are more likely than Type Bs to underestimate the length of a time interval, to get little or no exercise, to work long hours, and to travel as part of their job. Type As are also more likely than Type Bs to feel that their job is prestigious but are likely to be less satisfied with their work. Type As are also more likely to worry about their work quality and responsibilities. The job conditions most closely linked to the

Table 4.7
Type A: Behavior Quiz

To find out which type you are, circle the number on the scale below that best characterizes your behavior for each trait.

1. Casual about   Never late
   appointments   1 2 3 4 5 6 7 8

2. Not competitive   Very competitive
                          1 2 3 4 5 6 7 8

3. Never feel rushed   Always rushed
   even under pressure   1 2 3 4 5 6 7 8   .

4. Take things one   Try to do many
   at a time   1 2 3 4 5 6 7 8   things at once,
                                               think about what
                                               I am going to
                                               do next.

5. Slow doing things   Fast (eating,
                          1 2 3 4 5 6 7 8   walking, etc.)

6. Express feelings   "Sit" on
                          1 2 3 4 5 6 7 8   feelings

7. Many interests   Few interests
                          1 2 3 4 5 6 7 8   outside work

Total your score: _____ Multiply it by 3: _____

The interpretation is as follows:

Number of points	*Type of Personality*
Less than 90	B
90 to 99	B+
100 to 105	A-
106 to 119	A
120 or more	A+

Adapted from Bortner (1966).

Type A pattern are supervisory responsibility for persons, competition, heavy work loads and conflicting demands.

Figure 4.4 presents a summary of the relationships identified. A major unanswered question about the Type A behavior pattern concerns causal relationships among the variables associated with Type A. Type A individuals may possess personality traits (e.g., ambition,

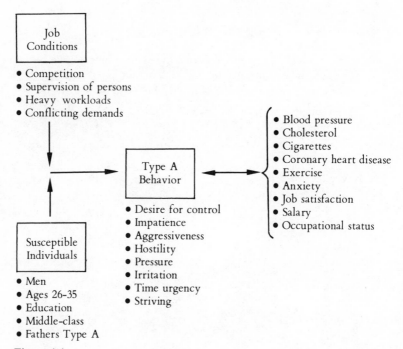

Figure 4.4
Relationships of Type A Behavior to Other Variables. (Adapted from Howard, Cunningham, and Rechnitzer 1977)

impatience, aggressiveness) which motivate self-selection into jobs with high potential rewards and high levels of stress, and they may then react to the stressful job conditions with the Type A physiological symptoms. On the other hand, the Type A individual may be more sensitive than Type B persons to the stressful conditions identified in Figure 4.4, and may attempt to cope with this stress by living the Type A lifestyle, which results eventually in coronary heart disease.

AN OVERVIEW

First, it was shown that three groups of organizational characteristics, which are partly a consequence of perceptions of the environment, can be a source of job stress. Increased organizational size results in a more complicated social system with coordination problems and unsatisfying work relationships which lead to stress. The contribution of technology to stress was outlined, and shift work was identified as a cause of physiological stress and disrupted social relationships. Lack of participation in decision making, caused by a mechanistic, centralized structure, results in stress and can cause alienation or the use of dysfunctional power tactics by employees who have little legitimate power in organizations.

Secondly, role-related stress, job demands, and working conditions were discussed as sources of job stress. Specifically, it was shown that role conflict is associated with boundary-spanning roles and supervision of other persons. Potential causes of role ambiguity were identified as substitutes for leadership and the information leaders can provide. Stressful job demands were briefly characterized as those that give the employee either little decision latitude—but entail high pressure and routine, nonchallenging tasks—or that give the employee more complexity, pressure, and other demands than the person can handle. Stressful working conditions were illustrated by reviewing the consequences of excessive noise.

Thirdly, it was noted that individual characteristics can contribute to job stress, and the potential contributions of employee needs and expectations to job stress were outlined. Finally, the Type A behavior pattern as a source of job stress was described.

The intent of this chapter was not to be exhaustive. Rather, we aimed to demonstrate linkages between work and stress through examples. As you move through the remainder of the book, you will want to refer to Table 4.1 as a quick reference for a more comprehensive list of job stressors.

REFERENCES

Adams, J.S. 1976. The structure and dynamics of behavior in organizational boundary roles. In *Handbook of industrial and organizational psychology*, M. D. Dunnette, ed., pp. 1175-99. Chicago: Rand-McNally,

Bortner, R.W. 1966. A short rating scale as a potential measure of Pattern A behavior. *Journal of Chronic Diseases* 22:87-91.

Brief, A.P., Aldag, R.J., Van Sell, M., and Melone, N. 1979. Anticipatory socialization and role stress among registered nurses. *Journal of Health and Social Behavior* 20:161-66.

Burns, T., and Stalker, G.M. 1966. *The management of innovation*. London: Tavistock Publications.

Cooper, C.L., and Marshall, J. 1978. Sources of managerial and white collar stress. In *Stress at work,* C.L. Cooper, and R. Payne, eds., pp. 99-136. Chichester: John Wiley and Sons, Ltd.

Etzioni, A. 1964. *Modern organizations.* Englewood Cliffs, N.J.: Prentice-Hall.

Gillespie, D.F., and Mileti, D.S. 1977. Technology and the study of organizations: An overview and appraisal. *Academy of Management Review* 2:7-16.

Hage, J. 1965. An axiomatic theory of organizations. *Administrative Science Quarterly* 10:289-320.

Haus, Erhand. 1976. Pharmacological and toxicological correlates of circadian synchronization and desynchronization. In *Shift work and health,* R.G. Rentos, and R.D. Shepard, eds., pp. 43-67. Washington, D.C.: HEW Publication No. (NIOSH) 76-203.

Howard, J.H., Cunningham, D.A., and Rechnitzer, P.A. 1977. Work patterns associated with Type A behavior: A managerial population . *Human Relations* 30:825-36.

Karasek, R.A. 1979. Job demands, job decision latitude, and mental strain: Implications for job redesign. *Administrative Science Quarterly* 24:285-308.

Kerr, S. Substitutes for leadership: Some implications for organizational design. In *Organizational design: Theoretical perspectives and empirical findings,* E.H. Burack and A.R. Reghandhi, eds., pp. 135-146. Kent, Ohio: The Kent State University Press, 1977.

Perrow, C. 1970. *Organizational analysis: A sociological view.* Belmont, Calif.: Wadsworth.

Rizzo, J.R., House, R.J., and Lirtzman, S.I. 1970. Role conflict and ambiguity in complex organizations. *Administrative Science Quarterly* 15:150-63.

Schuler, R.S., Aldag, R.J., and Brief, A.P. 1977. Role conflict and ambiguity: A scale analysis. *Organization Behavior and Human Performance* 20:111-29.

Winget, C.M., Hughes, L., and LaDou, J. 1978. Physiological effects of rotational work shifting: A review. *Journal of Occupational Medicine* 20:204-10.

Woodward, J. 1965. *Industrial organization: Theory and practice.* London: Oxford University Press.

Zaleznik, A., Ket de Vries, M.F.R., and Howard, J. 1977. Stress reactions in organizations: Syndromes, causes and consequences. *Behavioral Science* 22:151-62.

Chapter 5

Personal Mechanisms
for Coping with Job Stress

Bob is a wonder to his colleagues. He and several other engineers have been assigned to a project team of a large consulting firm. The team is working on some design problems encountered in the construction of a nuclear power plant. The construction of the plant is 30 months behind schedule, and the project team has been receiving almost daily pressure from the client and the consulting firm's vice-president of operations to speed things up. On the other side, the Nuclear Regulatory Commission and the project team's manager have been urging caution, that the team move slowly and carefully to be sure the design problem is resolved precisely. The team has been putting in ten-hour days including working on the weekends. Each of the team members except Bob has been showing signs of the strain; but Bob just keeps smiling and plugging along. He just seems to have an amazing tolerance for living with conflicting demands and coping with the pressure. In fact, Bob's pleasant and supportive personality has been the key factor in keeping the team together.

Jane is the first female surgeon on the staff of Memorial Hospital. Lately, her case mix has been particularly dismal. This morning, for example, she had to tell the parents of a child born with a severe heart defect that the child did not survive an attempt at corrective surgery. What makes the situation worse for Jane is that she is new to town and has no friends, and she hasn't been receiving any social support from the other doctors on the staff. In fact, she is treated like an outcast. Jane knew the staff wasn't particularly excited about working with a woman, but she didn't think things would be as bad as they are. Nevertheless, Jane is coping. Every day after work she makes a point of relaxing. She goes home, changes into comfortable clothing, dims the light in her living room, and lies down on the couch. She then systematically tenses and relaxes virtually every muscle in her body. She learned this progressive relaxation technique during medical school while on rotation in psychiatry. Over the years she has found it really helps. Jane completes her evening by jogging three miles. She hits her bed tired but relaxed— ready for a good night's sleep and even eager to face tomorrow's challenges.

Dr. Stuart Klein is the Dean of the College of Education at a major midwestern university. He's good at what he does and feels comfortable with his performance as dean during the last three years. About six months ago, however, Betty Summers was appointed the new president of the university. Dr. Summers is known as a hard-charging, aggressive, action-oriented administrator. During the first three months of Dr. Summer's appointment, she and Dr. Klein used to meet or talk over the telephone at least two or three times a week, but the dean became progressively frustrated by these contacts. Yes, indeed, the president wanted results; however, she never clearly communicated what results she wanted from Dr. Klein or where he was to get the resources necessary to implement her ambiguous plans. Worse yet, when he finally thought he understood what the president wanted, she would change her mind completely or say something in conflict with what she had said the previous week. The dean decided the only way to effectively deal with the new president was to avoid her. Thus, he delayed as long as possible in returning her phone calls and even arranged to be out of town when he was scheduled to meet with her. The president didn't seem to notice his evasive tactics, and Dr. Klein was much happier with the arrangement.

The above examples illustrate how people respond to and cope with job stress, which is the focal point of this chapter. Earlier, we examined the personal and organizational consequences of job stress, noting that job stress can be costly and that certain clues help us to identify particular sources of stress in work organizations.

If it is assumed that job stress can be a detriment to the well-being of the individual and to the health and vitality of the organization, it is important to discuss effective, as well as ineffectual, ways of responding to stress on the individual level. It has already been noted that two people can be exposed to the same stressful situation, yet actually experience quite different levels of discomfort. To quote Shakespeare, "There is nothing either good or bad,/But thinking makes it so." Thus, the first topic to be addressed concerns individual differences in the response to stressful conditions at work.

Secondly, it will be demonstrated that social support may be essential to effective coping methods. The third topic to be covered in the chapter focuses on how people cope with the job stress they experience and which strategies appear to be most individually productive. Finally, the chapter concludes with a brief summary.

Before entering the text of the chapter, two points should be noted. First, the following discussions do not consider generally what organizations can do as social entities to combat undue levels of job stress experienced by their members, since Chapter 6 focuses on managerial and organizational strategies for coping with employee stress. This chapter centers on individual approaches that ultimately may or may not have a positive impact on the effectiveness of an organization. Second, although numerous authors have popularized an array of strategies for coping with stress, this chapter avoids the so-called "pop psych" approaches because many of them have not been analyzed closely enough or objectively enough. The strategies to be offered have been drawn mainly from the clinical, counseling, and social psychological areas where evaluative information is more readily available.

INDIVIDUAL DIFFERENCES IN RESPONDING TO JOB STRESS

Chapter 2, "Job Stress and the Quality of Life," noted that a number of unspecified individual characteristics help to determine a person's psychological responses to stress at work. Principal among those individual characteristics are various personality traits. *Personality* is the dynamic organization within the individual of those psychophysical systems that determine a person's unique adjustments to the environment (Warren and Carmichael 1930). This definition of personality implies that several aspects need to be taken into account (Allport 1937).

1. Dynamic organization. The "normal" personality is thought to be in an organized, constant state of change and evolution. Disorganization, therefore, implies "abnormality."

2. Psychophysical systems. The traits (that is, habits, attitudes, and sentiments) which make up an individual's personality are neither exclusively mental nor exclusively neural, but are involved with the operation of both body and mind fused into a personal entity.

3. Determination factor. Personality is something and does something. It controls specific acts of the individual.

4. Uniqueness. Every adjustment of every person is unique, in time and place, and in quality.

5. Adjustments to the environment. Personality is a mode of survival. Adjustments entail a great amount of spontaneous, creative behavior toward the environment.

Of particular interest are the personality traits that determine an individual's unique adjustment (response) to the stresses in the work environment. Research has identified a number of personality traits that are potentially relevant to this environment, such as authoritarianism, rigidity, masculinity, femininity, extroversion, supportiveness, spontaneity, emotionality, tolerance for ambiguity, locus of control, neurotic anxiety, and achievement orientation. This chapter highlights only a few of the traits that have been explored.

Extroversion/Introversion. Because this trait orients the individual toward the external, objective world, extroverts are said to be in touch with their environment, outgoing, active, and zestful. Conversely, *introversion* orients the person toward the inner, subjective world, and introverts are self-oriented, introspective, serious, quiet, constrained, inhibited, solitary, shy, and retiring. In general, introverts are more sensitive to their environments and respond more negatively to strong stimulation. For example, introverts have lower pain thresholds than extroverts (Wilson 1976). Given these findings, it would be expected that introverts would respond more negatively to job stress than extroverts, as was noted by Kahn et al. (1964), whose intensive study of fifty-three individuals in six industrial locations found that introverts experiencing levels of role conflict similar to those of extroverts reported more job-related tension. Apparently, the introvert under job stress reduces his or her contacts with others and is seen by others as unsociable and overly independent. These circumstances thus contribute to the high levels of tension the introverted person experiences. Kahn's et al. findings are consistent with the general literature concerning the behavior of introverts; however, the study stands as the singular investigation of the role of extroversion/introversion in responding to job stress.

Flexibility/rigidity. Another cluster of personality traits investigated by Kahn et al. (1964) is formed by flexibility or its converse, rigidity. Some questionnaire items reflective of rigidity are presented in Table 5.1. In the literature on personality this cluster of traits is commonly labeled authoritarianism or dogmatism.[1]

Table 5.1
Example Items Used to Measure the Rigid Personality Type

I dislike to change my plans in the midst of an undertaking.
I do not enjoy having to adapt myself to new and unusual situations.
I try to follow a program of life based on duty.
I think it is usually wise to do things in a conventional way.
I always put on and take off my clothes in the same order.[a]

---

[a]"True" responses are reflective of the rigid person.

Source: Drawn from Wesley (1953).

Authoritarianism. An authoritarian person rigidly adheres to conventional middle-class values and has an exaggerated concern with those values, is submissive toward the moral authorities of their in-groups, condemns and rejects persons who violate conventional values, is preoccupied with power and status considerations, tends to identify with powerful figures, and is generally hostile towards members of out-groups.

Dogmatism. Closed-minded, dogmatic persons see themselves as alone, isolated, and helpless in the face of environments that are hostile and dangerous; thus, they tend to appraise many situations as threatening.

The above definitions might at first lead us to expect that the rigid, authoritarian, and dogmatic personality type would more readily succumb to job stress. But Kahn et al. (1964) found the flexible individual to be in a more precarious position. Rigid persons were shown to be wholeheartedly dedicated to the responsibilities assigned to them by official agents of the organization and they preferred such responsibilities to be well defined, mutually compatible, and relatively stable. Rigid persons, therefore, tended to gravitate toward more stress-free working conditions. On the other hand, flexible persons in the process of seeking recognition and appreciation from others were shown not to say "no" to requests from others and thus experienced higher levels of role conflict. Further, flexible persons generally responded more negatively (that is, with higher levels of anxiety) to the job stresses that they did experience, possibly

[1]Kahn et al. (1964) also included Riesman's (1950) inner-other-directedness personality trait as part of the flexible/rigid cluster.

because in facing role conflict, flexible persons continued to say they would comply to role expectations which they could no longer fulfill.[2]

Internal/external control. This factor has received somewhat more attention from job stress researchers than the previous examples of personality traits. *Internally* oriented persons believe that reinforcements (i.e., rewards), in their lives are under their control and are contingent upon their behavior, in contrast to *externally* oriented persons who believe that reinforcements are not under their control and are not contingent on their behavior. Externals, thus, are believers in fate and luck. In their reactions to stress in general, internals experience more anxiety when they do not in fact have some control over the occurrence of stressful events; and externals experience more anxiety when they do have control over the occurrence of stressful events (Houston 1972; Pittman and Pittman 1979). What emerges is a picture of person-situation fit. When an individual's personality in terms of locus of control is congruent with the actual locus of control in the environment, less negative consequences occur in response to stress. Several studies concerned with job stress per se extend this line of reasoning. For instance, Anderson's study (1977) of 102 owner-managers of small businesses found that internals adjusted better to an uncontrolled stressful event. This event was a flood that caused extensive damage to a Pennsylvania community. After the flood, it was found that internals perceived less stress and responded with much more task-oriented coping behaviors than externals. These task-oriented coping behaviors included such acts as obtaining resources to counter their initial losses. In contrast, externals withdrew and expressed feelings of anxiety, hostility, and anger. It therefore appears that internals experience less job stress and respond in a more functional manner than do externals, who respond emotionally when confronted with similar job stresses, possibly because externals assume they have little power to repair the damage caused by external forces.

Research into hardiness in human beings supports the notion that internals cope with stress more effectively. *Hardiness* is a cluster of personality traits that encompasses the locus of control trait. Hardy persons are thought to believe that they can control or influence the

---

[2]It should be noted that these results run counter to the finding that measures of dogmatism and anxiety have been found to be positively related to each other (Lazarus 1966).

Table 5.2
Measure of Tolerance for Ambiguity

How important is it to you to know, in detail, what you have to do on a job?
How important is it to you to know, in detail, how you are supposed to do a job?
How important is it to you to know, in detail, what the limits of your authority on a job are?
How important is it to you to know how well you are doing [a]

[a] Affirmative responses (i.e., very important) to each item are reflective of a low tolerance for ambiguity.
Source: Adapted from Lyons (1971).

events they experience (i.e., to be internally oriented), to have the ability to feel deeply involved in or committed to the activities of their lives, and to anticipate change as an exciting challenge to further developments. Kobasa's study (1979) of 200 middle-and upper-level executives exposed to high levels of stress found hardy individuals experienced less ill health[3] and thus concluded that hardy persons are better able to cope with the stresses they experience.

Ambiguity tolerance. The last example of personality traits to be discussed here, *tolerance for ambiguity* is the tendency to perceive ambiguous situations as desirable, without feeling compelled to structure those situations in meaningful, integrated ways. The obvious expectation that persons with a high tolerance for ambiguity will respond less negatively to high job stress conditions than persons with a low tolerance has been confirmed by several studies. For example, Lyons (1971) investigated tolerance for ambiguity and reactions to role ambiguity among 156 staff nurses. He found that nurses having high tolerance for ambiguity experienced less tension in response to role ambiguity than did low-tolerance nurses. Further, it was shown that nurses having high tolerance for ambiguity experienced lower levels of voluntary turnover—a form of withdrawal from stress. Lyon's measure of tolerance for ambiguity is presented in Table 5.2.

Some recent research thus indicates that extroverted, rigid, internally oriented individuals with a high tolerance for ambiguity are

[3] The material in Chapter 2, "Job Stress and the Quality of Life," regarding stress-health relationships presents further discussion of health status as a consequence of job stress.

likely to suffer less from job stressors than their opposites in personality structure. This is probably the case because such persons (1)
perceive less stress in their work environments and/or expose themselves to less stressful conditions, (2) in the face of job stress they respond with less tension and other dysfunctional psychological reactions, and (3) engage in task-oriented coping behaviors in response to
job stress. These relationships are depicted in Figure 5.1. Other individual characteristics could be added to the list of traits discussed;
but the point has been sufficiently demonstrated that individual
characteristics are important determinants of how people respond to
job stress.

Individual Stress Control

How might this information about individual characteristics be used
to control stress? Obviously people cannot readily alter their personality structures or other individual traits. Rather, the lesson to be
learned is "To know thyself." It is not being suggested that one engage in extended self-analysis, but that people should reflect on their
own nature, needs, wants, and desires, as well as their typical means
of coping with job stress. If it is found that they suffer great levels of
anxiety and tension in response to job stress, for example, then stressful working conditions should be avoided. This notion of "self-
selection" is a possible key to experiencing a higher quality of working life. Humans, more than any other animal, are capable of changing their environments. Realistically, one is not forced into a stressful
working environment. It is freely selected. The execution of a well-

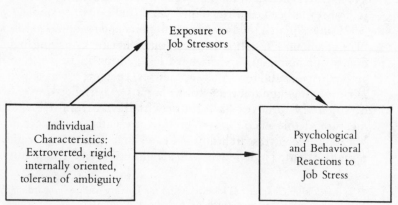

Figure 5.1
Individual Characteristics and Reactions to Job Stress.

planned self-selection process can help people who are particularly susceptible to the dysfunctional consequences of job stress to avoid harmful work environments. People make choices (conscious or otherwise) about careers and jobs they pursue, and to make these decisions without conscious forethought is foolhardy. Later in this chapter, the notion of "self-selection" will be examined further as an effective coping mechanism.

Social Support

Having someone to turn to in a time of need obviously is beneficial to anyone experiencing distress. In the case of job stress, social support can be viewed as a buffer against the dysfunctional consequences of stress emanating from the workplace. *Social support* can be defined as the friendly, approachable, trustworthy, cooperative, and warm attitude of members of the social network to which a person belongs. In simple terms, someone is there to turn to for help. This someone may be found in a social network at work or off the job. Networks at work include subordinates, peers, and superiors. Nonwork networks may consist of friends, neighbors, and family members.

One's family network would seem a likely source of social support; however, this clearly is not always the case. A program of research undertaken at the London School of Business (Handy 1978) provides a tentative framework for understanding when a person's family can be expected to serve as a buffer against job stress. The study investigated the marriages of twenty-three successful male executives. Each husband and wife was characterized as "involved," "thrusting," "existential," or "caring." *Involved* persons are said to be achievement and dominance oriented, with a desire to be a part of a strong relationship. *Thrusting* persons also are described as high achievers who need to dominate others; unlike involved persons, they are willing to act on their own without regard for the feelings of others. *Existential* persons are said to be loners who have little desire to control others or to look after others. *Caring* people gain their satisfactions from looking after others and from belonging rather than dominating. Among the twenty-three couples, four prevalent marriage patterns emerged:

	HUSBAND	WIFE
Pattern 1	Thrusting	Caring
Pattern 2	Thrusting	Thrusting
Pattern 3	Involved	Involved
Pattern 4	Involved	Caring

Pattern 1. The husband works and the wife minds the home. The wife is very supportive of her husband in his work although she may not be interested or involved in its details. The husband's need to dominate and achieve is no problem to the wife, particularly if he satisfies these needs in the work arena. The wife's task, as she sees it, is to absorb her own problems and not to burden her husband. In the husband-wife relationship she expects to be dominated. Furthermore, she manages their joint social network. The couple's home is regulated with routines, rules, tidy rooms, and disciplined children. Conversations within the relationship are more often ritualistic or logistic rather than issue raising. There are few arguments. When intramarital tension occurs, these couples move away from each other. In general, the relationship is secure—a safe harbor. In terms of providing social support as a buffer against the husband's job stresses, it would be expected that the "traditional" marriage reflected in Pattern 1 would function effectively.

Pattern 2. Typically both the husband and wife seek to fulfill their achievement and dominance needs in the work arena, with the wife generally working part-time. When there are children, the wife shifts fulfillment of these needs to the home arena, creating competition rather than support within the family. With both marriage partners working, home life is disorganized, even chaotic, and becomes irritating to both; one blames the other and they generate conflict. When they feel tension, they move against one another in recriminatory arguments. Survival of the marriage without children is most likely and each partner generally establishes separate spheres of activity. Typically, Pattern 2 is not a supportive environment for either partner and generally would not be expected to serve as a buffer against job stress.

Pattern 3. Each person's needs for achievement and dominance are tempered or confused by the high value placed on caring and belonging. Conversations are about issues and values as well as logistics and rituals. Social networks are shared. Because both partners are sensitive, tension is high and initially leads to withdrawal. Following withdrawal, however, both partners move toward one another and develop an intense relationship with the potential for considerable support. Thus, the Pattern 3 marriage may serve as a barrier against the dysfunctional consequences of job stress.

Pattern 4. The Pattern 4 marriage generally approximates the comfortable Pattern 1 marriage. The husband-wife relationship, however, is more intense and emotional, more questioning and flexible, than in the "traditional" marriage. If the wife works, she does so principally to earn money or to provide companionship for herself. Like Pattern 1, the Pattern 4 marriage provides a safe harbor for the husband and is likely to serve as a buffer against his job stresses.

The research conducted by the London School of Business clearly demonstrates that one's family may not always provide the social support necessary to withstand the hazards of job stress. This is particularly true if two thrusting type persons are paired. It should also be noted that the research focuses on the married male, though it does not totally ignore the stresses of the working wife. The unique problems of working women are explicitly addressed in Chapter 7, "Stress and the Working Woman." The social support emanating from work and friendship networks was not fully addressed in the present chapter either, but Chapter 6 will elaborate on the potential buffering effects offered by relationships with subordinates, peers, and superiors.

The issue previously raised in Chapter 4 concerning the relevancy of individual characteristics can be related to this discussion of social support by asking: "How might an individual prone to work stress use social support to control discomfort?" It may sound trite, but the ideal response to this question, for both married and single persons, is to seek out friendships actively both at work and away from work. Most certainly, belonging to an open, trusting, and warm social network can serve as a defense against the stresses experienced at work. Such relationships provide another perspective and new ideas, as well as a means of engaging in "serious talk" about one's life (Schein 1978). For example, upon entry into a new organizational setting, one should actively seek out others also involved in the process of adjusting to their new environment.

In one study of the initiation of graduates into industry, it was found that new organizational members reduced the stress associated with the "identity crisis" they experienced by befriending peers in the same situation (Mansfield 1972). Reciprocal relationships were established, and each graduate contributed to and drew strength from the friendship. Away from work, the family stands as a principal source of support, a source that is often discounted. Other traditional networks which should not be ignored are church groups, social clubs, and various voluntary public service groups. The idea is to become socially integrated as rapidly as possible into the work organization and the community. This cannot be accomplished by adopting a passive posture—a "let them come to me" attitude.

Social support serves as a buffer against job stress only when such support is available. Of course, in lieu of reliance on informal linkages, one may seek out the aid of counselors and other professionals trained to help people cope with stress. Such a strategy, however, typically is not adopted as a preventive mechanism and is turned to only in time of great need. Thus, one's established network of friends, family, and colleagues remains the primary safeguard.

Personal Strategies for Coping with Job Stress

Choosing Success: Transactional Analysis on the Job; Elements of Encounter; Personal Vitality, Trust: A New View of Personal and Organizational Development; Direct Decision Therapy, Reality and Career Planning: A Guide for Personal Growth, Assert Yourself!; How to be Your Own Person; Teaching People to Love Themselves: A Leader's Handbook of Theory and Technique for Self-Esteem and Affirmation Training—these are all representative of the thousands of books, magazine articles, and cassette titles concerned with various self-improvement strategies. Consumers of learning materials aimed at developing personal skills for coping with job stress will find themselves confronted with an almost endless array of choices. The following presentation does not attempt to lay out all of these options or to spell out specific steps for self-improvement. Rather, it can be viewed as an abridged buyer's guide. In this vein the costs and benefits of a few alternatives are highlighted. As will be shown, the old adage, "let the buyer beware," clearly is applicable in this case.

Strategies for coping with job stress can be divided by and large into two categories, direct actions and palliation (Lazarus 1966, 1976). *Direct actions* are personal behavioral strategies that attempt to deal with job stress by altering troubling relationships in the environment. *Palliation* is directed at reducing, eliminating, or tolerating the dysfunctional consequences of job stress once they have been aroused. Direct actions are aimed at the sources of job stress, whereas palliation is aimed at seeking comfort or dealing with the symptoms of job stress.

Direct actions. These mechanisms generally include: (1) preparing against harm, (2) aggression or attack, (3) avoidance, and (4) inaction or apathy. The direct action of preparing against harm typically is preceded by a forewarning that exposure to high levels of job stress is imminent (e.g., being informed ahead of time of a job transfer, promotion, layoff, or termination of employment). Before deciding to act, the person may institute a search to learn what is to be faced and to select an adequate alternative. For instance, Moore (1958) reported on the case of persons living in Waco and San Angelo, Texas, who were preparing against harm from a nonwork related source of stress, a tornado. In 1951, a tornado unexpectedly struck the area. During the following year, one-third of the families in a section of San Angelo built storm cellars. When subsequent storms occurred, fear was reduced as these families went into their shelters. In fact, friends and neighbors would gather in the cellars and the stressful storms became pleasant occasions rather than terrifying experiences.

The direct action of *aggression* was discussed in Chapter 2. It should be recalled that when this coping strategy manifests itself in the form of an attack on another person or persons at or away from work, the ultimate consequences for the aggressor (i.e., the person under job stress) are typically not positive. Instead, the preferred strategy is the expression of anger without aggression. A vivid example of this coping mechanism was depicted in the movie *Network* when millions of Americans were compelled to throw open their doors and windows and scream, "I'm mad as hell, and I'm not going to take it any more."

Avoidance reactions occur under circumstances similar to aggressive responses and also were addressed in Chapter 2. Avoidance commonly occurs in combination with feelings of fear when:

1. The source of job stress is appraised and located or specified

2. The source is judged to be overpowering and can be dealt with only by avoidance (i.e., refusal to put oneself in the situation that will produce stress)

3. The work environment constraints against avoidance (that is, social norms or other pressures) are weak or nonexistent and

4. The threatened person's values and beliefs against avoidance are weak or nonexistent.

Of course the fear commonly associated with avoidance is uncomfortable in and of itself. In addition, as suggested by the Anderson (1977) study discussed earlier in this chapter, avoidance behavior (escapist coping) may ultimately be related to more severe consequences for the person facing a stressful job situation.

Inaction is characterized as a pattern of hopelessness and despair. Inaction means the complete absence of any impulse to cope with job stress because no other alternatives are perceived. Persons apathetic in response to job stress do not struggle or panic; rather, inaction may lead to depression.

Palliation. Palliative forms of coping fall into two major subsets: *symptom-directed modes* and *intrapsychic modes.* Symptom-directed modes are any physiologically-centered ways of reducing the disturbances connected with job stress, including the use of alcohol, tranquilizers, and sedatives. Some of these dysfunctional modes were discussed in Chapter 2 as negative consequences of job stress; but symptom-directed modes also include various functional strategies such as training in muscle relaxation. Intrapsychic modes are defense mechanisms (previously addressed in Chapter 2 as negative consequences). It is important to note that defenses vary in the degree of their success. A successful defense mechanism shows no gaps, no evidence of emotional disturbances, that might point to a breaking through of threatening impulses or dangerous signals from the work environment. In sum, the more successful the defense, the less evidence there is of stress reactions.

The particular personal coping mechanisms discussed below fall into both the direct actions and palliation categories and include only those strategies purported to lead to functional outcomes. The preceding discussion provides a frame of reference for considering the various alternatives.

Relaxation techniques. Probably the most popularized form of relaxation therapy is meditation. *Meditation* involves sustained concentration on a single word, object, or idea while maintaining a quiet repose (Newman and Beehr 1979). The purported result of meditation is reduction of the levels of stress experienced through the restriction of physical and mental activity. Zen breath meditation, which is derived from the Eastern religious-philosophical tradition of Zen Buddhism, is an example of this strategy. The process can be described to have these five steps:

1. Focus on breathing pattern alters the pattern of breathing
2. Attention wanders
3. Focus returns to breathing but now "effortless breathing" occurs, accompanied by a relaxed, attentive awareness
4. New thoughts occur and are "watched" with relaxed awareness and continued focus on breathing
5. "Internal chatter" ceases, the mind becomes a "mirror"

Shapiro and Zifferblatt 1976

Generally speaking, meditation has been found to be a potentially effective means of controlling one's everyday life, thoughts and feelings. Thus, some form of relaxation technique might be expected to produce therapeutic effects that can help individuals cope with job stress. For instance, Roskies et al. (1978) employed a progressive relaxation training technique along with other strategies in an attempt to reduce the dysfunctional consequences experienced by twelve male professionals and executives whose behavior conformed to the Type A syndrome. The intervention reduced cholesterol and blood pressure levels without inducing changes in diet, exercise, smoking habits, or responsibilities and time spent at work. Some people may be wary of the mysticism commonly associated with various forms of meditation (e.g., Zen meditation or transcendental meditation); however, a number of techniques concerned purely with relaxation are available. Further, there is no research evidence to suggest that these more palatable forms of relaxation therapy are any less effective than their mystical counterparts.

Biofeedback. *Biofeedback* involves the use of instruments to mirror psychophysiological processes of which the individual is not normally aware and which may be brought under voluntary control: for example, muscle tension, skin surface temperature, brain wave activity, blood pressure, and heart rate (Fuller 1978). Because this feedback is said to enable the individual to become more active in maintaining his or her health, it provides a tentative strategy for coping with the arousals, fears, anxieties, and other dysfunctional consequences associated with job stress. One instrument used in biofeedback is the electromyograph (EMG), which measures muscular contraction and relaxation. The EMG amplifies the electrical activity originating in a muscle and translates it into an auditory or visual display. The information provided in the display allows persons to observe changes in muscle activity of which they previously had not been aware. This form of biofeedback has been used successfully in the treatment of tension headaches, which are thought to be caused by excessive, sustained contractions of the head and neck muscles. Indeed, various biofeedback strategies have been used to treat several symptoms thought to be associated with job stress.

Since relaxation techniques and biofeedback are directed at the same or similar job stress symptoms, a comparison is in order. Neither coping strategy appears to be superior in terms of which works best, which works faster, which produces longer lasting benefits, or which is likely to benefit a larger proportion of a treated population. However, relaxation techniques generally are superior to biofeedback in terms of convenience and cost (Silver and Blanchard 1978). It is probably slightly more convenient for a person not to be connected to a machine and cost differentials are significant, with the prices of biofeedback instruments ranging from several hundred to several thousands of dollars. Another factor is that the biofeedback therapist requires more training than the therapist who administers relaxation techniques.[4] Thus, it may be that one is more likely to encounter an undertrained biofeedback therapist than an undertrained relaxation therapist.

Psychodynamic therapies. The purpose of psychotherapy is to help people obtain deeper insight into the psychodynamics of their problems and to help them use this understanding to change their troubled ways of living and reacting (Lazarus 1976). Here, psychodynamic therapies are viewed as ways of helping people develop strategies for coping with job stress. There are several types of psychodynamic therapies: Freudian psychoanalysis, neo-Freudian approaches, Carl Rodgers's client-centered therapy, Rollo May's existential therapy, Victor Frankl's logotherapy, Fritz Perls's gestalt therapy, Albert Ellis's rational-emotional therapy, and group psychotherapy. As an example of these approaches, we will focus on "encounter groups," a subset of group psychotherapy. *Encounter groups* (sensitivity training groups or marathon groups) consist of small groups of people who are led to express how they actually feel about things and toward each other, and to interact on an emotional level that is usually concealed below the surface (Lazarus 1976). The assumed purpose of such an exploration of implicit emotional forces is to make group members more aware of how groups function, how they as individuals relate to others, and how others relate to them. In summarizing the research on the therapeutic effects of encounter groups, Back (1973) has concluded that the technique should be viewed as a form of recreational activity or a limited adjunct to other more specific forms of interpersonal skills training. Most certainly, this approach cannot be interpreted as one that favors the development of strategies for coping with job stress, because encounter groups may in fact be hazardous. Hartley, Roback, and Abramowitz (1976) reviewed the research on deterioration effects in encounter groups and found reported "casualty rates" to range from less than 1 percent to almost 50 percent. The magnitude of negative effects associated with psychodynamic therapies in general have been hotly debated. Until this

---

[4]It should be recognized that biofeedback and relaxation techniques can be and are used in conjunction with one another.

debate is resolved, it is probably wiser to seek some other mechanism for coping strategies for job stress.

Behavior therapies. The purpose of behavior therapies, like psychodynamic therapies, is to help people develop coping strategies, but the approach is radically different. Behavior therapists view unadaptive responses as learned behaviors—that is, as habits acquired at some time in the past which permitted an individual to avoid painful experiences but which are repeated in inappropriate situations. Thus, treatment involves confronting a person with conditions designed to produce "unlearning" of undesired behaviors with the substitution of desirable coping behaviors (Lazarus 1971). Unlike psychodynamic therapists, behavior therapists do not insist that people should gain insight into their problems; rather, they focus on altering future behavior patterns. Examples of behavior therapy techniques include desensitization (or counterconditioning), aversion training, assertive training, token economies, and modeling. Behavior modification techniques exemplify the behavior therapy approaches. *Behavior modification* can be defined broadly as a methodological approach derived from psychological research for developing, implementing and evaluating behavior-change techniques. This view of behavior modification implies that behavior modifiers undertake an experimental analysis of problem behaviors. Behavior modification techniques have been successfully applied in a wide variety of settings such as, educational institutions, health care facilities, homes, businesses, and prisons; and they have been implemented for an array of problems from anxiety to depression, sexual deviance, social skill difficulties, employee absenteeism, obesity, smoking, and marital disorders. The techniques and other forms of behavior therapy offer a viable set of options for developing effective coping mechanisms to the person who is experiencing unduly high levels of discomfort from job stress. One particularly effective option is the use of "self-reinforcement" techniques. *Self-reinforcement* encourages people to establish their own standards of coping effectiveness and to gauge their own behaviors against those standards. When actual coping behaviors meet or exceed self-defined standards, they may reward themselves with rewards that are generally freely available but that have been reserved for the period as special rewards. Consider a manager who finds himself becoming so anxious and tense before a monthly performance review meeting with his boss that he is unable to sleep the night before. The manager sets for himself the objective of sleeping the night through and, when he achieves that objective, rewards himself with a meal at the finest restaurant in town. Behavior therapies do work; but their success in all instances, as with any technique, cannot be guaranteed no matter how carefully it is applied. Each person must be diligent and search out the behavior therapy that is personally most effective.

Planning. The *planning* strategy involves looking ahead, identifying goals and potential job stressors, and developing strategies for achieving the goals, while minimizing the dysfunctional consequences of job stressors encountered. This approach sounds like a tactic based on common sense, and it is. It may be that the scarcity of research aimed at evaluating planning strategies results because the tactics seem so obvious. These approaches must be adopted or rejected, therefore, on the basis of intuition or experience. Schein's (1978) "constructive coping process" captures many of the components contained in other planning strategies and includes the following four steps:

1. Diagnosing the problem. A key to problem definition is the careful examination of one's internal reactions to the external events which are precipitating the stress.
2. Diagnosing oneself. Self-awareness requires that one critically assess personal resources, feelings, and needs.
3. Selecting a coping response. This step requires a redefinition of one's self-image and the invention of new options.
4. Diagnosing the effects of the coping response. Coping is a cyclical problem-solving process that requires evaluating whether the selected coping response has achieved its purpose.

One coping response that may be generated by Schein's process is withdrawal, opting to remove oneself from a situation. Planning strategies capitalize on the notion that people have at least some degree of control in selecting the organizations they work in, the jobs they occupy in those organizations, and the tasks that comprise those jobs. Effective coping may require the exercise of self-selection, which in this instance would be the planning ahead to leave one work environment for another. If well considered, withdrawal behavior should not be viewed as a form of escapism; rather, it is an option that is sensible to exercise under certain conditions. Employers should be chosen carefully and should be left at the individual's convenience and under the most pleasant circumstances manageable.

In summary, relaxation techniques, biofeedback, psychodynamic therapies, behavior therapies, and planning are personal mechanisms for coping with job stress. Collectively, the mechanisms comprise both direct action and palliation categories of coping strategies. Furthermore, hard and fast boundaries do not exist between the strategies reviewed, and the strategies commonly are used in conjunction with each other. Thus, one is not faced with an "either/or" decision. Appreciation of this point is important because the greater the variety of an individual's coping strategies, the more protection afforded by coping (Pearlin and Schooler 1978). Finally, one must recognize that there are limits to coping (Schalit 1977) and one should not allow the search for an effective coping mechanism itself to become a source of stress.

AN OVERVIEW

Figure 5.2 depicts the major relationships discussed in this chapter. First, it was shown that various characteristics of individuals predispose them to (1) perceive less stress in their work environments and/or expose themselves to less stressful conditions, (2) to respond to job stressors with less tension and other dysfunctional consequences, and (3) engage in task-oriented coping behaviors in response to job stress. For example, extroverted, rigid, internally oriented individuals who have a high tolerance for ambiguity are expected to suffer less from job stressors than their opposites in personality structure. As was seen, people should reflect on their own unique characteristics and how they typically cope with job stress; then, in light of this information, they should select work environments most suited to their predispositions.

Secondly, it was shown that social support can serve as a buffer against the consequences of job stress. Thus, it was recommended that persons actively seek out friendships both at work and away from work as a form of insurance against the hazards of job stress.

Subsequently, a "buyer's guide" to various strategies for coping with job stress was offered. Relaxation techniques, behavioral therapies, and planning ahead were recommended. Biofeedback and psychodynamic therapies were not judged to be as effective as the other three approaches. The reader also was urged to develop a large repertoire of coping strategies, because the greater the variety of coping strategies, the more protection coping affords. Finally, it was

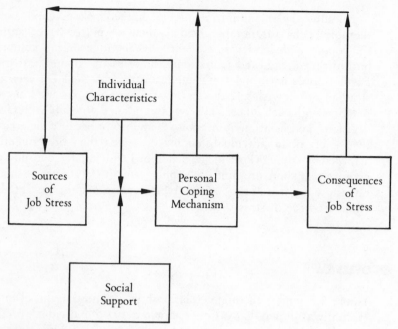

Figure 5.2
Coping with Job Stress.

recognized that there are limits to coping and that removal from a situation is then recommended.

This chapter focused exclusively on what individual employees can do to cope with their job stresses. The following chapter completes the discussion of coping processes by suggesting what managers and organizations can do to manage stress among their employees. As will be seen, many of the managerial and organizational approaches to be presented will have beneficial repercussions for the individual employee.

REFERENCES

Allport, G.W. 1937. *Personality: A psychological interpretation.* New York: Holt, Rinehart, and Winston.

Anderson, C.R. 1977. Locus of control, coping behaviors, and performance in a stress setting: A longitudinal study. *Journal of Applied Psychology* 62:446-51.

Back, K.W. 1973. Encounter groups and society. *Journal of Applied Behavioral Science* 9:7-20.

Fuller, G.D. 1978. Current states of biofeedback in clinical practice. *American Psychologist* 33:39-48.

Handy, D. 1977. The family: Help or hindrance? In *Stress at work,* C.L. Cooper and R. Payne, eds. pp. 107-126. Chichester, England: Wiley.

Hartley, D., Roback, H.B., and Abramowitz, S.I. 1976. Deterioration effects in encounter groups. *American Psychologist* 31:247-55.

Houston, B.K. 1972. Control over stress, locus of control, and response to stress. *Journal of Personality and Social Psychology* 21:249-55.

Kahn, R.L., Wolfe, D.M., Quinn, R.R., Snoek, J.D., and Rosenthal, R.A. 1964. *Organizational stress: Studies in role conflict and ambiguity.* New York: Wiley.

Kobasa, S.C. 1979. Stressful life events, personality and health: An inquiry into hardiness. *Journal of Personality and Social Psychology* 37:1-11.

Lazarus, A.A. 1971. *Behavior therapy and beyond.* New York: McGraw-Hill.

Lazarus, R.S. 1966. *Psychological stress and the coping process.* New York: McGraw-Hill.

.1976. *Patterns of adjustment.* New York: McGraw-Hill.

Lyons, T. 1971. Role clarity, need for clarity, satisfaction, tension, and withdrawal. *Organizational Behavior and Human Performance* 6:99-110.

Mansfield, R. 1972. The initiation of graduates in industry: The resolution of identity-stress as a determinant of job satisfaction in the early months of work. *Human Relations* 25:77-86.

Moore, H. E. 1958. *Tornadoes over Texas.* Austin, Texas: University of Texas Press.

Newman, J.E., and Beehr, T.A. 1977. Personal and organizational strategies for handling job stress: Review of research and opinion. *Personnel Psychology* 32:1-43.

Pearlin, L.I., and Schooler, C. 1978. The structure of coping. *Journal of Health and Social Behavior* 19:2-21.

Pittman, N.L., and Pittman, T.S. 1979. Effects of amount of helplessness training and internal-external locus of control on mood and performance. *Journal of Personality and Social Psychology* 37:39-47.

Riesman, D. 1950. *The lonely crowd.* New Haven: Yale University Press.

Roskies, E., Spevack, M., Sukis, A., Cohen, C., and Gilman, S. 1978. Changing the coronary-prone (Type A) behavior pattern in a nonclinical population. *Journal of Behavioral Medicine* 1:201-16.

Schein, E.H. 1978. *Career dynamics: Matching individual and organizational needs.* Reading, Mass.: Addison-Wesley.

Shalit, B. 1977. Structural ambiguity and limits to coping. *Journal of human stress* 3:32-45.

Shapiro, D.N., Jr., and Zifferblatt, S.M. 1976. Zen meditation and behavioral self-control: Similarities, differences, and clinical application. *American Psychologist* 7:519-32.

Silver, B.J., and Blanchard, E.B. 1978. Biofeedback and relaxation training in the treatment of psychophysiological disorders: Or are the machines really necessary? *Journal of Behavioral Medicine* 1:217-39.

Warren, H.C., and Carmichael, L. 1930. *Elements of human psychology.* New York: Houghton Mifflin.

Wesley, E. 1953. Preservative behavior, manifest anxiety, and rigidity. *Journal of Abnormal and Social Psychology* 48:129-34.

Wilson, G.D. 1976. Personality. In *A textbook in human psychology,* H.S. Eysenck, and G.D. Wilson, eds. Baltimore: University Park Press.

Chapter 6

Organizational Stress Management Strategies

Although job stress is often detrimental to organizational effectiveness, efforts to cope with or prevent stress can often result in substantial benefits for organizations. As one company president recollected:

> I think one of the best examples I can give you of trying to prevent stress from becoming a big problem was the relocation of some of our functions here at the main building to a service center which is in a much less desirable part of town. We were very concerned because we had people who were working on Fifth Avenue for up to forty years and suddenly they were switched from the nicest part of town to one that wasn't. It was traumatic for many. Because these people were older they worried about traveling back and forth and working in this kind of an area. So we realized that we had to embark on a selling campaign long in advance of the change.
>
> So instead of keeping this quiet, we made it an open secret and talked about it every chance we got. We also did all of the things that anyone would do in terms of enhancing and remodeling the physical surroundings. We air conditioned the building and we put in special elevators and many other things.
>
> But we also hired a writer and his assignment was to write about the history of the area and to romance it honestly. This writer told about the museums and special restaurants where employees could dine well for only a little amount of money, where they could go for a very special dinner. He also described the area's parks and the shopping avail-

able. He also tried to describe the function and the importance of what was going to be done in that center. Because all of our computers are down there now, it has really become the nerve center of the company. As a result of trying to handle this before it really took place, we transferred 800 people and only lost one. So we know it worked.

Kiev, *Handling Executive Stress* (1974).

This account of one organization's strategy to manage stress suggests the strategy was successful. Although this appears to be a rather straightforward management application, it really raises several important questions.

1. Could the organization have used any other strategies that would have been more successful?
2. Was the success of that strategy related to a particular stress condition or would it have been effective for any stress condition in the organization?
3. How was success of the strategy measured?
4. Was this a preventive or a curative strategy?
5. Did the strategy deal with organizational characteristics and conditions or with role and task characteristics and conditions?
6. Who in the organization should be responsible for the development of strategies to deal with stress?

Answers to these questions are important for students of stress as well as for managers who are concerned with effectively managing stress in their organizations. This chapter provides information that will help to answer these questions.

First, it is necessary to recall some points from Chapter 3 on stress and organizational effectiveness and Chapter 4 on the organizational conditions associated with stress. Those two chapters suggested strategies, their potential effectiveness, and methods by which to evaluate their effectiveness. The cure (strategies selected), after all, depends on the diagnosis (conditions associated with stress). Earlier we noted that concern about the management of stress in organizations is not widely shared by organizations, especially since stress may relate only to employee health. Even if an organization is concerned about managing stress, there are difficulties in developing and implementing stress programs, as was noted in Chapter 3, in the work of Katz and Kahn (1978). That study was cited to illustrate the influence of the employee's nonwork activities and individual differences in the employee's stress. In addition, Cooper and Marshall (1977) illustrate the potential internal contradictions that can occur in changing job characteristics related to stress:

> Few, if any, job areas can be identified as purely a source of one or the other (pressure or satisfactions) for the population as a whole, for the manager over time (short-term stress [pressure] is frequently a prelude to satisfaction) or even for the individual at an instant in time. In attempting to remove known causes of stress from the work environment, we could face danger of either (1) generating different pressures (worker participation while alleviating alienation at blue collar levels is, for example, putting added burdens on many managers) or (2) reducing job satisfaction (the growth-inducing potential of stress must particularly not be forgotten). Organizationwide reform, then, must be undertaken only with extreme caution and always be based on meaningful subgroup diagnosis and cater to individual needs. On whatever scale action is planned it should always incorporate the facility for modification, even complete reversal, if this becomes necessary in the light of feedback about its effect (from its own self-monitoring). The aim, in short, should be not to eradicate stress but to *manage* it.

> Cooper and Marshall, *Understanding Executive Stress (1977).*

TYPOLOGY OF ORGANIZATIONAL STRATEGIES FOR STRESS MANAGEMENT

To paraphrase from Newman and Beehr (1979), an organizational strategy for stress management is one intended to eliminate, ameliorate or change the stress-producing factors in the job context or intended to modify, in a beneficial way, the employee's reaction to the stressful job situation. Organizational strategies are those undertaken by the organization for the primary benefit of the organization; whereas individual strategies are those undertaken for the primary benefit of the individual. Organizational strategies can be implemented by the entire organization, any unit in the organization, or even by a manager vis-a-vis his or her employees (Newman and Beehr 1979).

The organizational strategies that can be implemented relate to seven major aspects of the organization:

1. Organizational structure
2. Relationships in the organizations
3. Roles in the organization

4. Change
5. Physical environment
6. Career development
7. Intrinsic job qualities.

These are the organizational conditions associated with stress that were identified in Chapter 4. Figure 6.1 presents those conditions again in the framework of organizational stress management strategy targets. Each condition can be a target for a stress strategy. Each category and condition is associated with stress because it is related to the desires of employees (that is, their needs and values); the employees' perception of opportunities, constraints, and demands; and/ or the employees' perception of the uncertainty for the resolution of those opportunities, constraints, and demands, which upon resolution result in valued outcomes. Although the extraorganizational sources of stress are crucial for understanding an employee's stress in the organization, they are by definition outside the boundary of the organization and will not be used here in the typology of organizational stress. A manager, however, should be aware of and sensitive to the possibilities of those extraorganizational conditions and the symptoms which may be evident inside the organization. The manager, of course, should also be aware of the individual strategies by which to deal with stress discussed in Chapter 5.

Strategy-target matching. The remaining seven categories, although not independent of each other, will form the typology of organizational strategies. The heading of each category identifies the general organizational condition being targeted by the stress strategy. Within each category, the strategy used will further depend on the specific organizational condition identified. The effectiveness of the strategy used therefore, depends partly upon the appropriateness of the strategy-target match, and needless to say, the criteria against which effectiveness is measured. The criteria will be discussed later, but finding the appropriate match is of initial importance. The first step in this process is to identify stress in organizations.

A group of researchers at the University of Michigan who have suggested that organizations should develop programs for the early identification of stress and stress symptoms recommend using questionnaires in combination with medical records to help diagnose the jobs, organizational units, and other organizational conditions in which stress symptoms exist. According to the University of Michigan team, measures of stress symptoms should include physical,

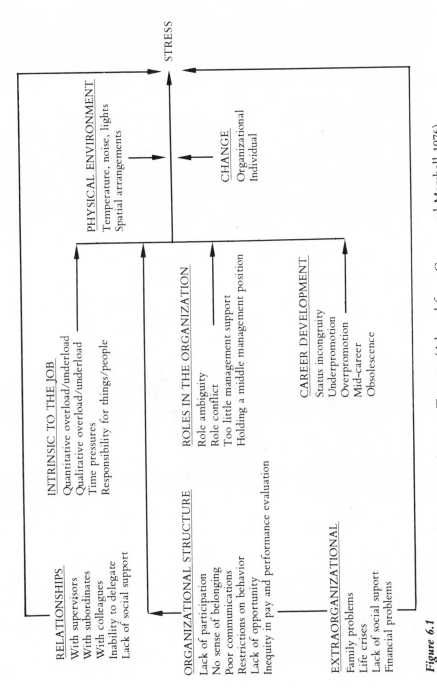

Figure 6.1
Organizational Stress: Management Strategy Targets. (Adapted from Cooper and Marshall 1976)

117

chemical, psychological, sociological, and behavioral indicators. Furthermore, programs with specific stress management strategies should be set up as field experiments to evaluate the effectiveness of each strategy. The researchers think that the strategies which are most "individualized," i.e., consider individual and situational differences, will be the most likely to succeed. For organizations to use strategies, however, requires that they perceive a need for them or that the organizations recognize that they have problems. Organizations, like people, are often unaware of what is really happening, as illustrated in the story of the ill-informed walrus:

The fable of the ill-informed walrus

"How's it going down there?" barked the big walrus from his perch on the highest rock near the shore. He waited for the good word.

Down below, the smaller walruses conferred hastily among themselves. Things were not going well at all, but none of them wanted to break the news to the Old Man. He was the biggest and wisest walrus in the herd, and he knew his business—but he did hate to hear bad news. And he had such a terrible temper that every walrus in the herd was terrified of his ferocious bark.

"What will we tell him?" whispered Basil, the second-ranking walrus. He well remembered how the Old Man had raved and ranted at him the last time the herd caught less than its quota of herring, and he had no desire to go through that experience again. Nevertheless, the walruses had noticed for several weeks that the water level in the nearby Arctic bay had been falling constantly, and it had become necessary to travel much farther to catch the dwindling supply of herring. Someone should tell the Old Man; he would probably know what to do. But who? and how?

Finally, Basil spoke up. "Things are going pretty well Chief," he said. The thought of the receding waterline made his heart feel heavy, but he went on: "As a matter of fact, the beach seems to be getting larger."

The Old Man grunted, "Fine, fine," he said. "That will give us a bit more elbow room." He closed his eyes and continued basking in the sun.

The next day brought more trouble. A new herd of walruses moved in down the beach, and with the supply of herring dwindling, this invasion could be dangerous. No one wanted to tell the Old Man, though only he could take the steps necessary to meet this new competition.

Reluctantly, Basil approached the big walrus, who was still sunning himself on the large rock. After some small talk, he said, "Oh, by the way, Chief, a new herd of walruses seems to have moved into our territory." The Old Man's eyes snapped open, and he filled his great lungs in preparation for a mightly bellow. But Basil added quickly, "Of course, we don't anticipate any trouble. They don't look like herring-eaters to me—more likely interested in minnows, and as you know, we don't bother with minnows ourselves."

The Old Man let out the air with a long sigh. "Good, good," he said, "No point in our getting excited over nothing, then, is there?"

Things didn't get any better in the weeks that followed. One day, peering down from the large rock, the Old Man noticed that part of his herd seemed to be missing. Summoning Basil, he grunted peevishly, "What's going on, Basil? Where is everybody?"

Poor Basil didn't have the courage to tell the Old Man that many of the younger walruses were leaving every day to join the new herd. Clearing his throat nervously, he said, "Well, Chief, we've been tightening things up a bit. You know, getting rid of some of the dead wood. After all, a herd is only as good as the walruses in it."

"Run a tight ship, I always say," the Old Man grunted. "Glad to hear that everything's going so well."

Before long, everyone but Basil had left to join the new herd band Basil realized that the time had come to tell the Old Man the facts. Terrified but determined, he flopped up to the large rock.

"Chief," he said. "I have bad news. The rest of the herd has left you."

The old walrus was so astonished that he couldn't even work up a good bellow. "Left me?" he cried. "All of them? But why? How could this happen?"

I can't understand it," the old walrus said. "And just when everything was going so well!"

From Management Review (Oct. 1961).

The fable illustrates that an important aspect of stress management is the establishment of methods by which managers can stay aware of what is happening in the organization. The awareness should be aimed at the stress symptoms and the seven organizational conditions related to those symptoms. The organizational structure condition will be considered first.

Organizational structure

The case history at the beginning of this chapter relates to an organizational structure strategy that was used to manage stress. An organizational structure strategy has as its target to improve the quality of the involvement with the arrangements and relationships among individuals and groups of employees. As Figure 6.1 shows, the actual stress structure targets include:

1. Lack of participation
2. No sense of belonging
3. Poor communications
4. Restrictions on behavior
5. Lack of opportunity for advancement
6. Inequity in pay and performance and evaluation.

Although this list is not exhaustive, it does indicate several aspects of the quality of employee involvement and attachment that are related to stress. Since the relationships between stress and effectiveness have already been examined in detail in Chapter 2, it should be apparent that organizational strategies which are to influence these targets in order to reduce stress should be related to employee and organizational effectiveness.

Some strategies said to be effective for these stress-related organizational structure targets are:

1. Clarification of policies regarding transfer and promotions
2. Decentralization and increased participation
3. Change in the selection and placement policies
4. Change in the communication procedures and networks in the organization
5. Change in the reward systems
6. Utilization of training and development programs
7. Statement of the performance evaluation system
8. Development and utilization of permanent and temporary work groups
9. Change in shift patterns and job rotation policies
10. Redesign of the organization, e.g., increasing span of control and creating lateral relations
11. Changes in retirement policies.

Although lack of space prohibits an examination of each of these strategies, it is important to examine a few in order to see how they are related to one or more of the organizational structure targets and thus to understand their relationship to stress, and to employee and organizational effectiveness.

Communications. The importance of organizational communications policies and practices was well illustrated in the employee relocation case at the beginning of this chapter. The relocation of several functions of the organization from the "nice" part of town to a less desirable part could have produced considerable stress and con-comitant ineffectiveness. (The company president used turnover as a measure of organizational ineffectiveness.) Notice that the content of the communication was both socioemotional (where the restaurants are) and task ("he also tried to describe the function and the importance"). Several researchers have shown the importance of both the socioemotional and task communications in the productivity and satisfaction of work groups (Goldhaber et al. 1978).

Socioemotional and task communications are related to employee stress in several ways. The socioemotional communication fulfills an employee's need for interpersonal respect and acceptance. The task communication facilitates an employee's task accomplishment, thus aiding the need for achievement, and increases the employee's level of certainty and predictability about events in the organization (House and Wells 1978; McLean 1979).

Increasing communications does not automatically imply an increase in socioemotional and task communications. Increasing those two types of communications, however, increases the probability of greater effectiveness. Some other types of communications are negatively related to effectiveness, such as communications that contain elements of regulation and control and those with elements of distortion or suppression. Increasing regulative or distortive communication has been found to be negatively related to employee satisfaction and performance. In fact, a vicious cycle is created such that lowered employee satisfaction and performance result in greater regulative or distortive communication, which in turn causes lowered employee satisfaction and performance (Schuler 1979). Regulative and distortive communications are probably stressful for most employees because they prevent employee achievement and also reduce employees' feelings of self-control.

An important aspect of organizational communication policies and practices is that employees often differ from their managers in perceptions of communications (Goldhaber et al. 1978). Employees report receiving fewer communications from their managers than the managers claim they send. We can conclude then, that one problem of improving communications in organizations is how the message is sent. That is only half the story. The other half is how the message is received, since we also communicate by listening:

> By constantly listening to a speaker you are conveying the idea that "I'm interested in you as a person, and I think that what you feel is important. I respect your thoughts, and even if I don't agree with them, I

know that they are valid for you. I feel sure that you have a contribution to make. I'm not trying to change you or evaluate you. I just want to understand you. I think you're worth listening to, and I want you to know that I'm the kind of person you can talk to."

But, the average person has only about 30% listening efficiency. This means we hear only 30% of what we listen to. We spend about 40% of our work day listening. Put these two things together and we find that the average person is only 30% efficient for 40% of his working day. From a business and personal standpoint this could be disastrous.

Huseman, Logue, and Freshly, Interpersonal and Organizational Communication (1977).

The following are a few typical stumbling blocks to effective listening and precepts as to how to remove these blocks:

1. *The Wandering Mind*—The average person talks at the rate of 125 words a minute and thinks at the rate of 300 to 400 words a minute. It is easy to see the problem here. It is very easy to allow our minds to wander while someone is speaking because of this rate difference.

   The precept here is to concentrate on what is being said. Try to give the speaker your attention.

2. *The Closed Mind*—We tend to hear only what we want to hear. A good example of this can be found in the political arena. There are people who support a candidate for political office when in reality that candidate may have a bad political record. The supporters tend to discount the negative things about the candidate because he or she may be good looking and have a nice personality. This becomes strictly an emotional response. We should put emotions aside and judge on the facts that are presented.

   The precept here is we'll listen to everything even if we don't want to hear it.

3. *Feedback Absence*—Everyone desires to know how he or she is being received by the other person, wants to know what the other person thinks about what we have just said. Although we have these desires, we often find that they are unfulfilled. Of course we often do the same thing to others, but that is not providing feedback. We often fail to receive or give feedback because we don't listen or others aren't listening to us.

   The precept here is that a committment to provide *responsible* feedback will increase the desire to listen.

Huseman, Logue, and Freshley (1977).

Selection and placement. Sleight and Cook (1974) report that selection and placement procedures can be preventive strategies for stress management. Implementation of these procedures for stress prevention must take into account the nature of the jobs and the susceptibility of the employee, but evaluating the nature of the jobs is difficult because one must decide how to measure this factor. Should the employee tell us about the job or should more objective measures be used? Determining the susceptibility or the vulnerability of the employees is also hard to do. Because of these conditions selection and placement have limited application as stress strategies:

> Until industry is able to rate its jobs in terms of the type and magnitude of stressors in each job and job situation, there is little scientific basis for selective employment and placement of "vulnerable" individuals. It should be added that considerable work needs to be done in measuring individuals in terms of the type and magnitude of stressors with which they are able to cope.
>
> McLean, *Work Stress* (1979).

One selection technique, however, that may help to reduce the possibility that an organization will select a vulnerable job applicant is the realistic job preview (Wanous 1977). The realistic job preview provides the job applicant with information about the actual job conditions in which the applicant would be working. Often the applicant is provided with more realistic job information by means of films of the job conditions or even a visit to the job location. The realistic job preview helps to reassure job applicants about their decision to either accept or reject a job offer and helps to reduce turnover and absenteeism of those who accept the offer (Van Maanan and Schein 1977).

Decentralization and participation. These two strategies decrease stress through their impact on the targets of the lack of participation, no sense of belonging, and unnecessary restrictions on behavior. Research on participation and decentralization suggests that the more employees are allowed to participate in decision making, especially decisions that have a direct bearing on their work, the more they experience job satisfaction and a feeling of self-esteem.

It would appear that strategies for greater participation should be implemented immediately. Locke and Schweiger (1979), however, suggest that cautious evaluation of organizational conditions and individual characteristics should precede increased participation. They indicate that participation research is far from conclusive on the consistency of benefits to performance from participation because some employees do not want it and some supervisors and managers see it as a threat (Locke and Schweiger 1979). Research and organizational realities indicate that a participation strategy should consider the plant and the work group, the task, and political contingencies. The implementation strategies related to participation and to communication policies and practices influences stress and effectiveness through their impact on organizational structure conditions and through their alteration of the roles in the organization (Schuler 1980b).

Role in the Organization

As shown in Figure 6.1, several stress-related targets fall under the heading "Role in the Organization": role ambiguity, role conflict, too little management support, and holding a middle-management position (Beehr and Newman 1978; Cooper and Marshall 1976). These targets essentially are the expectations that individuals receive from others in the organization.

Each employee in the organization is in a role network, that is, he or she receives expectations of behaviors and attitudes from several different people and groups. This situation can result in the employee not really understanding role expectations or the expected roles producing conflict. Those aspects or qualities of roles are stressful because in general they are associated with an individual's needs for achievement, productivity, certainty, and responsibility. Several organizational strategies that have been suggested are aimed at improving stressful roles in the organization. For example,

1. Change in role activities
2. Change in definition of role set or role network
3. Change in resources available for role performance
4. Increase in participation
5. Change in communications
6. Institutionalization of procedures for reducing stress when it occurs, for example, allowing the individual to convene the role senders who are sending conflicting or ambiguous expectations
7. Clarification of performance evaluation standards, defining goals and providing feedback
8. Development of effective leader behaviors.

Ambiguous or conflicting roles in the organization are closely related to employee stress, as discussed in Chapter 5. Accurate diagnosis of the links among sources of stress, roles in the organization, and one or more of the seven targets is essential for an effective strategy to manage role stress. Although the research suggests role stress is pervasive in many organizations, which target is most stressful, if indeed one is, remains to be determined. Role ambiguity is said to be more stressful than role conflict by some, but for others role conflict appears more stressful than role ambiguity. Consistent with our individualized approach, however, we recommend that few assumptions be made about which roles may be more stressful in a particular organization until evidence has been gathered and analyzed for that organization. Strategies that may be appropriate for stressful role targets are outlined below.

Role clarification. French and Caplan (1970) have suggested that an employee (the focal person) who is in a situation of role conflict or role ambiguity should be allowed to convene his or her set of role senders. Such a process may involve an actual meeting of all the role senders after they have listed individually what they expect of the focal person. The focal person should also try to determine the expectations of each of his or her role senders. These listings then provide an initial basis for discussion and clarification of ambiguities or for negotiation and resolution of conflict.

An example of an institutionalized role procedure is provided in the appendix to this chapter, "Mapping of Role Expectations." The institutionalized strategy can be effective in reducing role ambiguity and conflict, but it should be complemented by a high level of participation with informative communication between the focal person and the role senders in order for role clarification and conflict reduction to occur. The institutionalized meeting may become an occasion to vent frustrations rather than to resolve ambiguities or reduce conflicts, but the institutionalized strategy is still useful in times of rapid change, particularly for intersender conflicts.

Although institutionalized strategies are effective in reducing role conflict and ambiguity among employees in general, they are particularly helpful to the middle-management employee. It is the middle-management employee who often suffers the most role conflict because this position falls between top management and the employees, groups which may each have different values, goals, and motivations. Frequently the middle manager (or even more likely, the supervisor) is expected to encourage employees to do more work, which they do not want to do, for the same pay or with even fewer resources than before. An institutionalized procedure in which the person in the middle can discuss these conflicts would be useful for that person in managing role stress.

Setting performance standards, defining goals, and providing feedback. Role ambiguity arises from not knowing on what basis employees are evaluated and not knowing the goals and objectives of the job, the group, and of the organization. Although the majority of large organizations have formal performance evaluation systems, many employees indicate that they are really unaware of the performance criteria. Many new employees expecting to receive feedback on their performance soon experience the phenomenon of the vanishing performance appraisal (Hall 1976). They are often led to believe their performance will be evaluated frequently, whereas in actuality, the performance appraisal that was promised vanishes. This ambiguity regarding what to do and how to do it well is stressful because it creates a great deal of uncertainty about how to be productive, how to improve, what is fair, and what is rewarded in the organization. Some organizations defend this ambiguity by saying "that's policy," "that's the way things are," and "people are getting paid to tolerate uncertainty." Unfortunately, many employees are unaware that they are paid to tolerate uncertainty—but then again how could an organization actually tell its employees that and be consistent with its policy?

To minimize the stress associated with role ambiguity, it is necessary not only to have a formal performance evaluation system but also to relate the results of evaluations. The value of an evaluation system lies in how clearly it answers the two questions "What should I be doing?" and "How have I been doing?" An evaluation system should specify both of these points. Of course the actual importance attached to each will vary with the organization and particular jobs of the employees; the manner in which they are implemented, however, will generally be the same regardless. That is, the activities will be defined by behaviors and the results will be defined by goals and objectives. The content of the behaviors and the goals and objectives will be unique to organizations and jobs.

It is apparent that specifying behaviors, goals and objectives is important to allow for effective role-stress management. As indicated in the preceding paragraphs, each organizational strategy is related not only to individual stress but even more directly to organizational conditions that create stress and reduce effectiveness. The following fable exemplifies this. As you read, consider the confusion and stress on the part of the members of this organization.

The fable of the farmer's folly

Once upon a time, there was a young farmer who leased and operated a farm upon which he raised 16 chickens. The purpose of raising the chickens was to produce eggs and to make a profit for the young farmer.

The performance of the chickens was as follows:

One chicken laid one egg a day.
Two chickens each laid two eggs a day.
Three chickens each laid three eggs a day.
Four chickens each laid four eggs a day.
Three chickens each laid five eggs a day.
Two chickens each laid six eggs a day.
The champion hen laid seven eggs a day.

The plot (distribution) of the chickens' performance looked like this:

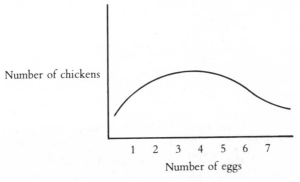

Now it came to pass that the absentee landlord who owned the farm required the young farmer to rate the ability of each chicken to perform. (The landlord was very fond of fried chicken. Need I say more?) For this purpose, the landlord gave the young farmer a "Performance Regarding Egg Production" (PREP) form. The young farmer was to rate each of his chickens on each of the five scales that comprised the form.

PREP			
POOR	O.K.	VERY GOOD	EXCELLENT
Attitude toward laying ⎯	⎯	⎯	⎯
Determination to nest ⎯	⎯	⎯	⎯
Courage to molt ⎯	⎯	⎯	⎯
Initiative to set ⎯	⎯	⎯	⎯
Loyalty to the Hen house ⎯	⎯	⎯	⎯
Rated by: _____			

Our young farmer rated each of his hens on the form. To him, most of his hens had loyalty, initiative, courage, and an attitude as good as that found on any other farms, so he rated his chickens fairly high. (He knew that the performance of some of his hens wasn't too good—BUT—let somebody else's hens get fried.)

The distribution of his rating looked like this:

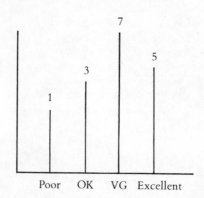

When the landlord saw the results of the rating, he said, "The rate of return of eggs to the amount of grain you feed is only 7 percent. Many of my other farms have a rate of return of at least 10 percent.

Obviously, you do not know how to use the rating form. From now on, you will give extra grain according to the following formula:

A maximum of 12 percent increase in amount of grain per year will be allowed for excellent hens;

A maximum increase in grain of 8 percent per year will be allowed for very good hens;

O.K. hens will be allowed to receive up to a 5 percent increase in grain per year;

Poor hens will receive no increase in grain.

So the farmer did as he was told. He gave only two of the five hens rated excellent a 12 percent increase in grain (that's all the "raise" grain he could use). Only one of the seven very good hens could get the full 8 percent grain increase. And so it went.

Now the only thing madder than a wet hen is a hen who is rated excellent or very good, but who does not receive a raise equal to the raise that is received by some other hens who are rated as excellent or very good.

These hens were not too sympathetic to the farmer's feelings and problems. They had very little or no appreciation for how difficult it is to judge small differences in attitudes, initiative, etc., or how difficult the landlord could be.

So the farmer became a little wiser. He thought, "If I have to give a small percentage of excellent and very good raises, then I will give only a small percentage of excellent and very good ratings. Then I won't have to explain my ratings to the landlords or the raises I give to the chickens."

Suiting his thinking to his behavior, the young farmer soon had both the pay distribution and the rating distribution looking like this:

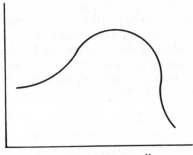

Poor   OK   VG   Excellent

At this time, all the hens became extremely competitive for the raises and ratings. Each thought this way, "If somebody gets a raise, it might as well be me. If some hen is going to the frying pan, it might as well be some other hen instead of me." But, no matter how hard each individual hen tried, only a certain number got more grain, and a few had to go to the frying pan.

On the surface, all was well. Apparently, the form was working well for both the landlord and the farmer. The landlord was getting plenty of fried chicken, and he thought, "Even if turnover is a little high, we might as well get rid of the deadwood."

But things weren't going as well for the hens. They were doing anything they could to compete successfully. Some followed the farmer around and rubbed against his legs constantly. Some hatched chicks. Some, radically, laid more eggs. And one hen actually "swiped" eggs from another hen's nest.

After a period of time, one of the hens died of hunger; five of the better hens got tired of going nowhere and left for other farms; two hens joined a commune in a duck sanctuary; and two other hens formed a corporation with the Easter Bunny.

Then hens who did not have the drive to get more grain, but who produced just enough to avoid the frying pan, thrived. Soon the performance distribution matched the pay and rating distribution. But once again, the landlord was not happy with the young farmer.

There is no telling what would have happened to our young farmer friend if it hadn't been for the white rat. One day, in the midst of his despair over being caught between the landlord and the hens, the young farmer found a white rat in a trap he had set in his kitchen.

As he approached the trap, the rat pleaded, "Please sir, don't hurt me. I haven't had much worldly experience at getting food because I have spent most of my life in a Skinner Box in a laboratory. However, while in the laboratory, I learned many things. You look worried and unhappy. Perhaps I can help you if you will help me and set me free."

So the farmer told the rat of his troubles.

"Aha!" said the rat. "As I see it, there are two main parts to your problems. First, you have fallen into a common managerial trap. You have been dealing with words rather than observable behaviors. The chickens are having trouble improving for the same reason you have trouble explaining your rating to them and to your boss. Attitude, determination, courage, initiative, and loyalty mean different things to different barnyards. How can a hen improve if she doesn't know what to do?"

"Secondly, there is little incentive to improve. Your pay system can tolerate only a few high achievers. The rest of the hens get nothing for improving. We rats worked our tails off in the laboratory when we were on 'ratio schedules of reinforcement.'

"With your chickens, this would mean that they would get a certain amount of grain per production unit (number of eggs), plus a certain amount of grain for improvement over past performance."

"But what if all my hens met the goals of excellence?" asked the farmer.

"That's o.k.," replied the rat. "Then your total production will be excellent. If you set your grain ratio carefully so that it is fair to the hens and still turns a profit, then everybody—hens, farmer, and land-lord—stand to gain."

"I see it now!" cried the farmer. "A pay and rating system built on observable behavioral objectives! I'll reward the hens for what is important—egg laying!"

Then the farmer turned the rat loose to scurry on his way to his final destination—Walden II.

The farmer presented his new plan to the hens, the landlord's staff, and the Egg-layer's Union. The hens liked it, but they were the only ones. The Union said it was a managerial trick and they wanted no part of it. The landlord's staff said, "Those chickens ought to have pride in their work. We don't need to bribe them. If they don't produce, we'll eat them." The staff all agreed and told the young farmer that he would make the existing Appraisal and Wage and Salary programs work if he just had a better attitude and showed more courage, determination, initiative, and loyalty.

The last that was heard of the farmer was that he was running a Kentucky Fried Chicken stand in Tahiti. As for the landlord, his staff, the former farmer's replacement, and the hens, they were still on the same old roost.

The moral of the fable: The moral of this fable is perfectly obvious to all those with a proper attitude, courage, determination and so forth.

Ely, Personnel Journal (1974).

Even if you have specified the behaviors, goals, and objectives, the results or the evaluation of performance must be fed back to the employees. This process, however, will be much easier with the evaluation made against the clearly specified behaviors, goals, and objectives. There are nonetheless a number of aspects of feedback that should be considered even when the behaviors, goals, and objectives are part of the evaluation system.

The characteristics of effective feedback include the following:

1. It is specific rather than general. To be told that one is "dominating" will probably not be as useful as to be told that "just now you were not listening to what the others said, but I felt I had to agree with your arguments or face attack from you."

2. It is focused on behavior rather than on the person. It is important that we refer to what a person does rather than to what we think or imagine he is. Thus, we might say that a person "talked more than anyone else in this meeting" rather than that he is a "loudmouth." The former allows for the possibility of change; the latter implies a fixed personality trait.

3. It takes into account the needs of the receiver of the feedback. Feedback can be destructive when it serves only our own needs and fails to consider the needs of the person on the receiving end. It should be given to help, not to hurt. We too often give feedback because it makes us feel better or it allows us to "cut a man down to size."

4. It is directed toward behavior which the receiver can do something about. Frustration is only increased when a person is reminded of some shortcomings over which he had no control or a physical characteristic which he can do nothing about.

5. It is solicited, rather than imposed. Feedback is most useful when the receiver himself has formulated the kind of question which those observing him can answer, or when he actively seeks feedback.

6. It involves sharing of information rather than giving advice. By sharing information, we leave a person free to decide for himself, in accordance with his own goals, needs, etc. When we give

advice we tell him what to do and to some degree take away his freedom to decide for himself.

7. It is well-timed. In general, immediate feedback is most useful (depending, of course, on the person's readiness to hear it, support available from others, etc.)

8. It involves the amount of information the receiver can use rather than the amount we would like to give. To overload a person with feedback is to reduce the possibility that he may be able to use what he receives effectively. When we give more than can be used, we are more often than not satisfying some need of our own rather than helping the other person.

9. It concerns what is said or done, or how—not why. Telling a person what his motivations or intentions are, more often than not, tends to alienate the person, and contributes to a climate of resentment, suspicion, and distrust; it does not contribute to learning or development. It is dangerous to assume that we know why a person says or does something. If we are uncertain of his motives or intent, the uncertainty itself is feedback, however, and should be revealed.

10. It is checked to ensure clear communication. One way of doing this is to have the receiver try to rephrase the feedback he has received, to see if it corresponds to what the sender had in mind. No matter what the intent, feedback is often threatening and thus subject to considerable distortion or misinterpretation.

Luthans and Kreitner, Organizational Behavior Modification (1975).

The use of the role strategy of clarifying performance standards, setting goals and providing feedback not only relate to the "Role in the Organization" but also to the "Organizational Structure." As indicated in some recent research many components of the organization are highly interdependent. Because of this, the role targets of responsibility for things and people will be discussed under the "Intrinsic to the Job" strategies, and the role the strategy of effective leader behaviors will be combined with communications and discussed under "Relationships in the Organization."

Relationships in the Organization

As discussed in the preceding chapter, relationships in the organization have a considerable effect on stress. As shown in Figure 6.1, several qualities of relationships are targets of stress strategies: with one's supervisor or manager, with one's employees, with one's coworkers or colleagues; or where there is inability to delegate and lack of social support (Cooper and Marshall 1976). These targets relate to stress in several ways. As discussed in Chapter 4, relationships with one's supervisor, employees, and colleagues can influence several needs, such as those for certainty, achievement, social recognition and acceptance and knowledge of results. Inability to delegate can result in overload, which is related to achievement for the supervisor, and to self-control, responsibility and achievement for the employee. Lack of social support can intensify the stress effects. Employees under similar stress environments experience less serious levels and symptoms of stress if they work in a supportive group, than if they work alone or in an unsupportive group. The supportive group provides an outlet for an employee to discuss and analyze situations that may be stressful, and aids in developing individual strategies for managing stress.

Aimed at these targets of stress in relationships in organizations are several strategies which, when appropriately applied, can help an individual to manage stress. These strategies include:

1. Training for effective leader communication behaviors

2. Development of delegation skills

3. Development of cohesive work groups

4. Group selection and recruitment of new employees

5. Development of group autonomy and participation and

6. Increase of interpersonal skills and sensitivities—with supervisors, colleagues and employees.

Effective leader communication behaviors. Many leader behaviors serve as essential forms of communication, and as such they affect several aspects of the relationship between the supervisor and the employee, as well as other roles in the organization. There are many categories of leader communication behaviors, but seven are important here because of their effect on employee stress (House and Mitchell 1974; Schuler 1979). All of these behaviors can be practiced by supervisors or managers; stress management in this case is just a matter of being aware of the effects of these behaviors of the employee.

Achievement communication behavior by the supervisor conveys to the employee statements of goals, challenge, confidence, and high expectations. Such a statement may be, "Sam, you know, that I really feel you can do this job, even though it is especially complex and difficult." A nonverbal communication of achievement would be allowing the employee freedom to do the job the way he or she thinks best, not the way the supervisor thinks best.

Achievement communication behavior builds the self-worth of the employee by expressing confidence in the employee's ability to do the job (House and Mitchell 1974). Knowing one has the ability to do the job can reduce or eliminate a potentially stressful situation. This communication behavior is especially important to new employees, to employees whose job demands may exceed their abilities, or to employees facing new or unpredictable job situations. the specific effect of this behavior is to reassure and recognize ability to do a job well if the effort is made to do so.

Ego-deflation communication behavior is the reverse of achievement communication behavior. As suggested by the title, this leader behavior reduces the employee's feeling of self-worth, reduces the employee's self-confidence, and makes the employee feel incapable of doing a job. Ego-deflation communication is captured in this statement of a supervisor to an employee: "You know, I can never trust you to do it right!" A nonverbal communication of ego deflation would be closely watching or checking up on the employee. The phrase "He's always on my back" typifies ego-deflation communication by a supervisor.

Contingent-approval communication behavior helps the employee determine what is expected and how well he or she is doing. The supervisor communicates a contingent approval by praising or otherwise rewarding the employee when performance is good. The approval or reward given by the supervisor is contingent on the employee's performance (Schuler 1979b). The phrase "That's excellent, Mary" when Mary's performance is outstanding is an example of contingent-approval communication. That phrase lets Mary know how well she is doing relative to the supervisor's standards.

Contingent communication behavior tends to be historically oriented, not future oriented. If jobs are constantly changing, the employee who receives only contingent approval may be in a state of uncertainty about future expectations, since past behaviors or rewards may not continue. Generally however, contingent approval communication clarifies the employee's perceptions of what is expected and rewarded, especially in situations that do not change much. These perceptions in turn will help reduce stressful situations.

Contingent-disapproval communication behavior lets the employee know what is not rewarded, or what results in punishment or disapproval. A supervisor engaging in this communication behavior may tell an employee, "You didn't finish that job," or "The quality of this work is substandard." It is important that the supervisor be specific enough for employees to know why they were reprimanded. In addition to being related to specific behavior, the contingent disapproval should be aimed only at the behavior or performance of the employee, not at the employee personally—as in "You're really a crummy worker."

Contingent-disapproval communication and contingent-approval communication require the supervisor to be aware of the employee's accomplishments. The employee may be left to decide how to do the job, but the supervisor should appraise the final results so that appropriate rewards or punishments can be applied. For contingent communications to be effective, performance indicators must exist and be known by both the supervisor and the employee. Taking time to develop performance standards and to observe employee achievements is well worthwhile. Effective contingent behaviors minimize stress levels of the employee.

Participative communication behavior of the supervisor can help the employee establish goals or decide how best to do a job. This behavior is especially useful when the employee is faced with a difficult job or when the job changes and new performance levels and goals must be established. Used in these conditions, participative communication behavior can clarify what is expected and rewarded, and can reduce stress-producing conflicts because the supervisor and employee discuss and iron out inconsistencies or uncertainties (Schuler 1980a).

There are occasions, however, when an employee would prefer to be told what to do (Schuler 1976). For example, when there is only one correct decision and the supervisor has all the relevant information. Of course, some employees prefer not to participate. Little or no participative communication may then be in order. A supervisor, therefore, needs to appraise both the situation and the employee before using participative communication. However, when the situation warrants participation, the supervisor benefits as much as the employee because of insights and skills that the employee can provide to the decisions being made. When the employee wants to be told what to do, then directive or instrumental communication is appropriate.

Directive communication behavior is especially appropriate when the employee wants directions and guidance or when circumstances warrant it. Appropriate circumstances are when an employee is entering the organization, when changes are being made by others and need to be communicated to an employee, and when time may preclude participation. Directive communication also may prove to be appropriate when the employee is not performing well because the desired performance is unclear.

Directive communication behavior may refer both to performance goals and methods, for example, "Here's what I want you to do today (goals), and here's how I want you to do it (methods)." When the employee is provided with the information about what to do or how to do something, the result is a decrease in role ambiguity. Directive communication can also help reduce stress when directions take the form of ranking the importance of goals or identifying the time and resources to do what is expected.

If the leader communication behaviors are to clarify expectations, and ultimately to reduce stress, the communications have to be accepted by the employee. If the employee doesn't accept the communication, the positive effect on stress is lost. The employee's trust of the supervisor is necessary for acceptance. But what fosters trust? Considerate or supportive communication behavior does.

Supportive communication behavior conveys concern for the employee as a person, rather than as an instrument of production. This behavior helps increase the trust level between the supervisor and the employee. Supportive communication has nothing directly to do with an employee knowing what is expected, how to do something, or what is rewarded. Its impact on employee stress in indirect; by increasing trust between supervisor and employee, this support facilitates other leader communication behaviors, which do directly influence employee stress

The seven leader communication behaviors have been discussed independently of each other as though a supervisor could employ any of them above. Although this might be possible, in reality most supervisors engage in several communication behaviors. It should be emphasized that effective supervisors are distinguished from ineffective or less effective supervisors by their use of appropriate leader communication behaviors—and by a sufficiently high level of those behaviors—so that stressful conditions are reduced. For example, the more the employee wants participation and the more complex and changing the job conditions, the more appropriate is more participative leader communication behavior (See Locke and Schweiger 1979). Similarly, all other leader communication behaviors have a range or a number of levels. Effective communications are usually not just a matter of behaviors being used or not being used, but of responding to specific situational and employee conditions.

Delegation. Although delegation is an essential part of time management which is discussed in the "Intrinsic to Job" section, it is addressed here because of its importance to employee-supervisor relationships. Effective delegation by the supervisor not only contributes to the management of the supervisor's stress by removing some time constraints, but it also may contribute to the quality of the employee's job by providing challenging opportunities within an employee's ability range. Although the employee may initially experience some uncertainties and stress because of new opportunities, the uncertainties will probably diminish quickly as the employee gains experience and familiarity.

But what can the manager or supervisor delegate? Although there is no exact answer to this question, Stewart (1978) offers some general guidelines on what cannot or should not be delegated:

Planning—setting plans within larger plans or objectives.

Morale problems of considerable importance to the work unit.

Reconciling line and staff conflicts or differences.

Coaching and training subordinates, and reviewing the performance of subordinates.

Assignments that the manager's superior has given specifically to him or her that are not be to be redelegated.

Any part of a committee or task force assignment, especially if the information is confidential, and that the manager as a member has taken on as a personal commitment.

Certain pet projects, ideas, or activities, when these do not cut seriously into the manager's larger responsibilities.

Matters on which there is just not enough expertise around to delegate—or which involve too much of a risk.

All these involve problems and functions that the manager is expected to cope with personally. In general, according to Stewart, the things that can be delegated include: problems or issues that require exploration, study, analysis and recommendations for solution; activities beyond day-to-day operations but still within the scope of the subordinate's job and his or her abilities; projects that guide human talent in a positive direction, toward the company's goals and needs and toward the employee's continuing development and growth; and problems which, if well handled by the subordinate, would conserve the manager's valuable time. Effective delegation related to these points requires several important activities within the supervisor-employee relationship. Stewart lists some of the characteristics that the supervisor should cultivate.

Give the employee the "feel" for the problem or situation at hand.

Indicate to the employee that what is to be done should be done within existing policies, systems, and limitations (with exceptions as approved).

Clarify the objectives of the delegation, the volume of effort that may be involved, the expected completion date, and generally the end product desired.

Make known your standards and expectations; provide a yardstick by which you will judge the caliber of the completed staff work.

Assure the subordinate that you will be available as needed at times for further communication, but only within reasonable bounds.

Build the necessary authority into the delegated assignment and make it known to the subordinate and to others that such authority has been given.

Provide some checklist of control points, and arrange informal interim meetings for periodic discussion and evaluation of progress on the delegated project.

Be sure that the individual whom you have selected for the task is ready to take it on and to handle it well—that he or she has the experience, education, training, judgment, or other special abilities.

Be aware, finally, that there is always an element of risk involved, and be prepared to accept the risk of a wrong approach the employee may take, some unorthodox use of data, or some other development during the time of the assignment.

Cohesive Work Groups. This particular stress management strategy is actually a result of the two strategies outlined earlier: group selection and recruitment of new employees, and the development of group autonomy and participation. Cohesive work groups can be an effective strategy for the management of employee stress in an organization because they help remove constraints and reduce uncertainties associated with potential opportunities which any or all of the employees may confront. Existing evidence strongly suggests that social support can mitigate or modify the effects of stressors in general, and of occupational stress in particular, on physical and mental health. House and Wells (1978) found that individuals in groups with maximum levels of social support have few if any symptoms of stress under increased stress. Their results would suggest that organizations really do not need to reduce stress but need to build good cohesive groups. These authors warn against this conclusion, however:

> Work organizations have no right to expect supervisors and co-workers, much less spouses, friends, and relatives of workers to buffer employees against stresses which the organization could reasonably reduce or prevent entirely. If the effects of stress are sufficiently deleterious that social support is necessary to alleviate these effects, then we ought to be willing to attempt to reduce that stress as much as possible, utilizing social support primarily to buffer people against stresses we cannot reduce.
>
> *House and Wells, Reducing Occupational Stress (1978).*

Likert's (1967) assertions and description of the importance of the effective work groups in organizations are consistent with the effectiveness of the stress management strategy for developing and building cohesive work groups. The characteristics of effective groups as described by Likert are as follows:

The group has well established, relaxed working relationships.

The members and leaders have a high degree of confidence and trust in each other.

The values and goals of the group are a satisfactory integration and expression of the relevant values and needs of its members; they have helped shape these values and goals and are satisfied with them.

All the interaction, problem-solving, decision-making activities of the group occur in a supportive atmosphere.

Although the group may experience conflict, the conflict is resolved to member's satisfaction.

The group is eager to help each member develop to his or her full potential.

The leader and the members believe that each group member can accomplish the "impossible."

The organization can facilitate the development of cohesive work groups by structuring work groups around tasks where possible; when feasible, structuring tasks around groups of employees; and allowing the work groups to make decisions regarding work group membership and even pay.

Although these group-building efforts may encounter initial resistance, the resistance often stems from the fact that there is a change and the change has not been implemented well. Because changes are so frequently accompanied by uncertainty, as shown in the relocation example at the beginning of this chapter, because they influence so many needs of employees, and because change is occurring with increasing frequency, the management of change will now be examined more closely. It is important to consider change as a general target of stress management strategies and to recognize that change may even be at the base of much stress in organizations (Morano 1977).

Change

Change is inevitable. There is little or no escape from it. We are continuously immersed in it. Organizations must learn to adapt and flex with the times. Otherwise they will stagnate and fail.

But change creates stress, and stress puts a tremendous strain on the organization and on the people who make up the organization. Thus there is a dilemma: For organizations to remain viable in the marketplace, they must be organized to plan for and respond to change in an effective way. But the very flexibility that's required to allow organizations to grow creates stress that may slow the organization's momentum (Morano 1977).

Morano, Management Review (1977)

How can we manage to reduce the stress caused by necessary change? Although there are numerous organizational change techniques—for example, those aimed at changing an organization's structure, roles, relationships, tasks, and physical environment—the importance of all of these changes as stress management strategies is that they are associated with people's needs for certainty and predictability. The results of changes and what can be done about them are discussed in relation to the following change strategies: recognize stages of change, and increase employee involvement in all stages. Although these two strategies are listed separately, they will be treated as one here.

Stages of change and employee involvement. As Morano (1977) suggests, people experience five distinct phases after a significant change has affected the stability of their lives: denial, anger, bargaining, depression, and acceptance. These, of course, are also symptoms of stress. Most people have a need for some certainty and predictability, and most organizational and individual changes are accompanied by uncertainty and stress. As shown in the example at the beginning of this chapter, however, the uncertainty of change can be managed by discussion and open, informative communication.

The stress from change can also be minimized by a greater involvement of those expected to change with those who are designing the change. Without this mutual involvement employees will experience more stress and tend to resist change, and thereby will reduce the effectiveness of the organization.

It has been suggested that individuals and groups should go through three basic processes or stages to help ensure obtaining and maintaining change. Observing these stages will assist individuals and groups in perceiving that they are maximizing their gain by changing. It is important to point out that these stages must be carried out with integrity by the managers and the organization. For example, if rewards are promised for change, change should actually result in rewards. Managers should want the desired conditions to come about and the individual to perceive them correctly. Managers should not want only employee perceptions to change, but should want reality to change as well.

Hackman and Suttle (1977) list three stages of change:

1. *Unfreezing.* Analyzing an individual's current characteristics, namely values, beliefs, behaviors, and attitudes, and providing information and experience to the individual which will indicate that the present is not as good as he or she wants. Therefore, there is a reason for change: dissatisfaction. The model thus recognizes the importance of having a state of dissatisfaction, or reason to change, before real change can occur.

2. *Changing.* Developing and facilitating the acquistion of new values, beliefs, behaviors, and attitudes consistent with the change desired by the organization. If an individual is dissatisfied with the present situation, his or her current values, beliefs, attitudes, and behaviors should be changed to be consistent with the new situation in order for organizational change to be successful. The individual may be assisted by the organization in this change, for example by training programs, role playing, job rotation, and so forth, to provide the individual with new behaviors, values, attitudes and beliefs consistent with the organizational change requirements.

3. *Refreezing.* Stabilizing (through group norms, organizational policies and practices, technology, task, structure, or rewards) and continually reinforcing the new values, beliefs, behaviors, and attitudes. These changes must be reinforced, rewarded, supported, and maintained. If they are not, the past will look brighter than it really was, and it will certainly look better than the new situation. If this is the case, the individual will revert to original attitudes and behaviors.

If these stages are followed carefully and with integrity, everybody wins—employees, coworkers, and even supervisors (Hackman and Suttle 1977).

Strategic Issues in Change. There are several strategic issues that all managers face in the development and implementation of any change program, and the way these are addressed influences the success of the change program. The manner in which they should be addressed relates to the three stages of individual change. The term *changer* is used to denote the one wanting to make the change and *changee* is the one for whom the change is made. Traditionally it has been assumed that the manager was the changer and the employee the changee, and that the manager decided what should be done and the employee was the one by whom and to whom it was done (Schuler 1977).

1. *Power vs. Collaboration.* Should change be promoted by the changer selling, forcing, or threatening the changee, or should they work together on the desired change? Usually, the choice is somewhere between these two extreme approaches. But what is important is that a manager determine the extent to which the changer and changee work together. The decision may depend on the amount of information available, the nature of the problem, the manager's personal preference, the degree of trust between

the changer and the changee, or the extent they share the same goals—a goal like improved organizational efficiency. The greater the extent the changee is involved in the change, however, the more likely the unfreezing, changing, and refreezing stages will be implemented, and implemented in the best interests of the changer and changee. A manager who thinks the changee does not share the same goals may want to address the issue of building mutual goal sharing before making any other changes.

2. *Who's Changing Whom and How?* Closely related to power verses collaboration is this issue of who is instigating the change, who or what is being changed, and what method is being used. Is the change being initiated by the changee, out of self-interest, or is the changer making the changee adjust only for the best interest of the changer? The research on change programs suggest that the most successful changes occur when the changee is both the changer and the target of the change (Huse 1980). When this occurs, the changee has a feeling of "ownership" of the change, a good understanding of the change, dissatisfaction with the current situation, and a real desire to change and to maintain that change. Mutual change really requires those managers who want others to change to provide them access to the same information and concerns that management has and opportunities to suggest, initiate, and be responsible for changes the managers desire. That's quite a challenge, but it works.

Facts On Resistance To Change. The importance of and application of the three stages for individual change and the strategic issues in implementing change programs can be seen in some "facts" about why people have resisted and do resist change (Schuler 1977; Beer and Driscoll 1977).

First, people resist making changes that they do not fully understand. Generally people prefer certainty to uncertainty. Lack of clear understanding or knowledge creates very uncertain situations. It may also prevent people from having sufficient information to go through the unfreezing stage. Lack of clear understanding generally produces a feeling that a very unrewarding but certain situation will be far better than the unclear situation being proposed. Not involving the employee in the change process at an early stage may result in a lack of clarity about what is expected.

Even though information about a change program may be accurately related to an employee, the individual may distort the information, and may underestimate or overestimate the importance of the change. People tend to think that the positions or ideas of those who agree with them are more similar to their own positions or ideas than they really are and they tend to think that the ideas or positions of those with whom they disagree as more dissimilar than they really are. These are called assimilation and contrast effects (Zimbardo, Ebbesen, and Maslach 1977). These effects cause distortion which, of course, can influence all three stages in the individual change model. For example, these effects may prevent an employee from perceiving the present situation to be as bad as the manager sees it or from perceiving the rewards for change to be as attractive as the manager does. Having the employee involved in the initiation of change reduces the possibility that distortion will influence the change program.

Resistance to change occurs when an individual is caught between forces for change and forces against change. In other words resistance occurs when the reasons for maintaining the status quo are about equal to reasons for changing; when there are punishments for changing, although there are no rewards for the status quo; or when there are equivalent rewards for the status quo and for changing. It is important for each manager to examine the rewards and punishment conditions for the status quo and change situations as they are perceived by the changee and as they actually are. Employee initiation and participation in the change program will help ensure that the employee perceives more rewards from the change than from the present circumstances, and that the employee perceives that the rewards for change really exist.

Resistance to change programs is usually highest where participation by the changee in the development and implementation of the change program is lowest. Low participation usually results in a low feeling of "ownership," lack of understanding about the change program, and lack of motivation, especially if the program is being initiated by the changer, not by the changee. High levels of participation by the changee result in greater acceptance of the change program and greater support for the maintenance of the change. The change program is not only more successful if the changee has high participation, but usually the quality of the program is enhanced through the contribution of more ideas and suggestions. Participation can help reduce uncertainty resulting from the change program and will also increase acceptance and maintenance of the change, even if the change may have been initially an undesirable one for the changee. Participation is also valuable to the change program because it can highlight areas of disagreement or difficulty. Participation ensures that all three stages of the individual change model are covered. Employee participation means that the roles of changer and changee will be distinct, that managers must become changees as well as changers.

It should be kept in mind that appropriate amounts of time are necessary to proceed through the three stages of the individual change model. If the change program proceeds too rapidly, the time needed to go through these stages may not be available. For example, the current values, attitudes, and beliefs of employees may not be sufficiently addressed to create dissatisfaction and desire for change.

In summary, lack of clear understanding, distortion of information, countervailing reward structures, levels of parrticipation, and pace of change all cause resistance to change. Each of these factors can make the change program unrewarding to the changee by forcing individuals to change when they are not dissatisfied with the present situation; by not assisting adaptation to the changes required, or not providing information that assists changes in attitudes, values, beliefs, or behaviors; by failing to provide support for the maintenance of the change; or by failing to provide rewards and feedback about individuals' attitudes, values, beliefs, or behaviors.

The important question then becomes what can be done to make the program rewarding or beneficial enough to ensure low resistance to change, acceptance, and maintenance of change? In other words, what can a manager do to maximize the gains from any change program?

Recommended strategies for maximizing gain in change programs. These strategies are based on the prior discussion of the three stages of the individual change model, the targets of change, strategic issues in change, and the factors causing resistance to change (Schuler, 1977). They are not necessarily in a specific order, but each should be addressed in any organizational change program.

> Be certain that all individuals involved in the change perceive themselves as much changer as changee. Individuals should be able to generate and suggest ideas for change. Managers may want to share information with employees so that everyone has the same facts.

> Be sure that the changer and the data—that is, the information provided to employees—are perceived as credible. The levels of motivation and reasons for change of the manager and employees will not be equal if the manager and employees are operating under information which is perceived to be substantially different. If the employees do not consider the manager to be credible, they will not believe that change

will benefit them. If the manager's credibility is low, the manager must find this out and use it as the first object of change.

Diagnose the organization. The employees may assist the manager with this. Know the sources of the problems and the possible interrelationships. Recall the targets of change model. It was suggested that it is unlikely that a manager can make a successful change by dealing with only one of the targets. Similarly, it is unlikely that only one target will be the source of a single problem.

Enlist top management support. This is extremely vital to the success of any change program because any change will involve several targets, and these targets may involve the top management of the organization. In the job enrichment example, it was suggested that if employees were given more discretion, there would be fewer rules and the compensation demands would change. This aspect will most likely influence top management. Almost any change will have the effect of a stone thrown into water: although the size of the stone may vary, the result is the same; it still sends its effects through all parts of the water.

Provide evidence that change is possible. It is important that employees perceive that successful change is possible. People are not going to try to change if they do not think their chances for success are very great. The manager may want to cite evidence from other organizations or part of the present organization where a similar change has been successful.

Enumerate the positive aspects of the change. This is much easier if the employees are participating in all aspects of the change program. The manager should insure that these positive aspects of change will continue after the change is implemented. Provide support for the change if employees need help in adapting to the change. If an employee appears to oppose the change, special diagnosis may be necessary to find out why. It is usually the case that the individual is not dissatisfied enough with the current situation, does not know how to change, or does not consider the new situation to be rewarding enough. These strategies of change are defined rather broadly in order that they can be applied to almost any change situation, such as one related to qualities intrinsic to the job.

STRESSORS INTRINSIC TO THE JOB

Stress management strategies related to the nature of the employee's job itself can be aimed at several targets (Cooper and Marshall 1976; Beehr and Newman 1978) quantitative overload/underload, qualitative overload/underload, time pressures and deadlines, employees' abilities and preferences, and job characteristics. The strategies proposed to deal with these targets include: implementation of time management skills, work analysis and redistribution, delegation, job-employee matching, training and development, and job design. All of these strategies are designed to manage the stress associated with five job targets, which results from, constraint on the employees and constraints regarding needs for achievement, certainty, responsibility, meaningfulness, and self-control. Because the two strategies of time management and job design are most capable of serving several targets; we will examine them in depth.

Time management. Time management is a process in which an individual identifies job responsibilities and determines priorities in order to accomplish or achieve needed or desired tasks or goals. These determinations in turn enable a person to be effective and satisfied in his or her job and career (Stewart, 1978). The essential object within this process is to identify needs and wants, attach value to them in terms of importance, and to match them with the time and resources available or potentially available. These tasks or goals an individual needs to achieve are defined as those prescribed by the organization for the individual to remain with the organization in his or her current position; the tasks or goals an individual wants to achieve are defined as those self-imposed by the individual because of a personal value system or because they are related to long-term career goals.

The real need for time management arises from the fact that many individuals have too many tasks they "need to do," and even if they can complete them, they still have things they desire or want to do but cannot find the time for. The relationship between stress and time management now becomes apparent. If an individual is not able to attain or fulfill a need or desire, according to the stress definition, the individual is under stress. (Time management will allow an individual to attain or fulfill a need or desire.) Before explaining this relationship further, however, it is important to examine the common obstacles to time management and then to discuss the steps necessary for effective time management.

Most individuals who claim they have time management problems, that is, who say they don't have enough time to do what they need or want to do, really think they are doing a good job or at least really trying hard. Our society tends to value individuals who really try hard to succeed but in fact don't more than individuals who appear not to try hard but nonetheless succeed. Thus time management problems are viewed by many individuals not as a need to manage time, but as a battle scar to be displayed proudly. It is assumed here, however, that individuals do desire to alleviate their time management problems. What are the stumbling blocks most of us encounter in achieving this goal?

A major stumbling block is the lack of awareness of one's job, duties, authority and responsibility levels. Upon closer inspection, the individual who is really trying hard to succeed is often performing the wrong tasks, either a task not a part of the job description or a task that is relatively unimportant. Often individuals fail to use the skillls or time of others because they do not recognize their power or authority to obtain their assistance. Time management problems, because of unawareness of responsibility levels, can occur when an individual finds out at the last moment he or she is really responsible for completing a task and is accountable for it, but there is no time left to do it. Time management problems related to authority and responsibility arise when an individual has to do two or more tasks and is responsible for both at the same time. In other words, the individual is in conflict and cannot finish what is really necessary in a given time period. The key phrase here is "given time period" because it highlights the fact that time management problems exist only in relation to a specified amount of time. If time were not a constraint, there would be no time management problems. Thus individuals who are comfortable with *manana* find time management to be a foreign word (Schuler 1979c).

Another serious stumbling block to effective time management suggested earlier is the lack of ability to attach priorities to tasks. Many individuals fail to attach priorities because they are unaware of their job duties; others fail because they are unaware of how priorities are given. An important first step is to categorize duties, for example, to group duties into trivial, routine, and innovative, or must do now, must do, desirable to do, and can wait. The next step is to identify those duties that only the individual can do and those that the individual can delegate. In the case of duties only the individual can do, it is necessary to rank their relative importance. Subsequently, time tables should be set up indicating time periods and extent of completion of the related duty. In briefly describing the practices of categorization, it is apparent why individuals may be unaware of them. Failure to decide priorities is a common source of time management problems, especially when combined with the Pareto Principle.

The *Pareto Principle* claims that eighty percent of the activities of most jobs accounts for only twenty percent of the results, while the other twenty percent of the activities accounts for eighty percent of the results. Most individuals spend eighty percent of their time performing duties that are related to only twenty percent of their results of the total job (Stewart 1978; Lakein 1973). That is, most individuals, perhaps because they fail to decide on priorities, spend much of their time on the wrong (less important) duties. Thus, if there is a time constraint, they are faced with doing the important eighty percent of the job in twenty percent of the total time. That is a real time management problem. The Pareto Principle is also evident in the fact that the eighty percent of duties performed are easy and quick to do. There is quick feedback in terms of whether a duty is completed or not completed. But even if an individual is working within the appropriate time allocation, "the best laid plans of mice and men often go astray."

An individual's plans often go astray because of time robbers. Time robbers are events, incidents, or situations that, if repeated often or with some frequency, tend to make one's time disappear quickly. Time robbers may be meetings, visitors, reports, telephone calls, and cancelled opportunities. They are not necessarily wasteful or undesirable, but they do cut into time that could be better spent. Again, many individuals encounter these time robbers every day and fail to do anything about them. As a result they fail to accomplish what they really need or want to do. A more extensive list of possible time robbers is shown in Table 6.1.

The stumbling blocks identified appear to be common sources of time management problems for many individuals in organizations. It is not unusual to find these individuals working at frantic paces, appearing to be in serious predicaments, drinking alot of coffee, and making themselves and others nervous and tense. What then can be done about these stumbling blocks? More specifically, what practices can lead to effective time management?

A key word is awareness: awareness of one's job duties, authority and responsibility and their importance; awareness of one's own skills, needs and abilities; and awareness of how one currently allocates time on the job. Every individual needs to develop this awareness. Suggested techniques for doing so involve keeping daily and weekly logs of activities and analyzing in detail what, who, where, and how much time are involved in each activity. Another technique is to review one's job description and its real meaning with one's supervisor, and perhaps coworkers and subordinates, if any. Occasionally, as previously discussed, individuals find it necessary to bring together all these persons, called "role senders," who send expectations or ask favors or make demands of them. These sessions can help

Table 6.1
Time Robbers

Meetings	Subordinates needing attention
Correspondence	Attempts to reach other managers
Visitors	for consultation
Reports	Need for discussion and correction
Travel (official trips)	of inadequate work by subordin-
Questionnaires and the like	ates
Committee work	"Breaking in" of new employees
Gripes, complaints, morale situations	Community activities
tions	"Standing by" for scheduled
Inaccessible records	meeting with bosses or other man-
Searches for needed information	agers
Emergency situations, trouble-	Clarification of misunderstand-
shooting	ings of policies, instructions, and
Overinvolvement in personal	the like
problems of a subordinate	New projects which seem to
Telephone	"break in" on the work load
Appointments—late arrivals, cancellations	Other time robbers

Adapted from Stewart (1978).

clarify job, authority, and responsibility expectations that these individuals have for the focal person and also can help reduce the conflict potential from these various "role senders."

Frequently time management problems arise because an individual just doesn't want to do but does the job. Lack of motivation may be due to a mismatch of individual's skills, needs, or abilities and those required by the job. Thus it may be necessary to analyze one's skills, abilities, and needs because an individual may be working for something he or she doesn't want.

A final technique related to awareness concerns the daily log of activities. An individual may be an ineffective time manager but in only certain situations (Bonoma and Slevin 1978). In the analysis of the daily log of activities, attention should be given to situations that can be regarded as particularly ineffectual and particularly effectual. The effectual situations may reveal use of effective time management practices that can then be applied to other situations. An example of a daily log is given in Table 6.2.

Assuming an individual has a high level of awareness in the areas discussed, it is important to use, or at least to consider, all of the as-

Table 6.2
Management Activities Daily Diary

LOCATION OF INCIDENT

My office	Starting time ———
Superior's office	Ending time ———
Subordinate's office	Duration ———
Other	

ALLOCATION OF TIME

WHO?		**HOW?**	
Superiors	—	Formal meeting	—
Peers	—	Informal meeting	—
Subordinates	—	Telephone	—
Other internal	—	Social	—
External contact	—	Reading	—
		Writing	—
		Reflecting	—

WHAT?		**FUNCTION?**	
Accounting/Finance	—	Planning	—
Marketing/Sales	—	Organizing	—
Production	—	Staffing	—
Personnel	—	Directing	—
Public Relations	—	Reporting	—
General Management	—	Budgeting	—

KIND OF INCIDENT

Is this incident an interruption	——— Yes ——— No
Could it have been delegated?	——— Yes ——— No

Adapted from Bonoma and Slevin (1978).

pects of the following three processes: (1) conserving time, (2) controlling time, and (3) making time. Each of these processes is too complicated for a general discussion here; however, one way of making time should be elaborated because of its importance: goal setting.

Goal setting involves setting down, on paper, the things that an individual really wants to, or needs to, achieve. Such a goal-setting procedure is as follows. First, list the desired lifetime goals—they can range from job-related goals such as being president of one's company, to several nonjob-related goals such as having a good family, a good marriage, a new vocation, and so on. Then make another list of short-term goals. Next, it is important to compare each set of these goals and identify any conflicts that may exist among the goals in each of these lists. Subsequently, specific behaviors that are needed to attain each of the goals should be listed. For example, in order to attain the goal of having a good family, an individual would say he or she needs to spend two nights a week with family. There may be several behaviors for each goal. After this, it is necessary to state the current strengths and weaknesses that will enable or prevent the individual from engaging in the behavior needed to reach each goal (MacKenzie 1975; McCay 1959).

Job Design. Although jobs may be designed or redesigned as simply as possible, most of the discussion and research in job design has focused on enlarging or enriching jobs, particularly by manipulating five job characteristics. These characteristics are skill variety, autonomy, significance, identity, and intrinsic feedback. *Skill variety* describes the number of skills needed by an individual to do the job. *Autonomy* represents the amount or degree of freedom or discretion the individual has in making decisions related to the task. *Significance* refers to how important the task is, or the extent to which it influences other people. *Identity* describes the degree to which the individual does an entire job from beginning to end, and *intrinsic feedback* refers to the extent the task itself tells the individual how well it has been done. All of these task characteristics are viewed from the perspective of the individual. When the individual considers these characteristics to be high, the task can be referred to as complex; and when they are considered to be low, it can be called simple.

These characteristics in turn are associated with the following individual needs: sense of responsibility, knowledge of results, and meaningfulness (Schuler 1980a). Therefore, increasing the five job characteristics should also increase an employee's sense of responsibility, knowledge of results, and meaningfulness. Aldag and Brief (1979) provide an excellent review of the research on the relationships between these job characteristics and employee needs and employee effectiveness. Their conclusions and suggestions are that not all employees respond the same to these five task characteristics and that job redesign programs should permit individualized response to employees.

Job design can also be applied as an effective stress management strategy when it is aimed at either quantitative or qualitative overload or underload. Situations of overload are associated with too much stimulation and situations of underload are associated with too little stimulation. Since either situation is stressful—especially qualitative overload, which implies being responsible for or dealing with too many people as opposed to things—it is important to deal with these underload and overload conditions. For the underload condition, adding responsibilities to the present job, for example, through delegation, may be an effective strategy, while reducing the responsibility for the number of people or reducing the responsibilities for things associated with a job may be effective strategies for the overload conditions.

Determination of the appropriate job design strategy is important since employees may exhibit similar stress symptoms even though some may have jobs with simple characteristics, whereas others may have jobs that are either overloaded or underloaded. At this time, little or no evidence exists to suggest the relationship among task design, overload, or underload stress. Thus research in this area would fill a significant void in the knowledge of stress management strategies.

There may be job situations that cannot be altered; for example, an underload situation may have to remain that way. An alternative strategy to job design then involves a special case of matching the employee to the job, for example, through a promotion or through selection practices. Of course stress may arise from promotions as well, particularly when they result in overpromotion or underpromotion. This discussion of promotion really leads us into the next major section: career development.

Career Development

Cooper and Marshall (1976) identify five major targets in career development, as shown in Figure 6.1: status incongruity, underpromotion, overpromotion, midcareer crises, and obsolesence—technical, professional and managerial.

Strategies related to these targets include:

1. Goals and value self-awareness
2. Skills, abilites and organizational awareness
3. Analysis of the job design characteristics and load qualities, vis-a-vis employees with promotion potential

4. Promotion policies with flexibility for upward, lateral, and downward moves.

Although all of these targets and strategies are becoming increasingly important, the midcareer crises and obsolescence targets are particularly crucial for many organizations. Therefore, we will examine only those two in depth. Implementation strategies for the targets should aid the organization's effectiveness through retention of employees having valued skills and abilities who will continue to remain up to date in those talents. Employee stress will be managed by these organizational strategies because they will allow the employee to continue to achieve and be productive.

> *Goal and Value Awareness.* John R. is a 38-year-old middle-level sales manager in a large corporation. He is considered hard-working, dependable, loyal, and productive by his superiors, who nevertheless feel that he does not have executive suite potential. This belief was formalized eight months ago when a key promotion was given to one of John's subordinates, instead of John. Since then his on-the-job behavior has gradually changed. His attention to detail has slipped. He has become withdrawn and seems to have lost enthusiasm for his superiors, who view his changed behavior as confirmation of their decision not to promote him.
>
> *Blau, Management Review (1978).*

Although John's situation at first reading may appear similar to that of Bob Lyons in Chapter 2, it is much different. Bob felt underutilized and wanted to do more but could not adjust to his new job demands. John on the other hand can not accept the fact that his mobility in the organization has stopped. In addition, he was passed over for one of his subordinates—probably a younger and more aggressive employee. John's case is typical of the increasingly common phenomenon called "midcareer stress."

The midcareer crises is a realization, as in the case of John, that there are younger and better employees in an organization. These employees, in fact, are the ones now valued by the organization. Another realization is that one may no longer be promoted, that one's skills may have become obsolete. Dreams of rising to the top now must come to an end. Many individuals at midcareer also realize that one's entire adult life has been focused on the career. The family as well as other outside interests may have been neglected. With the realization that one is at a career dead end, the question arises, "What should I do?" The question we must examine is: What can the organization and managers of employees at midcareer do to help reduce the impact of midcareer stress?

Recognition of midcareer stress is an essential first step. As Blau (1978) suggests:

> The recognition of midcareer stress must ultimately involve increased management insight into the role that job structure, selection, placement, and techniques of management will play in the future. While midcareer stress cannot be prevented by optimizing workplace perceptions and relationships, the severity of such stress can be reduced by minimizing the contribution of work-related factors. The quality of leadership in terms of human resource management must equal that of business and technical management.

A second important step in helping to reduce the potential for midcareer crises among some employees is the prevention of obsolescence. It should be noted that the potential for obsolescence is particularly acute among scientists, professionals, and engineers; but with the rapidly changing technology, almost everyone is susceptible to obsolesence (Margulies and Raia 1967).

Prevention of obsolescence. We emphasize here a strategy for the prevention of obsolescence rather than a strategy to deal with those individuals already obsolete, since those who have been identified by the organization as being obsolete may no longer be with the organization, and those who may become obsolete include most of the current employees of the organization.

Although career obsolescence and development are an important responsibility of the employee as well as the organization, the concern here is only with the organization. The organization can engage in two major sets of activities, one of which is related to the individual and the other of which is related to the organization.

The first set of activities involves making employees aware of their reactions to job circumstances. Specific types of awareness are shown in Table 6.3, which is a questionnaire organizations can use to measure their employees' awareness of these reactions.

The second set of activities contains suggestions for what an organization can do to help prevent employees' obsolescence. Such activities outlined by Rago (1973a) include:

1. Providing opportunities for frequent job assignment changes

2. Providing opportunities for employees to develop and utilize new skills and abilities, professional and managerial

Table 6.3
Personal Reactions to Job Circumstances

Here are some statements about the changing trends in one's personal experiences as influenced by one's job. Please circle the point on the scale next to each statement that most closely indicates the degree of change in the trends of your personal experience.

I feel …	STRONGLY TRUE	MODERATELY TRUE	NO CHANGE	MODERATELY NOT TRUE	STRONGLY NOT TRUE
1. I am becoming increasingly sure how one gets ahead in my organization.					
2. I have less energy in doing my work.					
3. I am learning new things about my profession at a decreasing rate.					
4. I am less aware of a variety of professional opportunities for me outside my company.					
5. I have fewer alternatives in the ways I can deal with the requirements of my job.					
6. I have increasing involvement in my work.					

Table 6.3 Continued
Personal Reactions to Job Circumstances

7. I am becoming less adept at making professional contact outside of my company.	—	—	—	—	—
8. My outside interests (e.g., sidelines, hobbies, or community activities) as compared to my job are becoming less important.	—	—	—	—	—
9. I am becoming less creative in my job.	—	—	—	—	—
10. I am increasingly meeting many new people in the context of my job.	—	—	—	—	—
11. My ability to deal with many things going on at the same time is decreasing.	—	—	—	—	—
12. My knowledge and skills are becoming increasingly general in nature.	—	—	—	—	—
13. I am increasingly worn down pushing the system to get things done.	—	—	—	—	—

157

158

Table 6.3 Continued
Personal Reactions to Job Circumstances

14. I have decreasing excitement in my job.	——	——	——	——
15. I devote an increasing amount of effort to searching out and adopting the newest trends in ideas, behaviors, and dress.	——	——	——	——
16. I am personally operating at an increasing pace of activity.	——	——	——	——
17. I am not experiencing increased discomfort within myself while on my job.	——	——	——	——
18. I am slower to change and learn new things to deal with new unfamiliar problems that I encounter.	——	——	——	——
19. I am decreasingly effective at making myself visible and influential within the company.	——	——	——	——
20. My tolerance toward the behaviors of others is increasing.	——	——	——	——

Drawn from Rago (1973). Used by permission of the author.

3. Training managers to recognize and reward outstanding performance
4. Rotating employees around into new, perhaps temporary work groups
5. Providing opportunities for employees to attend professional meetings
6. Training managers to recognize when and if their employees are tending to become obsolete.

If these aids are provided by the organization, according to Rago (1973a,b,c), the employees will be far less likely to become obsolete than if these activities did not exist. Of course, even though an organization may provide this help, some employees may not perceive their intent. One way that the organization can check the employees' perceptions is by having its employees complete the "Trends in Job Demands Experienced" questionnaire shown in Table 6.4. Combining the results of the employees' responses to the questionnaires shown in Tables 6.3 and 6.4 can provide a reliable indication of where the organization's potentially obsolete employees are. The list of six activities for use by the organization can then be used to help reduce the possibility of its employees becoming obsolete and perhaps reduce the levels of obsolescence in some of its employees.

Issues of obsolescence and development may not appear common to all employees in all organizations. We all know many people who have had the same job all their lives and who retired without ever experiencing obsolescence. Although this may still be possible in the years ahead, the probability of obsolescence occurring for many people appears to be growing rapidly. Thus the issue is perhaps more common to a great many more people than it once was.

Another important stress management strategy concerns the physical environment of the organization. This is the topic of the final section of this typology.

The Physical Environment

Oldham and Brass (1979) and Steele (1973) mention two major targets in the physical environment at which stress management strategies should be aimed: (1) the aspects of the physical environment not involving, though affecting, the employees (e.g., heat, light, noise,

Table 6.4
Trends in Job Demands Experienced

Here are some statements about the changing trends in requirements that might be experienced in a job. Please check the point on the scale next to each statement that most closely indicates the degree of change in the trends you find occurring in your job.

My job requires (involves) me ...

	STRONGLY TRUE	MODERATELY TRUE	NO CHANGE	MODERATELY NOT TRUE	STRONGLY NOT TRUE
1. To increasingly deal with persons who must use a narrow range of knowledge and skills in their jobs.					
2. To increasingly deal with unfamiliar situations.					
3. Receiving more encouragement from people outside my company.					
4. To make fewer contacts with people outside my company.					
5. To increasingly work with products or services that are changing at a slow rate.					

6.4 Continued
Trends in Job Demands Experienced

6. To deal with more new associates in short-term relationships.

7. To operate at a decreasing tempo of activity.

8. To take more actions for things to run smoothly. (Operations are less routine.)

9. To get increasing recognition of my contributions by my superiors.

10. To use my creativity less.

11. To have general knowledge and skills in more areas.

12. To expend decreasing amounts of energy and time pushing the system to get things done.

Table 6.4 Continued
Trends in Job Demands Experienced

13. To increasingly use knowledge and skills obtained from sources outside of my job experiences (e.g., courses, outside reading or data from people outside my work group).	—	—		—	—
14. Being subject to more control and direction from higher management.	—	—	—	—	—
15. To increasingly deal with people who have largely common characteristics (personalities, ages, and backgrounds).	—	—	—	—	
16. To spend increasing amounts of time on technical details.	—	—	—	—	—
17. To produce achievements seen by more people outside of my work group.	—	—	—	—	

Drawn from Rago (1973). Used by permission of the author.

toxic agents); and (2) the aspects of the physical environment involving the relationships among people, also referred to as the spatial arrangements (e.g., the size of one's office or work area, the amount of privacy one has, and one's location in regard to colleagues, supervisors, and subordinates).

They recommend that the organizational stress management strategies which may be aimed at these targets are: (1) monitoring, assessment, and adjustment of noise and light levels and the existence and levels of toxic agents such as chemicals and safety hazards; and (2) assessment of the spatial arrangements and their relationships with employees' effectiveness and, therefore, organizational effectiveness.

These are two major strategies by which organizations can manage stress related to physical environment of the organization. The first set of strategies is focused more on the stress from demands on employees, that is, aspects of the environment that will, or at least have the potential to, reduce or diminish the health or performance of employees. The existence of a safety hazard, for example, has the potential of severing a limb or otherwise harming employees. As noted in Chapter 4, noise in the environment also has a diminishing or destroying effect.

The second set of strategies is focused more on the stress conditions related to constraints and opportunities. There are essentially two major approaches to the effects of spatial arrangements in organizations: the social relations approach and the social-technical approach (Oldham and Brass 1979). Each of these suggests several ways the spatial arrangements can influence situations of constraints and opportunities for employees. On the other hand, the social relations approach suggests that open spatial arrangements (few partitions, walls, and private offices) are associated with employees' needs for social recognition and acceptance, achievement and productivity, and certainty because the open arrangements allow greater interaction, friendship opportunities, more feedback from others, and reduced interdepartmental conflict. On the other hand, the social-technical approach suggests that the more traditional private office and partitioned spatial arrangements are associated with employees' needs for meaningfulness, self-control, achievement and productivity, recognition and acceptance, and privacy and ownership because the office arrangements create clearly defined areas of work, privacy for meaningful conversation, and a greater sharing of ideas. Because of individual differences in needs, alternative spatial arrangements present themselves as constraints for some employees and opportunities for others.

The physical environment strategy. This strategy, of course, is encouraged by the Occupational Safety and Health Act (OSHA) of 1970 and various state acts and regulations regarding the work environment. These legal encouragements, however, tend to be directed at specific aspects of the physical environment such as noise, toxic agents, and safety hazards. They do not cover the spatial arrangements aspects of the physical environment. In addition, legal encouragements are generally based on the threat of punishment rather than the promise of reward and possibly can be enforced on only a limited basis.

It is important, therefore, that organizations regard the physical environment as an important source of stress for the employees and as such, it is related to organizational effectiveness. But even if safety hazards are removed, other stress-related decreases in effectiveness may be due to the noise or any of the other sources of stress discussed in the preceding chapter. Eliminating or at least reducing the physical sources of stress, is therefore, important. Each organization should be able to monitor its physical environment, for example, lighting, noise, and toxic agents. This monitoring should be done on a regular basis in coordination with collection of stress symptom data such as accidents, absenteeism, job satisfaction, and visits to the medical dispensary. The possible effects of the physical environment can thus be assessed. This assessment can then provide suggestions for adjustments to be made in the environment. These three processes should, of course, continue as changes are made in spatial arrangements and other aspects of the organization.

The spatial arrangement strategy. Results from spatial arrangements research are generally more supportive of the social-technical approach than the social relations approach (Oldham and Brass 1979). For example, although much research does indicate that open office arrangements (the social relations approach) increase the positive effect toward individual group members and toward the group as a whole, the research does not support many of the relationships between openness and employee needs and behavior hypothesized by the social relationists. In one of the few studies comparing open and traditional office arrangments, the results apear to support the hypothesized relationships of the traditional office arrangements. Oldham and Brass (1979) found that employee satisfaction and internal motivation declined substantially when an office, once traditionally arranged, went to the open office arrangement.

Thus the spatial arrangement strategy of the traditional office layout appears to be more effective than the open office layout. The research, however, is not conclusive, nor does the traditional office layout always prove better on all measure than the open office. The traditional office may be more costly and more permanent and it may provide status barriers, hence some communication barriers, between employees. As a result, some spatial compromises have been devised: the module design, the low walls and plant design (known as office landscaping design), the portable walls design, and combinations of all of these designs.

This discussion of the physical environment strategies raises an important issue related to all of the organizational stress management strategies we have examined. That is, if these strategies are to be designed, researched, and implemented, who or what department in the organization should be responsible for doing them?

DEVELOPMENT, IMPLEMENTATION AND ADMINISTRATION OF ORGANIZATIONAL STRESS MANAGEMENT STRATEGIES

Although some argue that employee stress is solely the employee's responsibility, the assumption we have made is that since several organizational qualities are potential contributors to stress and stress is related to organizational effectiveness, employee stress is also partly the organization's responsibility. Because employee stress is so closely associated with the management of human resources, a major part of an organization's responsibility for the development and implementation of stress strategies may lie with its personnel department or division of human resources. But since the line managers are the ones actively involved in the day-to-day management of employees, they are really the ones who must be responsible for the implementation and utilization of any stress strategies developed. Therefore we suggest that both the human resource people and the line managers together develop, implement, and administer organizational stress management strategies.

Top-level management, however, also must be a strong supporter and even a driving force for the organization to be committed to developing stress management strategies. Without the support and encouragement from the top management, the rest of the organization may think that such strategies and dealing with employee stress are not all that important. Top management's support should include an awareness of the issues related to stress contained in this book, and a familarity with stress management strategies. The relocation example at the start of this chapter illustrates the level of top management awareness and knowledge that together helped make a stress management strategy successful.

An important final phase of the development, implementation, and administration of stress management strategies is the evaluation of the strategies actually used by the organization. The evaluation should be made on the basis of the strategy and target selected and the symptoms of stress discussed in the first three chapters. For example, if a strategy of role clarification and awareness is selected and implemented, the first aspect of evaluation is whether the employees perceive more role clarificaiton than before the strategy. We are assuming here that an organization has already collected information related to all the stress management targets as well as information on its employees stress symptoms. The second aspect of evaluation is the measurement of the selected stress symptoms and the determination of whether a change has occurred and whether it has been due to the role clarification and awareness strategy. On the basis of these results, strategies can be revised, rejected and perhaps reimplemented. Additional strategies can be evaluated in the same manner for each organization. In this chapter we have talked about strategies as related to all organizations, but the actual development, implementation and administration must be regarded as unique to each organization. Each organization may have a different profile on the stress targets discussed, different levels of the symptoms of stress and even unique relationships between the stress targets and symptoms. Each organization may also have its own unique and best way to develop and implement strategies to gain maximum effectiveness from its efforts to manage stress.

AN OVERVIEW

In this chapter we have presented several stress strategies that an organization, part of an organization, or even individual managers can implement to help manage stress in the organization to the benefit of the organization's effectiveness. To organize these strategies, a typology of the targets of stress strategies was developed within the framework of seven general sections. Within these parameters we examined several targets and selected strategies related to them. The development of more strategies and perhaps more targets is left for the reader.

Because stress and its symptoms are becoming more pervasive in many organizations and at the same time the recognition of the importance of the human resource is growing, the development and implementation of stress management strategies by organizations is imperative. Although line managers are primarily responsible for work of their employees, they have limited time and skills to meet this imperative. Perhaps the principle responsibility should fall on the organization's human resource division, with assistance offered by line managers. Responsibility for employee stress, however, should also be shared with the employee. In the following chapter, we will direct our attention to ways that individuals can manage their own stress.

APPENDIX: MAPPING OF ROLE EXPECTATIONS

Goal of the Exercise

This exercise will introduce the concept of expectations, and teach a method of drawing or mapping expectations as a way to do the following:

1. Visualize the *pattern of relationship* among those who have expectations of you.
2. Explore the strengths and weaknesses of this network as regards potential stress in terms of role conflict and role overload.
3. Apply this way of thinking in your organizational role.
4. Suggest ways of reducing organizational stress.

Outline of the Exercise

1. Introduction: The importance of relationships and expectations. Social network as a way to think about *patterns of relationship* and how they affect you.
2. Mapping Your Personal Network: A structured process of network mapping and (optional) small group discussion of first impressions.
3. Theory and Discussion: Role conflict and role overload. Where they come from and what are the causes.

4. Application: Network Awareness and Problem-Solving for Self and Others: Discussion of how to use network ideas and techniques for improving your job role and for guiding your actions as a helper to others or your subordinates.

Mapping your Role Expectations

Materials.   Unlined sheets and Newspaper Magic Markers.

1. Listing Sectors: When thinking about how people are "clustered" with respect to use at work we can have generally three areas: (1) those people who are subordinated to us or who we have control over; (2) those people who are superiors or who have control over us; (3) those people who are peers or whom we interact with outside our hierarchical relationships.

2. Listing People: For each section list the people who expect something of you or whom you expect something from. They may have expectations in positive or negative ways or they may be important in getting things done. The "sectors" are meant to help you organize information; don't worry if some people fit in more than one (list them where they seem to fit best), or if they don't seem to fit any place, use an "other" category.

3. Preparing Your Map: Put a smaller circle at the center to represent you. Then draw lines out from that circle to divide the paper into "pie" sections, one for each sector may be used to list people. Label each sector at the edge.

4. Putting People on the Map: Starting with the people who have the most expectations of you, put them on the map using a small circle with their initials in it. Use the distance between their circle and yours to represent how close your relationship is. Work around the page, putting in the people who are closest to you in each sector, and slowly work outward until all the important people are included.

5. Connecting People and Describing Relationships: Draw lines between the people in your map who know each other. Use the thickness of the line to show how well they know each other. Draw connections across the sectors as well as within them. You do not need to draw lines between each of the people and yourself, unless you want to show something special about a relationship besides closeness. If you wish, you can show other qualities of

relationships with colors or special lines, for example, using a red or jagged line to show a negative relationship.

6. Changes: With small arrows you can show changes that have taken place or are happening or expected. If someone *has moved* in relation to you, draw an arrow from where they were to their circle. If you *expect them to move* from where they are, draw an arrow from their circle to where you think they are headed.

7. Ideal Network: You can sometimes get more perspective on your present network by imagining how you would *like it to be*. One way is to draw a new map on your ideal network. Another is to use a colored pencil to draw changes in your present network which would make it better, e.g., new people, new relationships, new patterns, changing old relationships.

Discussion Issues

1. Relationships and Support: What kind of relationships do you have? What's missing or too abundant?

2. Overall Network Structure: What is the overall structure of your network and how does that affect the relationships you get or need? Size? Diversity?

3. Key People: Who are the key people in your network and what role do they play. Are their links into your network appropriate for their role? Do they get what they need from you and are there "conditions" on their support?

4. Network Norms: What are the norms in your network for expectations? Give them when asked? Offer them when needed, whether or not they're asked for? Withhold them?

5. Personal Style: Do you accept help or reject it when it's offered, and seek it when you need it? How does your style "fit" with the norms of your network?

6. Overload: How many people have expectations of you? Are they close or distant? Do you have time to get your own work done? Which sectors do most of the expectations come from? What can you do to reduce the load?

7. Conflict: Do expectations conflict with one another? Where? Between which people? Are those conflicts from people who are close to you? What can you do to reduce the conflict?

8. Learning: What did you learn from this?

9. Change: What needs to change to reduce or clarify the expectations? What can you do? What can the organization do to help you?

This exercise was developed by Richard Leifer, Department of Management, University of Massachusetts, Amherst, MA. 01003 and is used here with his permission.

REFERENCES

Aldag, R.J., and Brief, A.P. 1979. *Task design and employee motivation.* Glenview, Ill.: Scott, Foresman and Company.

Beehr, T.A., and Newman, M.E. 1978. Job stress, employee health, and organizational effectiveness: A facet analysis, model and literature review. *Personnel Psychology* 31:665-699.

Beer, M., and Driscoll, J.W. 1977. Strategies for change. In *Improving life at work,* J.R. Hackman, and J.L. Suttle, ed. Santa Monica, Calif.: Goodyear Publishing Company, Inc.

Blau, B. 1978. Understanding midcareer stress. *Management Review* August:57-62.

Bonoma, T.V., and Slevin, D.P. 1978. *Executive survival manual.* Boston: CBI Publishing Company, Inc.

Cooper, C.L., and Marshall, J. 1976. Occupational sources and stress: A review of the literature relating to coronary heart disease and mental ill health. *Journal of Occupational Psychology* 49:11-28.

Cooper, C.L., and Marshall, J. 1977. *Understanding executive stress.* London: Macmillan.

Ely, D.D. 1974. The fable of the farmer's folly. *Personnel Journal* 579-82.

French, J.R.P., and Caplan, R.D. 1970. Psychosocial factors in coronary heart disease. *Industrial Medicine* 39:383-97.

Goldhaber, G.M., Porter, D.T., Yates, M.P., and Lesniak, R. 1978. Organizational communication. *Human Communications Research* 5:76-96.

Hackman, J.R., and Suttle, J.L., eds. 1977. *Improving life at work.* Santa Monica, Calif.: Goodyear Publishing Company, Inc.

Hall, D.T. 1976. *Careers in organizations.* Pacific Palisades, Calif.: Goodyear Publishing.

House, R.J., and Mitchell, T.R. 1974. Path-goal theory of leadership. *Journal of Contemporary Business* 3:81-97.

House, J.S., and Wells, J.A. 1978. Occupational stress, social support and health. In *Reducing occupational stress.* A. McLean, ed. DHEW (NIOSH), Publication No. 78-140. Cincinnati: National Institute for Occupational Safety and Health.

Huse, E.F. 1980. *Organization development and change.* 2nd ed. St. Paul: West Publishing Company.

Huseman, R.C., Logue, C.M., and Freshley, D.L. 1977. *Readings in interpersonal and organizational communication.* 3rd ed. Boston: Holbrook Press, Inc.

Katz, D., and Kahn, R.L. 1978. *The social psychology of organizations.* New York: John Wiley and Sons.

Kiev, A. 1974. *A strategy for handling executive stress.* Chicago: Nelson-Hall.

Lakein, A. 1973. *How to get control of your time and your life.* New York: Signet.

Likert, R. 1967. *The human organization: Its management and value.* New York: McGraw-Hill.

Locke, E.A., and Schweiger, D.M. 1979. Participation in decision-making: One more look. In *Research in organizational behavior,* Barry M. Staw, ed., pp. 265-339. Greenwich, Conn.: JAI Press.

Luthans, F., and Kreitner, R. 1975. *Organizational behavior modification.* Glenview, Ill.: Scott, Foresman and Company.

MacKenzie, A. 1975. *The time trap.* New York: McGraw-Hill Book Company.

Margulies N., and Raia, A.P. 1967. Scientists, engineers and technological obsolescence. *California Management Review* 10:43-48.

McCay, J. 1959. *The management of time.* Englewood Cliffs, N.J.: Prentice-Hall.

McLean, A.A. 1979. *Work stress,* Reading, Mass.: Addison-Wesley.

Morano, R.A. 1977. Managing change to reduce stress. *Management Review* November:21-25.

Newman, J.E., and Beehr, T.A. 1979. Personal and organizational strategies for handling job stress: A review of research and opinion. *Personnel Psychology* 32:1-43.

Oldham, G.R., and Brass, D.J. 1979. Employee reactions to an open-plan office: A naturally occurring quasi-experiment. *Administrative Science Quarterly* 24:267-84.

Rago, J.R., Jr. 1973a. Managerial obsolescence: Job-person interaction change and one's marketability. *The Cleveland State University Working Paper No. 1* Cleveland.

_____. 1973b. A program method for assessing client behavioral difficulties. Paper presented at the 81st Annual Convention of the American Psychological Association, Montreal.

_____. 1973c. Executive behavioral cages: is escape possible? *Business Horizons* February:29-36.

Schuler, R.S. 1976. Participatory supervision and subordinate authoutarianism: A path-goal theory reconciliation. *Administrative Science Quarterly* 21:320-25.

_____. 1977. Organizational and individual dimensions of change. *Bulletin of Business and Economic Research* November:4-8.

_____. 1979a. A role perception transactional process model for organizational communication-outcome relationships. *Organizational Behavior and Human Performance* 23:268-91.

_____. 1979b. Effective use of communication and employee stress. *The Personnel Journal* 24:40-48.

_____. 1979c. Time management: A stress management technique. *Personnel Journal* 58:851-54.

_____. 1980a. A role and expectancy perception model of participation in decision making. *Academy of Management Journal* 23:331-340.

_____. 1980b. Definition and conceptualization of stress in organizations. *Organizational Behavior and Human Performance,* 24:184-215.

Sleight, R. B. and Cook, K. G. 1974. *Problems in occupational safety and health: A critical review of select worker physical and psychological factors.* HEW Publication No. (NIOSH) 75-160. Cincinnati, Ohio: National Institute for Occupational Safety and Health.

Steele, F. I. 1973. *Physical settings and organization development,* Reading, Mass: Addison-Wesley.

Stewart, N. 1978. *The effective woman manager.* New York: Wiley-Interscience.

Van Maanen, J., and Schein, E. 1977. Career development. In *Improving life at work*, J.R. Hackman, and J.L. Suttle, eds. pp. 30-95. Santa Monica, Calf.: Goodyear Publishing Company, Inc.

Wanous, J.P. 1977. Organizational entry: Newcomers moving from outside to inside. *Psychological Bulletin* 84:601-18.

Zimbardo, P.G., Ebbesen E.B., and Maslach, C. 1977. *Influencing attitudes and changing behavior*. 2nd ed. Reading, Mass.: Addison-Wesley.

Chapter 7

Working Women and Stress

Dr. Frances Sachs, a new assistant professor in the College of Education, walked across the faculty lounge with a cup of coffee toward the four men seated around the table. She introduced herself as a new colleague and was invited into the group by the well-known writer, Professor John Anderson. "Sit down, sweetie," he said. I'm delighted Dean Huniboldt's hired such a good-looking girl." With mixed feelings, Frances declined the invitation and walked back to her office.

Later that afternoon Hugo King, who had been a part of the group in the lounge, stopped by Dr. Sach's office to apologize for Professor Anderson's sexist remark. "We're not all chauvinists around here, you know. Myself, I think it's fine that we've hired a competent woman."

Peggy was feeling very proud of herself as she cashed her first paycheck and drove home. With prices going up, George's salary just didn't cover their expenses any longer. Peggy had been happy at home when the children were babies but, now that the children were older, she had resumed her career as an elementary school teacher.

When she got home Peggy found 6-year-old Beth crying over a broken glass and the babysitter bathing 4-year-old Adam. By the time Peggy had comforted Beth and dressed Adam, George was home. Peggy ran to him with a smile to show him the money she'd earned. "Terrific!" George said, turning on the TV and sinking into a chair. "You're doing my job, and have stopped doing yours. Why don't you just quit rubbing it in and get my supper ready?"

Kathy Sullivan picked up her briefcase and walked into the rest-room. Today she had presented the results of her work to her boss, the district sales manager, and representatives from a prospective custo-mer. Kathy thought the presentation had gone well and was happy with the way she had handled herself. Pausing to comb her hair at the mirror, Kathy heard two secretaries talking in the next room.

The first one said, "That Kathy Sullivan sure spends a lot of time in Mr. Elliot's office. I can't believe it's all work."

The other replied, "I know. It's all over the building. I can't blame her though. If I were as ambitious as she is, I wouldn't mind spending my days and nights with our most successful sales manager."

Kathy grabbed her briefcase and rushed into the hall, walking quick-ly to her office. She had no idea of how to deal with a rumor like this but needed to collect her wits.

Women who work outside the home are likely to experience stress from other sources besides those identified in Chapter 4.[1] This chapter focuses on sources of job stress specific to women. First, traditional sex-role expectations for women are described. Current changes in women's life patterns have created conflicts between cultural images about women and the realities of most women's lives. Next, the sex-typing of occupations and the sources of stress for women in traditional and nontraditional jobs are described. Fi-nally, role conflicts between women's work and home roles are identified. Throughout the chapter, suggestions are offered for alleviating or coping with the stresses identified.

The following discussion of stress and traditional sex-role stereo-types does not attempt to gauge how extensively our traditional images of women's roles have changed. This is difficult to estimate. We are living in a period of social transition when women who ac-cept or reject traditional sex roles as appropriate for themselves meet with strong approval as well as strong disapproval. In our judgment, it is a rare individual who, or corporation which, is untouched by the issues discussed here.

SEX-ROLE STEREOTYPES AS CONSTRAINTS

Women are usually more patient in working at unexciting, repetitive tasks. . . . Women on the average have more passivity in the inborn core of their personality. . . . I believe women are designed in their deeper

---

[1]Throughout this chapter, the term "working women" is used interchangeably with the term "women who work outside the home" for the sake of variety. This is not meant to suggest a judgement that women who are not employed outside the home do not work.

instincts to get more pleasure out of life—not only sexually but socially, occupationally, maternally—when they are not aggressive. To put
it another way I think that when women are encouraged to be competitive too many of them become disagreeable.

Spock, Sisterhood is Powerful (1970).

Though there is no society in which a substantial percentage of the
work force is not made up of women, there are only a few which match
the fact with cultural images and ideals which facilitate and foster
women's work.

Epstein, Woman's Place (1970).

Roles were defined in Chapter 4 as sets of expectations or prescribed patterns of behavior attached to positions in organizations.
Similarly, *sex roles* are culturally prescribed behaviors expected
from, and differentiating, women and men. People's sex roles channel their life choices. Sex-role stereotypes, the traditional sex-role
expectations for women, cause job stress for women because:

1. They provide minimal social validation of career goals in that
   adult achievement for women is defined as successful marriage
   and motherhood.

2. Traditional sources of power for women are those which are ineffective in many job settings.

3. Only a small subset of vocationally relevant interests and capacities are traditionally considered appropriate for women.

In essence, sex-role stereotypes can cause work stress for women because they act as constraints on women's life goals.

In fact, it is equally true that masculine sex-role stereotypes
cause stress. Men's traditional sex roles constrain them from display-
ing emotions (other than anger), from "giving in" to feelings of
weakness and dependency, and from pursuing "feminine" interests
and skills as a career or a serious avocation. The consequences of
male stereotypes, however, appear to impact primarily on men's
physical health, emotional maturity, and on their nonwork roles,
rather than on career and goals achievement. The impacts of sex-role
stereotypes for women are considered in the following sections.

Traditional Portrait of the "Successful Woman"

Traditionally, a woman's life is centered around the needs of others,
especially those of her husband and children. Women are expected to
attain social graces, achieve beauty or stylishness in appearance, find
the right man, marry, and, if possible, have children. Having attained

adult status at marriage, according to the stereotype, women spend the last forty-plus years of their lives suppporting their husbands' careers, raising children, and keeping house. Depending on the socioeconomic status of their husbands, women may work intermittently after the children are in school. Sociologist Jesse Bernard (1971) identifies the functions that women are traditionally expected to perform in our society as: (1) bearing children; (2) homemaking, which includes doing housework, hostessing, and economic consumption; (3) child rearing; (4) contributing glamor, maintaining an alluring appearance; (5) augmenting industrial production, particularly as a reserve labor force; and (6) psychological stroking, that is, supporting others by raising their status, giving help, rewarding, agreeing, complying, or passively accepting.

Fulfillment of these expectations—being housekeeper, mother, and wife—is success for women, as traditionally defined. Girls are raised to want to achieve these goals. In other words, for women who wish to succeed in life and who subscribe to traditional role expectations, work outside the home is irrelevant. In fact, a strong, life-long career commitment conflicts with traditional role achievement for women.

It is by now a cliche to assert that the woman who lives out the traditional expectations is in the minority. The stereotype represents few actual women's lives. Furthermore, as more women participate in the labor force, as women marry later and have fewer children, as laws mandating equal opportunity for education and employment opportunities are enforced, socially validated expectations for women will slowly change.

The importance of sex-role stereotypes to job stress, however, lies in the fact that stereotypes are internalized by children as a major part of their socialization into adult roles. Stereotypes may become part of the self-image, as well as the goals, of women. This means that sex roles are an emotional, not a logical issue (Larwood and Wood 1977).

Thus, while it may be true that girl babies who are born in 1980 and afterwards may grow up as most boys do now (encouraged and expected to make work outside the home a central, fulfilling part of their identities and lives) all women now to some extent are affected by traditional stereotypes. Consequently, many women are ambivalent about career achievement. One indication of traditional sex-role expectations is shown in Table 7.1. The nationwide Gallup opinion poll in 1976 found that approximately 30 percent of the 1500 persons surveyed disapproved of a married woman earning money if she

Table 7.1
Responses to the Question: "Do you approve of a married woman earning money in business or industry if she has a husband capable of supporting her?"

	APPROVE	DISAPPROVE	NO OPINION
Nation-wide	68%	29%	3%
Among men	65%	31%	4%
Among women	70%	28%	2%

Source: Drawn from the Gallup opinion index, *Women in America* (1976).

has a husband capable of supporting her. Slightly more men than women said they disapproved. This response indicates that in 1976 about 30 percent of Americans believed that a woman's place is in the home.

In sum, the primary adult role that women traditionally have been socialized to anticipate is that of wife and mother. Women's vocational decisions have generally been made contingently, on the basis of marital status or plans, age and number of children, and economic need, rather than as their primary life-shaping decisions. Women have not been expected to take work roles as seriously as family roles, nor have they been expected to have consuming career goals. In fact, many people disapprove of women working voluntarily outside the home at all. This absence of positive, supportive cultural images of women who work outside the home means that throughout a woman's career strong norms suggest that she should stay home. This conflict between women's traditional and occupational roles causes stress.

Traditional sex-role attitudes and career decisions. Given that many married women have the options of joining or avoiding joining the labor force, it is interesting to note recent evidence suggests that women who internalize female stereotypes tend to place less importance on work in their lives, and to choose traditional "women's" jobs more frequently than do women with nontraditional attitudes.

At least two conceptualizations of the importance of work in life have been examined in the organizational and vocational literature: central life interests and career salience. Dubin, Hedley, and Taveggia (1976) report that persons who see their work as a central life interest have positive attachments to work while persons who see their

work otherwise have negative attachments to work. This evidence
suggests that women with traditional sex-role attitudes who are
forced to work by economic necessity may face the double stress of
working in the lower-paying, "female" jobs and of being unable to
live the traditional life-pattern they believe in. (Forty-four percent
of women who work are unmarried; in 1977 the median yearly income for families with a working wife was $22,128.) This situation is
a classic example of the person-role conflict discussed in Chapter 4.

   In addition to the stress caused from conflicts between traditional
sex-role expectations and the choice of a full range of life goals,
women's career achievement can be limited by the personality traits
attributed to the members of each sex and by the occupations men
and women traditionally choose.

Femininity and Masculinity as Influence Styles

Attached to the life patterns traditionally expected of women and
men are two complementary sets of personality traits, interests, and
competencies. Those prescribed for women are consensually defined
as "feminine" and those for men as "masculine." The "feminine"
woman is seen as selfless, dependent, concerned with others, non-
competitive, passive, emotional, sensitive, and supportive; the
"masculine" man is stereotyped as competitive, active, self-asser-
tive, insensitive, independent, and unconcerned with others. Table
7.2 provides examples of items used to gauge self-images of mascu-
linity/feminity. It has often been noted that "feminine" personality
traits are congruent with women's traditional adult roles (i.e., wife,
mother, housekeeper). It is equally the case that sterotypes of women's and men's personalities represent two sets of influence (or
power) tactics. A list of sex stereotypes of power tactics is displayed
in Table 7.3 While influence based on force, rewards, knowledge,
and legitimate authority is "masculine," women are traditionally
expected to use indirect means of influence (e.g., gossip), or to get
their way through personal relationships or attributes (e.g., sexuality, appearance). Finally, women often are expected to trade on their
weaknesses to influence others. The links between traditional power
tactics and work stress for women lie in the masculine power styles
expected from incumbents of managerial and professional jobs. In
other words, the influence styles of managers are masculine.

Good managers are pictured as masculine.   Schein (1975) has found that
both women and men describe "men in general" and "successful

Table 7.2
Typical Items Used to Measure the Masculinity or Feminity of a Person's Self-Image [a]

1.	Not at all aggressive	A B C D E	Very aggressive
2.	Very submissive	A B C D E	Very dominant
3.	Very home oriented	A B C D E	Very worldly
4.	Very little need for security	A B C D E	Very strong need for security
5.	Never cries	A B C D E	Cries very easily
6.	Feelings not easily hurt	A B C D E	Feelings easily hurt
7.	Indifferent to others' approval	A B C D E	Highly needful of others' approval

[a] Instructions: Choose a letter which describes on the scale where you fall between the two extremes for each item. Feminine responses are "A" for items 1 through 4, and "E" for items 5 through 7.

These items are drawn from the Personal Attributes Questionnaire of Spence and Helmreich (1978).

middle managers" in similar stereotypically masculine terms (e.g., competitive, self-confident, aggressive, objective). "Women in general" are thought to possess few characteristics attributed to successful managers. To the extent that this association between sex-role stereotypes and managerial characteristics fosters the idea that all women are less qualified than all men for managerial positions, sex stereotypes are likely to cause stress for women managers, who will be seen as less competent than their male peers.

Stereotypes vis-a-vis Women's Self-Confidence and Fear of Failure

Although there are few actual sex differences in capacities, considerable evidence indicates that women are less confident about their capacities than are men. This lack of confidence could cause women to avoid careers and work assignments appropriate to their actual abilities, resulting in stress from a lack of fit between the woman's job and her abilities. In her recent review of the literature on women's self-confidence in achievement settings, Lenney (1977) finds that

Table 7.3
Sex Stereotypes of Power Tactics

FEMININE
Appearance; Likeableness
Helplessness
Indirect Information; Gossip
False Information
Sexuality
Nagging
Emotionality; Moodiness

MASCULINE
Rewards
Coercion
Legitimate Authority
Information
Expertise
Aggression; Confrontation

MASCULINE AND FEMININE
Ingratiation

Source: Adapted from Frieze et al. (1978).

the nature of sex differences in self-confidence depends on the specific ability area, the availability of performance feedback, and the emphasis placed upon evaluation. For example, she finds in particular that when people are provided with clear information on their task-specific abilities, men and women report equal levels of self-confidence in their expected performance on that task.

It has been proposed that in addition to having low self-confidence women are afraid of succeeding; that is, women have been supposed to be motivated to avoid success, on the theory that femininity and achievement based on a woman's intellectual competence or leadership skills are inconsistent. To the extent that women are "feminine," they avoid success in achieving "masculine" (i.e., career) goals since they expect social rejection following such success (Horner 1972). Experiments investigating this hypothesized motive have found that both men and women "fear success" in occupations considered appropriate only for the opposite sex. The social costs expected when people succeed in tasks that are defined by sex-role stereotypes as inappropriate cause both women and men to avoid such success. Perhaps women fear success more than men do since women typically conform more readily than men to social pressure (Eagly 1978) and since traditional sex stereotypes place involvement in any job in conflict with the wife, mother, and housekeeper roles.

Vocational achievement support groups. A creative and productive approach to coping with the stress of making career decisions is the formation of vocational achievement support groups for women. In such groups, women address sex stereotypes, their own beliefs and feelings, and other obstacles to achieving their own goals. Such groups offer social support, encouragement, information, and feedback to women who can then proceed at their own pace toward confident career decisions (Fleming 1978).

Beyond stereotypes: the androgynous personality. As the effects of traditional stereotypes become clear, an alternative to the polarized and constraining feminine and masculine cultural images is developing. That alternative, *androgyny*, pictures women and men as possessing personalities that contain both "masculine" and "feminine" traits. A woman may be assertive or yielding, cooperative or competitive, whichever is required in a given situation. Recent investigations of androgyny among college students have revealed that about one-third of college women and men are androgynous. Items used to gauge androgyny are shown in Table 7.4.

The significance of androgyny to job stress is that according to some evidence "feminine" women avoid "masculine" tasks, whereas androgynous women adapt comfortably to situations and tasks that are labeled both masculine and feminine (Bem 1976). Thus, a "feminine" woman may experience high levels of stress in situations that are socially defined as "masculine." In addition, androgynous women are more likely than feminine women to choose a nontraditional occupation, such as business management or engineering, to aspire to higher-level occupations, and to have high self-esteem. Thus, it appears that androgynous women may not be as likely as stereotypically feminine women to limit their job choices to those endorsed by sex-role stereotypes, or to feel the person-role conflict inherent in the clash between women's traditional life goals and career achievement goals.

To summarize, there are as yet very few direct investigations of links between sources and symptoms of work stress for women. Instead, building on evidence presented in Chapter 4 that role conflicts cause stress, it has been argued that sex-role stereotypes cause role conflicts for women who work outside the home. Since stereotypes

Table 7.4
A Measure of Androgyny[a]

Describe yourself: How often is it true that you are[b]:

1. Ambitious	11. Analytical
2. Cheerful	12. Gentle
3. Forceful	13. Athletic
4. Childlike	14. Loyal
5. Independent	15. Individualistic
6. Shy	16. Sympathetic
7. Self-reliant	17. Self-sufficient
8. Warm	18. Yielding
9. Dominant	19. Aggressive
10. Compassionate	20. Soft spoken

[a] Odd-numbered items are masculine and even-numbered items are feminine. An androgynous person is one who endorses both masculine and feminine items as equally self-descriptive. (See Spence and Helmreich, 1978).

[b] Responses are measured on a 7-point scale which ranges from 1 = never to 7 = always.

Source: These items are from the Bem (1974) Sex Role Inventory.

(1) devalue career achievement, (2) limit women to an indirect, personal, and dependent power style that is ineffective in at least managerial jobs, and (3) are associated with "the fear of achieving job success," it is asserted that traditional stereotypes are a cause of job stress for women who work, or who wish to work, outside the home.

Changes in sex stereotypes toward androgyny proceed slowly. Meanwhile, most women currently work outside the home at least part of their lives and must cope not only with their own beliefs about appropriate sex roles, but also with the stressful jobs and attitudes that sex-role stereotypes create for women employees. These sources of work stress for women are addressed next.

JOB SEX-TYPING AND DISCRIMINATION

Faith in ourselves, like every other faith, needs a chorus of consent.

Hoffer, *The Passionate State of Mind (1955)*.

The fact that men earn more than women is one of the best established and least satisfactorily explained aspects of American labor-market behavior.

Fuchs, *Monthly Labor Review (1971)*.

Work stress for women results from:

1. The sex-typing of occupations, which segregates most women into a small subset of poorly paid occupations and results in role strain for women in "male" jobs

2. The stresses associated with traditional and nontraditional jobs for women

3. Discrimination against women in hiring, performance evaluation, pay, and promotion practices.

Each point is documented in the following sections and suggestions are offered for reducing the stresses identified.

Sex Stereotypes of Occupations

The distribution of sexes across occupations clearly is not proportional to the number of males and females in the labor force. For example, the ratio of males to females between the ages of fourteen and sixty-four in the labor force is 1.48 to 1.00, but the male-female ratio for managers and administrators (except farm managers) over fourteen years of age is 5.00 to 1.00, and for craft and kindred workers over fourteen years of age it is 19.38 to 1.00 (U.S. Bureau of Labor Statistics 1977). Table 7.5 displays the ratio of women to men employed in several other occupations. Approximately three-fourths of all working women are employed in one of five occupations: registered nurse, paid household worker, clerical worker, elementary school teacher, or service employee (Keyserling 1976). The segregation of occupations falls into several categories. Tables 7.6 and 7.7 contrast the characteristics of sex-typed occupations and of sex-typed professions. These tables suggest, as many analysts assert, that women's occupations serve to channel women into an unstable, crowded, secondary labor market, whereas marginal workers they can be laid off and rehired with swings in the economy.

Other attempts to explain the sex stereotyping of occupations— like Schein's "successful executive" noted earlier—have tried to describe a job in terms of the "masculinity" or "femininity" of the behaviors and skills that the job requires, but the cases of occupations that have "changed sex" (e.g., secretaries, bank tellers) seem to deny that actual job skills and behaviors determine sex-types.

A third explanation posits an association between the status of an occupation and the proportion of males who enter it. Barnett (1975) found that girls between the ages of nine to seventeen had already learned to avoid high-prestige occupations, while boys of the same

Table 7.5
Ratio of Women to Men Employed in 1977 in Selected Occupations

TOTAL EMPLOYED [a]	.67
Engineers	.02
Mechanics	.02
Lawyers and judges	.05
Truck drivers	.10
Physicians, dentists	.09
Blue-collar supervisors	.09
Operatives—precision machinery	.10
Managers and administrators	.20
Teachers, college and university	.40
Sales clerks, retail	1.27
Teachers, except college and university	2.36
Bookkeepers	4.55
Health service workers (aides, orderlies)	7.46
Other health workers (nurses, technicians, therapists)	8.13
Operatives—sewers and stitchers	14.80
Telephone operators	16.74
Secretaries and typists	28.34
Private household workers (paid)	28.43

[a] Persons ages 14 and over, in all occupations
Source: U.S. Department of Commerce, Bureau of the Census, *Current Population Reports,* Series P-20, No. 274.

Table 7.6
Characteristics of Sex-Typed Occupations

"WOMEN'S" OCCUPATIONS	"MEN'S" OCCUPATIONS
Low wages	High wages
Limited opportunities for promotion	Reasonable chances for promotion
Few on-the-job training programs	On-the-job training
Job insecurity	Relatively secure employment
High turnover	Low turnover
Weak unions or no unions	Powerful labor unions

Source: Summarized from Power (1975).

Table 7.7
Characteristics of Sex-Typed Professions

"WOMEN'S" PROFESSIONS[a]	"MEN'S" PROFESSIONS[b]
Require large numbers of skilled but cheap workers.	Require limited numbers of highly skilled, expensive workers.
Do not require extensive schooling or great investments of time, energy, and devotion.	Require extensive schooling and great investments of time, energy, and devotion.
Most training acquired before employment and thus requires virtually no investment by the employer.	Additional professional training by employers often provided or contributed.
Do not require continuity in employment or long-term commitment.	Generally require continuity in employment and long-term commitment.
Do not generally expect overtime work (paid by employer or contributed by employee for professional development).	Often expect a lifetime of overtime work. The unpaid services of the employee's wife frequently presupposed.
Worker's mobility not important: jobs all over the country.	Mobility required for advancement.
Rarely place women in supervisory positions over men.	Frequently place men in supervisory positions over women.

[a] For example, nursing, teaching, librarianship.
[b] For example, law, engineering, medicine.
Source: Drawn from Gullahorn (1977).

age had learned to prefer them. The process by which women conclude that prestigious occupations are inappropriate is unclear, but one is led to predict that in general women are less likely to aspire to a high-status occupation than are men. It may be that conforming to strong socially reinforced expectations is less stressful for women than fighting stereotypes by choosing a nontraditional occupation.

A final rationale for forming occupational sex-types is caused by having a high percentage of workers in the occupation who are male. Women, anticipating discrimination, are likely to choose occupations such as bookkeeping and teaching, which have substantial proportions of women employed in them, and to avoid mostly "masculine" occupations.

In any case, those occupations and the specialties within occupations which are considered appropriate for one sex or the other are clearly defined and held in common by both men and women. For example, Table 7.8, which displays data from a 1976 nationwide Gallup poll, reveals that both men and women agree that women make better nurses, grade school teachers, secretaries, and hairdressers than do men. Responses to a similar question about the occupations in which men excel show that the occupations of police officer, auto mechanic, airline pilot, truck driver, and firefighter are stereotyped as male, and that doctors, lawyers, bankers, stockbrokers, executives, U.S. senators, judges, and veterinarians are considered to be in an interesting "undifferentiated" category. These data are shown in Table 7.9.

In summary, most occupations are sex-typed. The reasons for occupational stereotypes are not entirely understood, but they serve to

Table 7.8
Responses to the Question: "Which of these occupations or professions, if any, do you feel *women would be better than men?*"

OCCUPATIONS	RESPONDENTS	
	MEN	**WOMEN**
Police officer	2%	3%
Doctor	12%	17%
Lawyer	7%	9%
Banker	8%	7%
Nurse	66%	60%
Auto mechanic	1%	2%
Stockbroker	5%	5%
Airline pilot	1%	3%
Truck driver	2%	2%
Corporate executive	4%	9%
U.S. Senator	8%	14%
Grade-school teacher	56%	50%
Secretary	57%	53%
Firefighter	<1%	1%
Hairdresser	53%	43%
Judge	12%	19%
Veterinarian	16%	13%

Source: Drawn from The Gallup opinion index, *Women in America* (1976).

Table 7.9
Responses to the Question: "Which of these occupations or professions, if any, do you think *men would be better than women?*"

OCCUPATIONS	RESPONDENTS	
	MEN	WOMEN
Police officer	64%	58%
Doctor	33%	29%
Lawyer	37%	32%
Banker	31%	28%
Nurse	1%	1%
Auto mechanic	58%	52%
Stockbroker	28%	27%
Airline pilot	50%	45%
Truck driver	58%	54%
Corporate executive	35%	29%
U.S. Senator	31%	27%
Grade-school teacher	4%	4%
Secretary	3%	1%
Firefighter	58%	55%
Hairdresser	2%	5%
Judge	32%	27%
Veterinarian	25%	26%

Source: Drawn from the Gallup opinion index, *Women in America* (1976).

channel three-fourths of the women who are employed outside the home into five occupations, whereas men are spread into all the occupations not defined as women's work.

Integrating the workforce.   Remedies for sex-typing of occupations include nation-wide and state-wide mandates promoting equality of educational and occupational opportunity and affirmative action plans. Within organizations, practices such as wide advertisement of opportunities in all occupations, and freely hiring women into formerly male jobs has been suggested to alleviate sex-typing. These measures are unlikely to change perceptions of sex-types in the short run but offer hope for long-term change.

Work Stress for Women in Sex-typed Jobs

In Table 7.5 and Table 7.6, characteristics of sex-typed jobs for women and men were compared. The sources of stress for women employed in each type of occupation are, for the most part, quite different. Although it would not be possible to detail the sources of stress for every occupation women occupy, two representative examples—secretary and manager—are selected for attention.

Clerical workers and secretaries. Often the top-level clerical job in an organization, the group makes up 32 percent of women in the labor force; 94 percent of clerical workers and secretaries are women. The secretary's job is perhaps the closest organizational analog to many of the functions performed by a wife; her official tasks are routine, her relationship with her (usually male) boss is generally personal. She derives her status in the organization from the rank of her boss, rather than from her own job duties or skills. She is expected to do housekeeping chores, and often to provide devotion and emotional, as well as task, support to her boss. Her pay is low. According to a national survey of 19,000 secretaries, the average salary of a secretary in 1979 was about $8,500 (*Iowa City Press Citizen* 1979). She is expected to desire and be satisfied by her boss's attention and appreciation.

One of the myths about working women is that while men want career-related work outcomes such as promotions and high pay, women prefer rewards associated with the social aspects of work, like pleasant coworkers and attractive surroundings. This myth has been used to justify keeping women in low-paying, low-level jobs. Kanter (1977) explains that this supposed sex difference in preferred work rewards is actually a response of women and men who are stuck in a job that has no potential for advancement. Since such people have no possibility of ever being promoted to a more responsible, higher-paying position, they quite naturally make the best they can of the work rewards available to them. These rewards tend to be primarily the social satisfactions women are supposed to prefer.

The sources of work stress reported in a 1979 survey of 19,000 secretaries by at least forty percent of the respondents were (1) inadequate pay; (2) boring jobs; (3) no opportunity for training or advancement; and (4) jobs that don't use their skills. Twenty percent or less of the secretaries reported stressful working conditions and treatment by bosses, recent layoffs and unemployment, and job difficulty (*Iowa City Press Citizen* 1979). The stressful combination of a dead-end clerical job and an unsupportive boss has been linked to an increased risk of heart disease for women (*New York Times* 1980). The "Office Procedures Memo" in Figure 7.1 offers a humorous but

MEMO TO: Professional Group

FROM: Secretaries

SUBJECT: Office Procedures

GENERAL

1. Never give us work first thing in the morning—we much prefer a terrific rush in the late afternoon.
2. Whenever possible, please endeavor to keep us late. We have no homes to go to and are only too thankful for somewhere to spend the evening.
3. Should work be required urgently (a most unusual occurrence) it aids us considerably if you will rush in at intervals of 30 seconds to see if it is done.
4. When we stagger out carrying a pile of files, please do not open the door for us; we should learn to crawl under it.
5. Send us out to cash your checks, buy your cigars, etc., in all weather—walking is exhilarating and, as we sit down all day the exercise does us good.
6. Do walk out of the office without telling us where you are going or how long you might be. We enjoy telling people who wish to contact you urgently that we have no idea where you are.

USE OF DICTAPHONE AND GENERAL WRITING PROCEDURES

1. When dictating, please parade up and down the room and practice your golf strokes. We can understand what is said more distinctly.
2. Please lower your voice to a whisper when dictating names of people, places, etc., and under no circumstances spell them to us—we are sure to hit on the right way of spelling sooner or later, and we know the name and address of every person, firm, and place in the world.
3. Should a letter require a slight alteration after it is typed, score the word heavily through about four times and write the correct word beside it, preferably in ink or heavy pencil. Always make the alteration on the top copy.
4. Please dictate a paragraph and change your mind, with the corrected version following—it adds variety to our typing.
5. Hours for dictation: (a) During the lunch hour (b) Any time between 4:30 p.m. and 5:00 p.m.
6. Should you wish to write out a letter or report, please write with a blunt pencil in the left hand, and use plenty of arrows, balloons, and other diagrams. If figures are altered, please write directly over those previously inserted.

USE OF TELEPHONE

1. Remember when asking us to place a long distance call, you must be very fast on your feet to get out of the office before the call comes through.
2. If possible, always pick up your calls on your secretary's call director. This makes sure that we cannot pick up calls for any of our other people, or on your own phones. It also helps to keep us company—we miss you during the day.
3. When you have given us a rush project be sure to use your intercom line frequently, at intervals of every 60 seconds or so, to ask us to get minor items, call someone, go for coffee, etc.
4. If you are paged, please ignore it—we usually have no particular reason for wanting to locate you and enjoy hunting you down or taking messages.
5. Do interrupt us while we're speaking on the phone—we've got two ears so might as well use them.

Figure 7.1

Office Procedures Memo. (From McLean and Crawford 1979)

pointed sketch of the thoughtless behavior common toward secretaries and clerical workers. The relationships of these experiences to job stress have been described in Chapter 4.

Managerial jobs. Among the lures for women into managerial jobs are that more money and responsibility are available than in many jobs. The median salary for women managers and administrators in 1977 was $9,804, compared to a median salary of $16,674 for men. The difference is largely due to women's lack of seniority and concentration in lower-level managerial jobs (*U.S. News and World Report* 1979).Currently, six percent of women are employed as managers or administrators. Approximately seventeen percent of all managers are women, but few women have middle- and top-level managerial positions. If secretaries fill organizational positions analogous to the family roles of the wife, then the manager's position is somewhat analogous to that of the husband. It has already been shown that "successful executives" are seen as masculine. Responses to a 1976 nationwide Gallup poll, shown in Table 7.10, reveal that sixty percent of both women and men say they would prefer to work for a male boss. A breakdown of responses by age shows that older respondents report the strongest preferences for a male boss. Typical items used to gauge attitudes toward women as managers are shown in Table 7.11.

Attempts to explain the basis of negative attitudes toward women as managers have focused on the discrepancy between the masculine sterotype of managerial work and the feminine personal-

Table 7.10
Responses to the Question: "If you were taking a new job and had your choice of a boss, *would you prefer to work for a man or a woman?"*

RESPONDENTS	MAN	WOMAN	NO DIFFERENCE	NO OPINION
Women	60%	10%	27%	3%
Men	63%	4%	32%	1%
BY AGE				
Total under 30	51%	14%	34%	1%
18-24 years	45%	17%	38%	<1%
25-29 years	61%	10%	27%	2%
30-49 years	63%	5%	30%	2%
50 and older	68%	5%	25%	2%

Adapted from the Gallup opinion index, *Women in America* (1976)

Table 7.11
Sample Items Used to Gauge Attitudes Toward Women as Managers

1. It is less desirable for women than men to have a job that requires responsibility.
2. Challenging work is more important to men than it is to women.
3. The possibility of pregnancy does not make women less desirable employees than men.
4. To be a successful executive, a woman does not have to sacrifice any of her femininity.
5. Women are less capable of learning mathematical and mechanical skills than are men.
6. Women would no more allow their emotions to influence their managerial behavior than would men.
7. Women are not competitive enough to be successful in the business world.
8. On the average, a woman who stays at home all the time with her children is a better mother than a woman who works outside the home at least half time.

Responses are measured on a 7-point scale which ranges from 1 = strongly disagree to 7 = strongly agree. Items 1, 2, 5, 7, and 8 are reverse scored so that a high score is associated with a favorable attitude toward women as managers.
Source: The items are drawn from The Women as Managers Scale (Terborg, et al. 1977).

ity and sex-role stereotypes attached to women. Women are seen both as incomprehensible and unpredictable and—paradoxically— as performing also under more internal (e.g., personality) and external (e.g., responsibilities for family role) constraints than are men. In addition, women bosses are stereotyped as extremely demanding, controlling, detail oriented, discriminatory and guilty of partiality. Kanter (1977) points out that this operating style is a result of powerlessness, which is more often the fate of female than male managers in organizations. Men appear to have more power for similar levels of authority than women do, at least partly because, compared to women, men tend to be unquestioningly supported in authority positions by their supervisors and peers.

Organizational strategies for supporting female managers. The stresses experienced by competent female managers, then, can be reduced by increasing the support they receive from their supervisors and peers. Three ways by which this can be done are for organizational managers to:

1. Avoid tokenism. Hire groups of women—rather than one woman and several men—into open positions formerly held by men. Kanter (1977) has detailed the processes by which solo women in professional peer groups become isolates or deviates. Defuse the situation for role innovators by hiring more than one at a time.

2. Include women in peer ("old boy") networks. Take care that women are included in the informal socializing that is an important source of information and assistance.

3. Encourage senior executives to sponsor women as protégées. The importance of mentors or sponsors to advancement in managerial careers has long been recognized. Sponsoring a woman may be seen by men as a risky activity, however, since women in a predominantly male group are particularly visible and their failures will be noticed, and since a sponsor's interest in a female protégée can be interpreted by third parties as a sign of sexual involvement.

Sexuality and work stress. Throughout the history of western culture sexuality has been seen as a (curiously) unilateral source of power for women over men. The image of Woman as Temptress, enticing men to intoxication and often to disastrous commitments, is as old as our myths and stories of creation. In our modern world, advertising uses the image of Woman as Temptress to sell everything from house slippers to farm implements. Moreover, the reciprocal picture of Man as Seeker and Conqueror is also central in our set of human images.

Throughout adolescence and adulthood, much of the social interaction between pairs of women and men revolves around sexuality. When a woman comes into a formerly all-male preserve, not as a supporter or helper but as a peer or supervisor, and is in frequent contact with a male, it is an adjustment for some people to think of this pair of workers as supervisor-subordinate or as colleagues. Male-female interaction still, in our traditions, evokes primarily sexual connotations.

As a result, proximity to women is sometimes avoided by men so as not to provoke "the wrong idea" in the minds of third parties. For example, women may not be sent on overnight business trips with a male colleague; or a male supervisor, perhaps fearing negative reactions from his wife, may avoid dining alone with a promising female subordinate. Men may request not to share an office with a female colleague. In time, this kind of avoidance can cause serious harm to women's careers. The practice of avoiding informal interactions with women employees reinforces sex stereotypes and rejection of women as colleagues.

Dealing maturely with sexuality at work means, in the view of the authors, keeping it out of work relationships. Books of career advice for women, such as those listed in the bibliography, concur with this, partly because the consequences of sexual relationships at work impact more negatively on the woman than on the man involved. Moving beyond the confines of sex stereotypes for both men and women also means seeing male-female interactions in nonsexual terms.

Self-help for managerial women. In the past few years, several excellent books have been written in response to the needs of women who hold, or wish to hold, managerial positions. The focus of these books has been to orient women to the "male culture" within organizations, train women in specific management skills, and increase women's general confidence and effectiveness. In addition, many institutions offer training programs or classes that cover the skill requirements of specific positions or that convey information on the three topics listed above. Some examples are listed in the bibliography.

Sexual harassment. According to several recent surveys (Farley, 1978, Lindsay, 1977; and MacKinnon, 1979), from seventy to ninety percent of working women report they have been subjected to unwanted, repeated, and coercive sexual advances at work. Sexual harassment can take the form of innuendoes, lewd comments, sexual gestures and touching, demands for dates, and outright demands for sexual involvement. Often, promises of career advancement in return for sexual favors, or threats of harm if demands are rejected, are implicitly or explicitly made.

Like rape, sexual harassment is a manifestation of domination and aggression against women as a group, rather than of sexual attraction to an individual woman. Regardless of age, attractiveness, or occupation, women are likely to be sexually harassed when they are economically dependent on the men who enact the harassment. The consequences for individual women can be personally devastating. For women as a group, the dynamics of sexual harassment contribute to job turnover—since often the only way to stop the harassment is to quit—and result in low wages and downward mobility.

Coercive sexual pressures at work are beginning to receive the attention of lawmakers. In April 1980 the U.S. Equal Employment

Opportunity Commission published regulations that make sexual harassment of employees by their supervisors a civil rights violation. According to the rules, which apply to all government offices and to private firms having fifteen or more employees, sexual harassment becomes illegal if the employee's submission is an implicit or explicit condition of employment, the employee's response is a basis for employment decisions, or sexual advances create a hostile or offensive work environment that interferes with workers' performance. Employers are charged by the regulations with an "affirmative duty" to prevent and eliminate physical and verbal sexual harassment (*New York Times* 1980). In several states, bills are pending that would make sexual harassment a criminal violation. Until such bills are law, a woman who loses or quits her job because she refuses the sexual advances of her employer may be refused unemployment compensation unless she has carefully documented her case, as recommended below.

Handling sexual harassment.   A woman who is sexually harassed on the job has several options. The following suggestions are offered to help women deal with harassment in a way that minimizes stress and harm to their careers:

1. Understand that sexual harassment is not a personal response to you, or a comment on your competence, but a manifestation of the stereotypes attached by some people to women as a group. You have a right to complain and take action, to put a stop to the harassment.

2. Make it very clear to the offender that you don't like his sexual attentions and want them to stop. If the harassment is repeated, repeat your complaints in front of witnesses.

3. Talk to other women at work and gather support. Chances are that if a man has harassed you, he has others also. You are more likely to be believed, and less likely to be fired, if you are not alone.

4. Keep a diary of the times, places, and witnesses present whenever the abuse occurs. Write down exactly what happened or what was said.

5. Complain to your supervisor (or his supervisor, if you are being harassed by your boss) in writing, asking for an investigation of your charges. Request a written reply. Move up the organizational structure if you don't get results.

6. If your complaints don't work, or if you are fired or refused promotion because of those complaints, you can file an official complaint with your city or state Human Rights Commission or Fair Employment Practices Agency, or with the federal Equal Employment Opportunity Commission. Be forewarned that settlement of your complaint can take months or years.

7. If you decide to quit, apply for unemployment benefits. State clearly that you quit because of sexual harassment. If your claim is denied, contact the Equal Employment Opportunity division of your state Employment Security Commission.

8. While you are coping with the stresses caused by this career threat and with your own feelings of violation, be especially good to yourself. Use the coping mechanisms identified in Chapter 6 of this book to reduce the effects of stress on your life.

Sex Discrimination in Organizational Practices and Policies

Sex discrimination refers to nonjob-related limitations placed on women in hiring, performance evaluations, pay, and promotions. Every time that a woman is not hired or paid less, rated lower, or not promoted when a man of equal qualifications and performance would be favorably evaluated, the woman has been subjected to sex discrimination. For example, in addition to the concentration of women in low-paid occupations, discrimination is another cause of the low pay women receive.

Recent attempts to understand discrimination suggest that the reasons evaluators give for women's successes differ from the reasons given to explain men's successes in the same tasks. Women's successes are attributed to luck or to an easy job (external factors) rather than to internal factors such as women's efforts or abilities. Positive attitudes toward women as managers have been identified as significant predictors of the belief that women's successes are due to their abilities and efforts, rather than to luck or the ease of the job. By the same token, women's successes can be discounted by attributing them to luck when the evaluator believes women to be "unsuitable" as a worker in a masculine task.

In addition, it has been found that although personal attractiveness is an advantage for men, attractiveness in women is an advantage only for women seeking nonmanagerial positions. Attractive female applicants for managerial positions are rated lower in qualifications, are less highly recommended, and receive lower starting salaries than unattractive applicants. Attractive women are seen as more feminine—therefore, less qualified for a managerial job—than are unattractive women. In sum, sex discrimination is based on both sex-role stereotypes about women and on sex stereotypes of occupations.

COPING WITH WORK AND HOME ROLES

> Most husbands harbor deeply ambivalent feelings about working wives. A man may be proud of his wife's accomplishments, yet resent having to help out at home. He may welcome the money she earns, yet feel his masculine role as the breadwinner is being degraded . . . . He may be grateful that she shares the financial burdens, yet reluctant to share major family decisions with her.
>
> *Lobsenz, Humanity as a Career (1979).*

> How can you serve a husband, kids, an automatic washer, the Board of Health, and a cat who sits on top of the TV set and looks mad at you because you had her fixed and still have something left over for yourself?
>
> *Bombeck, I Lost Everything in the Postnatal Depression (1973)*

The following discussion deals explicitly with the problems of women who are married and today working outside the home. The millions of single, divorced, and widowed women—with or without children—who work confront some of the same problems. Lack of research on the nonwork sources of stress in the lives of these groups of women, as well as the fact that most women marry at some time in their lives, dictated this choice of topics.

At the beginning of this chapter, traditional sex-role expectations for women were described. Women's successes are traditionally defined as being good wives, mothers, and housekeepers. Work outside the home is given a peripheral position, if any, in this cultural image, so women who do work outside the home must define their own criteria for a successful life. Currently, in the United States, over fifty percent of households are made up of working couples, in which both husband and wife have paid jobs. This percentage is expected to continue to increase; seventy to eighty percent of married women are expected to be in the work force by the end of the 1980s. Such a massive change in the activities of married women has not yet been accompanied by a cultural shift away from the traditional picture of women's or men's roles at home. Some women are trying to integrate their "extra" job into their traditional role expectations. Other couples who are sharing housework, child raising, and support for two careers are working out their own patterns.

For a household to operate, each couple must resolve three issues: (1) what is the relative importance of the woman's and man's work, (2) how is child care (if any) shared, and (3) who does the housework? Each issue, and its relationship to women's stress, is considered next.

Relative Career Involvement

Earlier in this chapter, an association was documented between the importance of work in a woman's life and the woman's rejection of traditional sex stereotypes as appropriate for herself. This relationship suggests that women who are highly involved in their careers may also be comfortable with nontraditional marital patterns. Women's job involvement has been found to be independent of involvement with their families. A career woman is just as likely as any other woman to attach great importance to her family.

The dual-career couple, made up of two people who are both highly involved in their careers, has resulted in such lifestyle patterns as couples who commute long distances or live temporarily in separate cities to pursue their careers. The partners in dual-career couples tend to share child care and household chores on a more egalitarian basis than do traditional couples. In addition, their relatively high family incomes make it possible to afford day care tuition and to pay to have the house kept clean. Time is the resource in shortest supply among such couples, particularly when work schedules conflict.

Among all couples, there is a substantial amount of evidence to indicate that the degree of stress and the level of career achievement experienced by married women is related to their husbands' needs for power and attitudes toward their wives working. Women with supportive husbands experience significantly less stress than women whose husbands believe the "women's place is in the home."

Child Care

When time is scarce, caring for children takes precedence over housework, which can be postponed. Arranging for child care, when both parents work outside the home, also takes high priority and is usually done by women. According to recent surveys, the most frequently used child care arrangements are: care by a relative at home (grandparent), care at home by someone other than a relative, or care in another home. Day care centers and other formal child care institutions are used by only about ten percent of working couples. In order to avoid stress, it is important to find child care patterns that satisfy people's beliefs about being good parents.

It has recently been discovered that working women with several children are significantly more likely than single working women or housewives with children to develop stress-linked heart disease. The stresses associated with raising three or more children are so great, in fact, that single working women face lower risk of heart disease than do housewives with large families. If the demands of a career are added to the duties of raising a family, the resulting stress can literally help precipitate heart disease (*New York Times* 1980).

Housekeeping

Conflict over which family members are responsible for, and do, household chores can be a source of stress for working women. There is little information on associations between stress and specific divisions of household labor, but total responsibility for housework or lack of help has often been identified as a source of stress by women who are employed. In 1975, married women employed outside the home spent an average of twenty-five hours a week on housework and shopping, while married men spent, on average, ten hours a week. There is some evidence that divisions of household labor are passed from one generation to the next within families (Thrall, 1978). Thus, it appears that in most marriages women do most of the housework themselves and that such patterns may be resistant to change. Housework is defined as the woman's responsibility and family members are seen as helping her (note the wording of the first quotation introducing this section) when doing housework. To the extent that women do most of the housework and maintain high standards of housekeeping, they experience stress because of severe time pressures on their other life roles.

The patterns that working couples develop to cope with the role conflict between women's traditional family tasks and their job reflect, among other things, the relative priority of the wife's work, the husband's support for her working, the number and ages of children, child care arrangements, and divisions of household labor. To the extent that women must shoulder responsibility for children and housework themselves, the role overload from home roles is a source of stress for working women.

AN OVERVIEW

This chapter has discussed sources of work stress for women. First, the constraints and conflicts caused by traditional female sex-roles to women's career goals, power tactics, and self-confidence were shown. Androgyny was proposed as an alternative to sex stereotypes. Secondly, sources of work stress were said to be the stereotyping of occupations, the sex structuring of organizations, and sex discrimination. Sexual harassment was identified as a sign of aggression and dominance. Thirdly, conflicts between women's work and home roles were discussed. Throughout the chapter, suggestions have been offered for alleviating or coping with the stresses identified.

There is a very old Chinese curse that reads, "May you live in interesting times!" The fact that it is a curse suggests that periods of rapid, major transition in social roles and institutions snatch from us all some of the certainties and life patterns we know and force us to change, or at least to expend energy resisting change. The resulting conflicts and ambiguities subject us all to stress.

When our comfortable roles and valued institutions change, we are driven back on ourselves. To cope with the stresses caused by social change, we may reevaluate our habitual responses and our unquestioned values. We may adapt our organizations, our families, and ourselves to new values while trying to preserve the best of the old. We are pressured, in other words, to rebuild important parts of our lives around new opportunities, problems, and constraints. This pressure to change is both the curse and the potential blessing of living and working in interesting times. It is our hope that this book helps you turn the "curse" of these interesting times into the blessing they can be in your life.

REFERENCES

Barnett, R.C. 1975. Sex differences and age trends in occupational preference and occupational prestige. *Journal of Counseling Psychology* 22:35-38.

Bem, S.L. 1974. The measurement of psychological androgyny. *Journal of Consulting and Clinical Psychology* 42:155-62.

.1976. Sex-role adaptability: One consequence of psychological androgyny. *Journal of Personality and Social Psychology* 34:1016-23.

Bernard, J. 1971. *Women and the public interest: An essay on policy and protest.* Chicago: Aldine Publishing Co.

Bombeck, E. 1973. *I lost everything in the post-natal depression.* Garden City, N.J.: Doubleday.

Dubin, R., Hedley, R.A., and Taveggia, T.C. 1976. Attachment to work. In *Handbook of work, organization and society*, R. Dubin, ed. Chicago: Rand McNally College Publishing.

Eagly, A.H. 1978. Sex differences in influenceability. *Psychological Bulletin* 85:86-116.

Epstein, C. 1970. *Women's place: Options and limits in professional careers.* Berkeley: University of California Press.

Equal employment commission outlines harassment regulations. *New York Times,* 12 April 1980, p. 20.

Farley, L. 1978. *Sexual shakedown: The sexual hararssment of women on the job.* New York: McGraw-Hill.

Fleming, P.J. 1978. *Beyond coping: How to form a vocational achievement support group for women.* Cambridge, Mass. Unpublished manuscript, 12½ Tufts St.

Frieze, I.H., Parsons, J.E., Johnson, P.B., Ruble, D.N., and Zellman, G.L. 1978. *Women and sex roles: A social psychological perspective.* New York: W.W. Norton and Company.

Fuchs, V.R., 1972. Differences in hourly earnings between men and women. *Monthly Labor Review* May, 1971: 9-15.

Gullahorn, J.E. 1977. The woman professional. In *Women: A psychological perspective,* E. Donelson, and J.E. Gullahorn, pp. 87-103. New York: Wiley.

Heart risk less in some working women. *The New York Times,* 15 April 1980, p. C2.

Hoffer, E. 1955. *The passionate state of mind.* New York: Harper & Row.

Horner, M.S. 1972. Toward an understanding of achievement—related conflicts in women. *Journal of Social Issues* 28:157-175.

Kanter, R.M. 1977. *Men and women of the corporation.* New York: Basic Books.

Keyserling, M.D. 1976. The economic status of women in the United States. *American Economic Review* 66:205-12.

Larwood, L., and Wood, M.M. 1977. *Women in management.* Lexington, Mass.: Lexington Books.

Lenny, E. 1977. Women's self-confidence in achievement settings. *Psychological Bulletin* 84:7-14.

Lindsey, K. 1977. Sexual harassment on the job and how to stop it. *Ms.* November: 48-51, 76-78.

Lobsenz, N.M. 1979. How husbands really feel about working wives. In *Humanity as a career: A holistic approach to sex equity,* G.N. McLean and J.S. Crawford, eds. pp. 90-98. Rehoboth, Mass.: Twin Oaks Publishing Company.

MacKinnon, C.A. 1979. *Sexual harassment of working women.* New Haven: Yale University Press.

McLean, G.N., and Crawford, J.S. 1979. *Humanity as a career: A holistic approach to sex equity.* Rehoboth, Mass.: Twin Oaks Publishing, Inc.

Power, M. 1975. Women's work is never done—by men: A socio-economic model of sex-typing occupations. *The Journal of Industrial Relations* 17:225-39.

Secretaries' day Wednesday. *Iowa City Press Citizen,* 24 April 1979 p. 7A.

Schein, V.E. 1975. Relationships between sex role stereotypes and requisite management characteristics among female managers. *Journal of Applied Psychology* 60:340-44.

Spence, J.T., and Helmreich, R.L. 1978. *Masculinity and feminity: Their psychological dimensions, correlates, and antecedents.* Austin: University of Texas Press.

Spock, B.M. 1970. Quoted by R. Morgan, Know your enemy: A sampling of sexist quotes. In *Sisterhood is powerful: An anthology of writings from the women's liberation movement,* R. Morgan, ed. New York: Vintage Books.

Terborg, J.R., Peters, L.H., Ilgen, D.R., and Smith, F. 1977. Organizational and personal correlates of attitudes toward women as managers. *Academy of Management Journal* 20:89-100.

Thrall, C.A. 1978. Who does what: Role stereotypy, children's work, and continuity between generations in the household division of labor. *Human Relations* 31: 249-265.

U.S. Bureau of Labor Statistics 1977. *Employment and earnings November 1977.* Washington, D.C.: U.S. Government Printing Office.

Women in America. The Gallup opinion index, March, 1976. Report no. 128.

Working women: Joys and sorrows. *U.S. News and World Report,* 15 January 1979 pp. 64-68.

Chapter 8

A Topical Bibliography

The purpose of this bibliographic chapter is to identify additional reading materials for the person wishing to gain further insights into the topics discussed in this book. These materials should be viewed as supplements to the references cited at the end of the chapters. Under each topical heading, arranged in alphabetical order, one or more bibliographic entries are provided. The entries were selected because they are considered to be "classics" in the particular topic or because they represent current writings in the area. Some entries are marked by an asterisk (*) to denote that they are generally less technical than the other entries and, therefore, of particular value to the reader who is seeking a lay treatment of the subject matter.

Aggression

Bandura, A. 1973. Social learning theory of aggression. In *The control of aggression: Implications from basic research,* J.F. Knutson, ed. Chicago: Aldine.

Berkowitz, L. 1969. The frustration-aggression hypothesis revisited. In *Roots of aggression,* L. Berkowitz, ed. New York: Atherton Press, Inc.

Knutson, J.F., ed. 1973. *The control of aggression: Implications from basic research.* Chicago: Aldine.

Aging and the Relative Importance of Life Domains

Lowenthal, M.F., Thurnher, M., and Chiriboga, D. 1975. *Four stages of life.* San Francisco: Jossey-Bass.

Alcohol Consumption and Job Stress

Caplan, R.D., Cobb, S. and French, J.R. 1975. Relationships of cessation of smoking with job stress, personality, and social support. *Journal of Applied Psychology* 60:211-19.

Chafetz, M.E., Blaue, H.T., and Hill, M.T. 1970. Frontiers of alcoholism. New York: Science House.

Margolis, B.L., Kroes, W.H., and Quinn, R.R. 1974. Job stress: An unlisted occupational hazard. *Journal of Occupational Medicine* 16: 659-61.

Roman, P.H., and Trice, H.M. 1972. Psychiatric impairment among "Middle Americans." Surveys of work organizations. *Social Psychiatry* 7:157-66.

Anxiety and Job Stress

Caplan, R.D., Cobb, S., and French, J.R. 1975. Relationships of cessation of smoking with job stress, personality, and social support. *Journal of Applied Psychology* 60:211-19.

Cherry, N. 1978. Stress, anxiety, and work: A longitudinal study. *Journal of Occupational Psychology* 51:259-70.

House, J.S., and Harkings, E.B. 1975. Why and when is status inconsistency stressful? *American Journal of Sociology* 81:395-412.

Authoritarianism

Adorno, T.W., Frenkel-Brunswik, E., Levinson, D.J., and Stanford, R.W. 1950. *The authoritarian personality.* New York: Harper & Row.

Behavior Therapies

Ayllon, T., and Azrin, B.H. 1968. *The token economy: A motivational system for therapy and rehabilitation.* New York: Appleton-Century-Crofts.

Bandura, A. 1974. Behavior theory and the models of man. *American Psychologist* 29:859-69.

Eysenck, H.J. 1964. The outcome problem in psychotherapy: A reply. *Psychotherapy* 1:97-100.

Krasner, L. 1971. The operant approach in behavior therapy. In *Handbook of Psychotherapy and Behavior Change: An Empirical Analysis*, A.E. Bergin and S.L. Ganfield, eds. New York: Wiley.

Krasner, L. 1976. On the death of behavior modification: Some comments from a mourner. *American Psychologist* 31:387-88.

Lazarus, A.A. 1971. *Behavior therapy and beyond.* New York: McGraw-Hill.

———. 1977. Has behavior therapy outlived its usefulness? *American Psychologist* 32:550-54.

Locke, E.A. 1971. Is "behavior therapy" behavioristic? (An analysis of Wolfe's psychotherapeutic methods). *Psychological Bulletin* 76:318-27.

Mahoney, M.J., Kazdin, A.E., and Lesswing, N.J. 1974. Behavior modification: Delusion or deliverance? In *Annual Review of Behavior Therapy, Theory, and Practice*, 2 vols., New York: Bruner/Magel.

Ullman, L.P., and Krasner, L.A. 1975. *Psychological approach to abnormal behavior.* 2nd ed. Englewood Cliffs, N.J.: Prentice-Hall.

Wolfe, J. 1974. *The practice of behavior therapy.* 2nd ed. New York: Pergamon.

Biofeedback

Benson, H., Shapiro, D., Tursky, B., and Schwartz, G.E. 1971. Decreased systolic blood pressure through operant conditioning techniques in patients with essential hypertension. *Science* 173: 740-42.

Blanchard, E.G., and Epstein, L.H. 1978. *A biofeedback primer.* Reading, Mass.: Addison-Wesley.

Blanchard, E.G., Young, L.D., and Haynes, M.R. 1975. A sample feedback system for the treatment of elevated blood pressure. *Behavior Therapy* 6:241-45.

Epstein, L.H., and Abel, G.G. 1977. A analysis of biofeedback training effects for tension headache patients. *Behavior Therapy* 8:34-47.

Fuller, G.D. 1978. Biofeedback: Methods and procedures in clinical practice. *Psychologist* 33:39-48.

Goldman, H., Kleinman, K.M., Snow, M.V., Bidus, D.R., and Korol, B. 1975. Relationship between essential hypertension and cognitive functioning: Effects of biofeedback. *Psychophysiology* 12:569-73.

Hume, W.I. 1976. *Biofeedback: Research and therapy.* Montreal: Eden Press.

Kleinman, K.M., Goldman, H., Snow, M.V., and Korol, B. 1977. Relationship between essential hypertension and cognitive functioning. II. Effects of biofeedback training generalize to non-laboratory environment. *Psychophysiology* 14:192-97.

Kristt, D.A., and Engel, B.T. 1975. Learned control of blood pressures in patients with high blood pressure. *Circulation* 51:370-78.

Phillips, C. 1977. The modification of tension headache pain using EMG biofeedback. *Behavioral Research Therapy* 15:119-29.

Whitehead, W.E., Renault, P.F., and Goldiamond, I. 1975. Modification of human justice acid secretion with operant-conditioning procedures. *Journal of Applied Behavior Analysis* 8:147-56.

Boundary-Spanning Roles

Leifer, R., and Delbecq, A. 1978. Organizational/environments interchange: A model of boundary-spanning activity. *Academy of Management Review* 3:40-50.

Miles, R.H. 1976. Role requirements as sources of organizational stress. *Journal of Applied Psychology* 61:172-79.

————. 1977. Role-set configuration as a predictor of role conflict and ambiguity in complex organizations. *Sociometry* 40:21-34.

Miles, R.H., and Perrault, W.D. 1976. Organizational role conflict: Its antecedents and consequences. *Organizational Behavior and Human Performance* 17:19-44.

Parkington, J.J., and Schnieder, B. 1979. Some correlates of experienced job stress: A boundary role study. *Academy of Management Journal* 22:270-81.

Cardiac Heart Disease and Job Stress

Brand, R.J., Rosenman, R.H., Sholtz, R.I., and Friedman, M. 1976. Multivariate prediction of coronary heart disease in Western Collaborative Group Study compared to the findings of the Framingham Study. *Circulation* 53:348-55.

Caplan, R.D., Cobb, S., and French, J.R. 1975. Relationships of cessation of smoking with job stress, personality, and social support. *Journal of Applied Psychology* 60:211-19.

Cooper, C.L., and Marshall, J. 1976. Occupational sources of stress: A review of the literature relating to coronary heart disease and mental ill health. *Journal of Occupational Psychology* 49:11-28.

House, J. S. 1974. Occupational stress and coronary heart disease: A review and theoretical integration. *Journal of Health and Social Behavior* 15:12-27.

Jenkins, C.D. 1976. Recent evidence supporting psychologic and social risk factors for coronary heart disease. *New England Journal of Medicine* 294:987-94, 1033-38.

Jenkins, C. D., Zyzanski, S. J., and Rosenman, R. H. 1976. Risk of new myocardial infarction in middle-aged men with manifest coronary heart disease. *Circulation* 53:342-47.

Rowland, K. F., and Sokal, B. 1977. A review of research examining the coronary-prone behavior pattern. *Journal of Human Stress* 3: 26-33.

Career Choice Process

Brief, A.P., Van Sell, M., and Aldag, R.J. 1979. Vocational decision making among women: Implications for organizational behavior. *Academy of Management Review* 4:521-30.

Jepsen, D.A. 1975. Occupational decision development over the high school years. *Journal of Vocational Behavior* 7:225-37.

*Osopow, S.H. 1973. *Theories of career development.* 2nd ed. Englewood Cliffs, N.J.: Prentice-Hall.

*Schein, E.H. 1978. *Career dymanics: Matching individual and organizational needs.* Reading, Mass. Addison-Wesley.

Wallace, J.L., and Leonard, T.H. 1971. Factors affecting vocational and educational decision-making of high school girls. *Journal of Home Economics* 63:241-45.

Career Obsolescence and Job Stress

*Burack, E.H., and Pati, G.C. 1970. Technology and managerial obsolescence. *MSU Business Topics* 18:49-56.

Ferdinand, T.N. 1966. On the obsolescence of scientists and engineers. *American Scientist* 54:46-55.

Kimblin, L.W., and Sounder, W.E. 1975. Maintaining staff productivity as half-life decreases. *Research Management* 18:29-35.

Levinson, D.J. 1977. The mid-life transition: A period and adult psychosocial development. *Psychiatry* 40:99-112.

Rago, J.R., Jr. 1973. Executive behavioral cages: Is escape possible? *Business Horizons* February:29-36.
Seifert, W.W. 1964. The prevention and cure of obsolescence in scientific and technical personnel. *Research Management* 7:143-54.
Shearer, R.L., and Steger, J.A. 1975. Manpower obsolescence: A new definition and empirical investigation of personal variables. *Academy of Management Journal* 18:263-75.

Career Planning Strategies

*Bolles, R.N. 1975. *What color is your parachute? A practical manual for job hunters and career changers.* Rev. ed. Berkeley, Calif.: Ten Speed Press.
*Hall, D.T. 1976. *Careers in organizations.* Pacific Palisades, Calif.: Goodyear.
*Hall, D.T., Bowen, D.D., Lewicki, R.J., and Hall, F.S. 1975. *Experience in management and organizational behavior.* Chicago: St. Claire Press.
*Jennings, E.E. 1971. *Routes to the executive suite.* New York: McGraw-Hill.
*Schien, E.H. 1978. *Career dynamics: Matching individual and organizational needs.* Reading, Mass.: Addison-Wesley.
*Wright, H.B. 1975. *Executive ease and disease.* New York: Halsted Press.

Career Salience

Greenhaus, J.H. 1973. A factorial investigation of career salience. *Journal of Vocational Behavior* 3:95-98.

Central Life Interests

Dubin, R. 1956. Industrial workers' worlds: A study of the "central life interests" of industrial workers. *Social Problems* 3:131-42.
Dubin, R., and Champoux, J.E. 1975. Worker's central life interests and personality characteristics. *Journal of Vocational Behavior* 6: 165-74.
Dubin, R., Hedley, R.A., and Taveggia, T.C. 1976. Attachment to work., In *Handbook of Work, Organization and Society,* R. Dubin, ed. Chicago: Rand McNally College Publishing.

Communication Processes

*Farace, R.V., Monge, P.R., and Russell, H.M. 1977. *Communicating and organizing*. Reading, Mass.: Addison-Wesley.

Festinger, L. Informal social communication. 1950. *Psychological Review* 57:271-82.

*Gibb, J.R. 1974. Defensive communication. In *Organizational psychology: A book of readings,* 2nd ed. D.A. Kolb, I.M. Rubin, and J.M. McIntyre, eds. Englewood Cliffs, N.J.: Prentice-Hall.

*Huseman, R.C., Lahiff, J.M., and Hatfield, J.D. 1976. *Interpersonal communications in organizations*. Boston: Holbrook Press, Inc.

*Kolb, D.A., and Boyatzis, R.E. 1974. On the dynamics of the helping relationship. In *Organizational psychology,* D.A. Kolb, I.M. Rubin, and T.M. McIntyre, eds., Englewood Cliffs, N.J.: Prentice-Hall.

*Rogers, C.R., and Roethlesberg, F.J. 1974. Barriers and gateways to communication. In *Organizational psychology: A book of readings,* 2nd ed., D.A. Kolb, I.M. Rubin, and T.M. McIntyre, eds. Englewood Cliffs, N.J.: Prentice-Hall.

Wofford, J.C., Gerloff, E.A., and Cummins, R.C. 1977. *Organizational communication*. New York: McGraw-Hill.

Dogmatism

Rokeach, M. 1960. *The open and closed mind*. New York: Basic Books.

Dual-Career Couples

*Hall, F.S., and Hall, D.T. 1979. *The two-career couple*. Reading, Mass.: Addison-Wesley.

*Rapoport, R.N., and Rapoport, J.M., eds. 1978. *Working couples*. New York: Harper & Row.

Enactment Processes in Organizations

Mitroff, I.I., and Emshoff, J.R. 1979. On strategic assumption making: A dialectical approach to policy and planning. *Academy of Management Review* 4:1-12.

Weick, K.E. 1977. Enactment processes in organizations. In *New directions in organizational behavior*. B.M. Staw, and G.R. Salancik, eds., Chicago: St. Clair Press.

————. 1979. Cognitive processes in organizations. In *Research in organizational behavior,* B.M. Staw, ed., 1:41-74.

————. 1979b. *The social psychology of organizing.* 2nd ed. Reading, Mass.: Addison-Wesley.

Wilensky, H. 1967. *Organizational intelligence.* New York: Basic Books.

Environmental Uncertainty

*Duncan, R., and Weiss, A. 1979. Organizational learning: Implications for organizational design. In *Research in organizational behavior,* B.M. Staw, ed. 1:75-123.

Emery, F., and Trist, E. 1965. The causal texture of organizational environments. *Human Relations* 18:21-32.

Miles, R.E., Snow, C.C., and Pfeffer, J. 1974. Organization-environment concepts and isssues. *Industrial Relations* 13:244-64.

Pfeffer, J., and Salancik, G.R. 1978. *The external control of organizations: A resource dependence perspective.* New York: Harper & Row.

Extroversion—Introversion

Eysenck, H.J. 1967. *The biological basis of personality.* Springfield: Thomas.

Jung, C.G. 1924. *Psychological types.* New York: Harcourt Brace & Co., Inc.

Kahn, R.L., Wolfe, D.M., Quinn, R.R., Snoek, J.D., and Rosenthal, R.A. 1964. *Organizational stress: Studies in role conflict and ambiguity.* New York: Wiley.

Family Life and Job Stress

Kanter, R.M. 1977. *Work and family in the United States: A critical review and agenda for research and policy.* New York: Russell Sage Foundation.

*Maccoby, M. *The gamesman.* 1976. New York: Simon & Schuster.

Family Life and Work

Bailyn, L. 1977. Involvement and accommodations in technical careers: An inquiry into the relation to work at mid-career. In *Organizational careers: Some new perspectives,* J. Van Maanen, ed. New York: Wiley.

Hall, D.T. 1971. A theoretical model of career subidentity develop-
ment in organizational settings. *Organizational Behavior and Human Performance* 6:50-76.

Kanter, R.M. 1977. *Work and family in the United States.* New York: Russell Sage.

Rapoport, R., and Rapoport, R. 1975. *Leisure and the family life-cycle.* London: Rathedge Kegan Paul.

*Schien, E.H. 1978. *Career dynamics: Matching individual and organizational needs.* Reading, Mass.: Addison-Wesley.

"Fear of Success"

Levine, A., and Crumrine, J. 1975. Women and the fear of success: A problem in replication. *American Journal of Sociology* 80:964-74.

Peplau, L.A. 1976. Impact of fear of success and sex-role attitudes on women's competitive achievement. *Journal of Personality and Social Psychology* 34:561-68.

Shapiro, J.P. 1979. "Fear of success" imagery as a reaction to sex-role inappropriate behavior. *Journal of Personality Assessment* 43:33-38.

Ward, C. 1978. Is there a motive to avoid success in women? *Human Relations* 31:1055-67.

Goal Setting

Carroll, S.J., and Tosi, H.L. 1970. Goal characteristics and personality factors in a management-by-objectives program. *Administrative Science Quarterly* 15:295-305.

*_____. 1973. *Management by objectives: Applications and research.* New York: MacMillan.

Kim, J.S., and Hamner, W.C. 1976. Effects of performance and goal setting on productivity and satisfaction in an organizational setting. *Journal of Applied Psychology* 61:48-57.

Locke, E.A. 1966. Toward a theory of task motivation and incentives. Organizational behavior and human performance. *American Journal of Psychology* 79:451-57.

_____. 1967. Motivation effects of knowledge of results on goal setting. *Journal of Applied Psychology* 51:324-29.

Locke, E.A., and Bryan, J.F. 1966. The effects of goal setting, rule learning and knowledge of score on performance. *American Journal of Psychology* 79:451-57.

Quick, J.C. 1979. Dyadic goal setting within organizations: Role-making and motivational considerations. *The Academy of Management Review* 4:369-80.

Hardiness

Kobasa, S.C., and Maddi, S.R. 1977. Existential personality theory. In *Current personality theories,* R. Corsine, ed. Itasca, Ill.: Peacock.
Maddi, S.R. 1976. *Personality theories: A comparative analysis.* 3rd ed. Homewood, Ill.: Dorsay Press.

Job Involvement

Lodahl, T.M., and Kejner, M. 1965. The definition and measurement of job involvement. *Journal of Applied Psychology* 49:24-33.
Rabinowitz, S., and Hall, D.T. 1977. Organizational research on job involvement. *Psychological Bulletin* 84:265-88.

Job-Life Satisfaction Linkages

Bass, B.M., and Bass, R. 1976. Concern for the environment: Implications for industrial and organizational psychology. *American Psychologist* 31:158-66.
Hulin, C.L. 1969. Sources of variation in job and life satisfaction: The role of community and job-related variables. *Journal of Applied Psychology* 53:279-291.
London, M., Crandall, R., and Seals, G.W. 1977. The contribution of job and leisure satisfaction to quality of life. *Journal of Applied Psychology* 62:328-34.

Job Satisfaction and Job Stress

Beehr, T.A. 1976. Perceived situational moderators of the relationship between subjective role ambiguity and role strain. *Journal of Applied Psychology* 61:35-40.
Beehr, T.A., Walsh, J.T., and Taber. T.D. 1976. Relationship of stress to individually and organizationally valued states: Higher order needs or a moderator. *Journal of Applied Psychology* 61:41-47.
Brief, A.P., and Aldag, R.J. 1976. Correlates of role indices. *Journal of Applied Psychology* 61:468-72.
Hamner, W.C., and Tosi, H.W. 1974. Relationships of role conflict and role ambiguity to job involvement measures. *Journal of Applied Psychology* 59:497-99.

House, R.J., and Rizzo, J.R. 1972. Role conflict and ambiguity or critical variables in a model of organizational behavior. *Organizational Behavior and Human Performance* 7:467-503.

Johnson, T.W., and Stinson, J.E. 1975. Role ambiguity, role conflict, and satisfaction: Moderating effects of individual differences. *Journal of Applied Psychology* 60:329-333.

Kahn, R.L., Wolfe, D.M., Quinn, R.P., Snoek, J.D., and Rosenthal, R.A. 1964. *Organizational stress: Studies in role conflict and ambiguity.* New York: Wiley.

Keller, R.T. 1975. Role conflict and ambiguity: Correlates with job satisfaction and values. *Personnel Psychology* 28:57-64.

Sales, S.M. 1970. Some effects of role overload and role underload. *Organizational Behavior and Human Performance* 5:592-608.

Job Stress Defined

French, J.R.P. 1974. Person role fit. In *Occupational stress,* A. McLean, ed., Springfield, Ill.: Thomas.

*French, J.R.P., and Caplan, R.D. 1973. Organizational stress and individual strain. In *The failure of success,* A.J. Murrow, ed. pp. 30-66. New York: AMACOM.

French, J.R.P., Jr., Rogers, W., and Cobb, S. 1974. Adjustment as a person-environment fit. In *Coping and adaptation: Interdisciplinary perspectives,* G.V. Coelho, D.A. Hamburg, and J.F. Adams, eds. New York: Basic Books.

Matteson, M.T., and Ivancevich, J.M. 1979. Organizational stressors and heart disease: A research model. *The Academy of Management Review* 4:347-58.

Schuler, R.S. In press. Definition and conceptualization of stress in organizations. *Organizational Behavior and Human Performance.*

Zaleznik, A., Kets de Vries, M.F.R., and Howard, J. 1977. Stress reactions in organizations: Syndromes, causes and consequences. *Behavioral Science* 22:151-61.

Leadership

Cherrington, D.J., Reitz, H.J., and Scott, W.E., Jr. 1971. Effects of contingent and noncontingent rewards on the relationship between satisfaction and performance. *Journal of Applied Psychology* 55:531-36.

Fossum, J.A. 1979. The effects of positively and negatively contingent rewards and individual differences on performance, satisfaction, and expectations. *Academy of Management Journal* 22:577-89.

House, R.J. 1971. A path-goal theory of leader effectiveness. *Administrative Science Quarterly* 16:321-38.

————. A 1976 theory of charismatic leadership. In *Leadership: The cutting edge,* J.G. Hunt, and L.L. Larson, eds. Carbondale, Ill.: SIU Press.

Kerr, S., and Jermier, J.M. 1978. Substitutes for leadership: Their meaning and measurement. *Organizational Behavior and Human Performance.* 22:375-403.

Schriesheim, C.A., and Murphy, C.J. 1976. Relationships between leader behavior and subordinate satisfaction and performance: A test of some situational moderators. *Journal of Applied Psychology* 61:635-41.

Schriesheim, C.S., House, R.J., and Kerr, S. 1976. Leader initiating structure: A reconciliation of discrepant research results and some empirical tests. *Organizational Behavioral Human Performance* 15:297-321.

Sims, H.P., Jr. 1977. The leader as a manager of reinforcement contingencies: An empirical example and a model. In *Leadership: The cutting edge.* J.G. Hunt and L.L. Larson, eds. Carbondale, Ill.: SIU Press.

Sims, H.P., and Szilagyi, A.D. 1975. Leader structure and subordinate satisfaction for two hospital administrative levels: A path analysis approach. *Journal of Applied Psychology* 60:194-97.

Vroom, V., and Yetton, P.W. 1973. *Leadership and decision making.* Pittsburgh: University of Pittsburgh Press.

Life Change and Health

Holmes, T.H., Hawkins, N.G., Bowerman, C.E., Clark, E.R., Jr., and Joffee, J.R. 1957. Psychosocial and psychophysiological studies of tuberculosis. *Psychosomatic Medicine* 19:134-43.

Rahe, R.H., and Arthur, R.J. 1978. Life changes and illness studies: Past history and future directions. *Journal of Human Stress* 4:3-15.

Life Stress

Becker, E. 1973. *The denial of death.* New York: The Free Press.

Dohrenwend, B.S., and Dohrenwend, B.P. 1974. *Stressful life events.* New York: Wiley.

Dohrenwend, B.S., and Dohrenwend, B.P. eds. 1974. *Stressful life events: Their nature and effects.* New York: Wiley.

*Galbraith, J.K. 1977. *The age of uncertainty*. Boston: Houghton-Mifflin.
*Kubler-Ross, E. 1969. *On death and dying*. New York: MacMillan.
Selye, H. 1976a. *The stress of life*. New York: McGraw-Hill.
———. 1976b. *Stress in health and disease*. Reading, Mass.: Butterworth.
*Toffler, A. 1970. *Future shock*. New York: Random House.

Locus of Control

Duffy, P.J., Shiflett, S., and Downey, R.G. 1977. Locus of control: Dimensionality and predictability using Likert scales. *Journal of Applied Psychology* 62:214–19.
Gregory, W.L. 1978. Locus of control for positive and negative outcomes. *Journal of Personality and Social Psychology* 36:840–49.
Joe, V.C. 1971. *Review of the internal-external control construct as a personality variable*. Psychological Reports. Monograph Supplement 3-V28, 619–40.
Rotter, J.B. 1966. *Generalized expectancies for internal vs. external control of reinforcement*. Psychological Monographs vol. 80. No. 609.

Managing Housework

*Impact at home when mother takes a job. *U.S. News & World Report,* 15 January 1979, pp. 69–71.
Olson, J.T. 1979. Role conflict between housework and child care. *Sociology of Work and Occupations* 6:430–56.
Thrall, C.A. 1978. Who does what: Role stereotype, children's work, and continuity between generations in the household division of labor. *Human Relations* 31:249–65.

"Masculine" and "Feminine" Influence Styles

Constantinople, A. 1973. Masculinity-femininity: An exception to a famous dictum? *Psychological Bulletin* 80:389–407.
*Deaux, K. 1976. *The behavior of women and men*. Monterey, Calif. Brooks/Cole.
Frodi, A., Macaulay, J., and Thome, P.R. 1977. Are women always less aggressive than men? A review of the experimental literature. *Psychological Bulletin* 84:634–60.
Johnson, P. 1976. Women and power: Toward a theory of effectiveness. *Journal of Social Issues*. 32:99–110.

Meditation

Benson, H., Rosner, B.A., Marzetta, B.R., and Klemchuk, H.P. 1974. Decreased blood pressure in borderline hypertensive subjects who practiced meditation. *Journal of Chronic Disease* 26: 163-69.

Epstein, L.H., Abel, G.G., and Webster, J.S. 1976. Self-managed relaxation in the treatment of tension headaches. In *Counseling methods*, J.D. Krumboltz, and C.E. Thoreson, eds. New York: Holt, Rinehard & Winston.

Stone, R.A., and DeLeo, J. 1976. Psychotherapeutic control of hypertension. *New England Journal of Medicine* 294:80-84.

Morbidity, Mortality, Accident Rates, and Occupational Grouping

Caplan, R.D., Cobb, S., French, J.R.P., Jr., Harrison, R.D., and Pinneau, S.R., Jr. 1975. *Job demands and worker health: Main effects and occupational differences.* Washington, D.C.: U.S. Government Printing Office.

Katz, D., and Kahn, R.L. 1978. *The social psychology of organizations.* 2nd ed. New York: Wiley.

Russek, H.I. 1965. Stress, tobacco, and coronary disease in North American professional groups. *Journal of the American Medical Association* 192:185-94.

Sales, S.M., and House, J.S. 1971. Job dissatisfaction as a possible risk factor in coronary heart disease. *Journal of Chronic Diseases* 23: 861-74.

Organizational Change

Alderfer, C.P. 1976. Change processes in organizations. In *Handbook of industrial and organizational psychology,* M.D. Dunnette, ed., pp. 1591-1638. Chicago: Rand McNally.

Coch, L., and French, J.R.P. 1948. Overcoming resistance to change. *Human Relations* 11:512-32.

*Cooper, C.L. 1973. *Group training for individual and organizational development.* Basel, Switzerland: S. Karger.

Organizational Commitment

Becker, H.S. 1960. Notes on the concept of commitment. *American Journal of Sociology* 66:32-42.

Brief, A.P., and Aldag, R.J. In Press. Antecedents of organizational commitment among hospital nurses. *Sociology of Work and Occupations.*

Buchanan, B. 1974. Building organizational commitment: The socialization of managers in work organizations. *Administrative Science Quarterly* 19:533-46.

Hrebiniak, L.C., and Alutto, J.A. 1972. Personal and role-related factors in the development of organizational commitment. *Administrative Science Quarterly* 17:555-72.

Mowday, R.T., Steers, R.M., and Porter, L.W. 1978. *The measurement of organizational commitment: A progress report.* Technical Report, University of Oregon.

Salancik, G.R. 1977. Commitment and the control of organizational behavior and belief. In *New directions in organizational behavior,* B.M. Staw, and G.R. Salancik, eds. Chicago: St. Clair Press.

Sheldon, M.E. 1971. Investments and involvements as mechanisms producing commitment to the organization. *Administrative Science Quarterly* 16:142-50.

Steers, R.M. 1977. Antecedents and outcomes of organizational commitment. *Administrative Science Quarterly* 22: 46-56.

Organizational Goals

Cyert, R.M., and March, J.G. 1963. *A behavioral theory of the firm.* Englewood Cliffs, N.J.: Prentice-Hall.

Georgious, P. 1973. The goal paradigm and notes toward a counter-paradigm. *Administrative Science Quarterly* 18:291-310.

*Pfeffer, J. 1978. *Organizational design.* Arlington Heights, Ill.: AHM Publishing Corporation.

Organizational Strategies for Managing Job Stress

*Jones, C.H. 1968. The money value of time. *Harvard Business Review* July-August: 94-101.

*Kahn, R.L., and Quinn, R.P. 1970. Strategies for management of role stress. In *Occupational mental health,* A. McLean, ed. New York: Rand McNally.

*Margolis, G.L., Kroes, W.H., and Quinn, R.P. 1974. Job stress: An unlisted occupational hazard. *Journal of Occupational Medicine* 16: 659-61.

Oldham, G. 1976. The motivational strategies used by supervisors: Relationships to effectiveness indicators. *Organizational Behavior and Human Performance* 15:66-86.

*Oncken, W., Jr., and Wass, D.L. 1974. Managing time: Who's got the monkey? *Harvard Business Review* November-December.

*Warshaw, L.J. 1979. *Managing stress.* Reading, Mass.: Addison-Wesley.

Organizational Structure

Berger, C.J., and Cummings, L.L. 1979. Organizational structure, attitudes, and behaviors. In *Research in organizational behavior*, B.M. Staw, ed. 1:169-208.

*Galbraith, J. 1977. *Organizational design*. Reading, Mass.: Addison-Wesley.

Hall, R.H., Johnson, N.J., and Haas, J.E. 1967. Organizational size, complexity, and formalization. *American Sociological Review* 32: 903-12.

James, L.R., and Jones, A.P. 1976. Organizational structure: A review of structural dimensions and their conceptual relationships with individual attitudes and behaviors. *Organizational Behavior and Human Performance* 16:74-113.

*Khandwalla, P.N. 1977. *The design of organizations*, New York: Harcourt Brace Jovanovich, Inc.

Kimberly, J.R. 1976. Organizational size and the structuralist perspective: A review, critique, and proposal. *Administrative Science Quarterly* 21:571-97.

*Mintzberg, H. 1979.The structuring of organizations. Englewood Cliffs, N.J.: Prentice-Hall, Inc.

*Pfeffer, J. 1978. *Organizational design*. Arlington Heights, Ill.: AHM Publishing Corporation.

Robey, D., Baker, M.M., and Miller, T.S. 1977. Organizational size and management autonomy: Some structural discontinuities. *Academy of Management Journal* 20:378-97.

Organizational Technology

Comstock, D.E., and Scott, W.R. 1977. Technology and the structure of subunits: Distinguishing individual and workgroup effects. *Administrative Science Quarterly* 22:177-202.

*Hall, R.H. 1977. *Organizations: Structure and process*. 2nd ed. Englewood Cliffs, N.J.: Prentice-Hall.

Thompson, J.D. 1967. *Organization in action*. New York: McGraw-Hill.

Person-Job Fit

*Hall, D.T. 1976. *Careers in organizations*. Pacific Palisades, Calif.: Goodyear.

Lofquist, L.H., and Dewis, R.V. 1969. *Adjustment to work: A psychological view of man's problems in a work-oriented society*. New York: Appleton-Century-Crofts.

O'Reilly, C.A. 1977. Personality-job fit: Implications for individual attitudes and performance. *Organizational Behavior and Human Performance* 18:36-46.

*Schein, E.H. 1978. *Career dynamics: Matching individual and organizational needs.* Reading, Mass.: Addison-Wesley.

Personality and Job Stress

Anderson, C.R. 1977. Locus of control, coping behaviors, and performance in a stress setting: A longitudinal study. *Journal of Applied Psychology* 62:446-51.

Cooper, C.L., and Marshall, J. 1976. Occupational sources of stress: A review of literature relating to coronary heart disease and mental ill health. *Journal of Occupational Psychology* 49: 11-28.

Gordon, F.E., and Hall, D.T. 1975. Self-image and stereotypes of femininity: Their relationship to women's role conflicts and coping. *Journal of Applied Psychology* 59:241-43.

Johnson, T.W., and Stinson, J.E. 1975. Role ambiguity, role conflict, and satisfaction: Moderating effects of individual differences. *Journal of Applied Psychology* 60:329-83.

Kahn, R.L., Wolfe, D.M., Quinn, R.R., Snoek, J.D., and Rosenthal, R.A. 1964. *Organizational stress: Studies in role conflict and ambiguity.* New York: Wiley.

McMichael, A.J. 1978. Personality, behavioral, and situational modifiers of work stressors. In *Stress at work,* G.L. Cooper, and R. Payne, eds., pp. 127-148. New York: Wiley.

Miles, R.H., and Petty, M.M. 1975. Relationships between role clarity, need for clarity, and job tension and satisfaction for supervisory and nonsupervisory roles. *Academy of Management Journal* 18:877-83.

Organ, D.W., and Green, C.N. 1974. Role ambiguity, locus of control, and work satisfaction. *Journal of Applied Psychology* 59:101-2.

Szilagyi, A.D., Sims, H.P., and Keller, R.F. 1976. Role dynamics, locus of control, and employee attitudes and behavior. *Academy of Management Journal* 19:255-76.

*Warr, P., and Wall, T. 1975. *Work and well-being.* Baltimore: Penguin.

Zalesnik, A., Kets de Vries, M.F.R., and Howard, J. 1977. Stress reactions in organizations: Syndromes, causes, and consequences. *Behavioral Science* 22:151-62.

Physical Working Conditions and Job Stress

Buskirk, E.R. 1978. Cold stress: A selective review. In *Environmental stress: Individual human adaptations,* L.J. Folinsbee, J.A. Wagner, J.F. Borgia, B.L. Drinkwater, J.A. Gliner, and J.B. Bedi, eds. New York: Academic Press.

Cameron, C. 1971. Fatigue problems in modern industry. *Ergonomics* 14:713-20.

Leithead, C.S., and Lind, A.R. 1964. *Heat stress and heat disorders.* London: Cassell and Company, Ltd.

Poulton, E.C. 1978. Blue collar stressors. In *Stress at work,* C.L. Cooper, and R. Payne, eds. Chichester: Wiley.

Schmidt, D.E., and Goldman, R.D. 1976. Physical and psychological factors associated with perceptions of crowding: An analysis of subcultural differences. *Journal of Applied Psychology* 61:279-89.

Stellman, J.M. 1977. *Women's work, women's health: Myths and realities.* New York: Pantheon Books.

Powerlessness in Organizations

Blauner, R. 1964. *Alienation and freedom: The factory worker and his industry.* Chicago: University of Chicago Press.

Crozier, M. 1964. *The bureaucratic phenomenon.* Chicago: University of Chicago Press.

*Kanter, R.M. 1977. *Men and women of the corporation.* New York: Basic Books.

Kanungo, R.M. 1979. The concepts of alienation and involvement revisited. *Psychological Bulletin* 86:119-38.

Mechanic, D. 1962. Sources of power of lower participants in complex organizations. *Administrative Science Quarterly* 7:349-64.

Protestant Work Ethic

Aldag, R.J., and Brief, A.P. 1975. Some correlates of work values. *Journal of Applied Psychology* 60:757-60.

Blood, M.R. 1969. Work values and job satisfaction. *Journal of Applied Psychology* 53:456-59.

Brief, A.P., and Aldag, R.J. 1977. Work values on moderators of perceived leader behavior-satisfaction relationships. *Sociology of Work and Occupation* 4:99-112.

Merrens, M.K., and Garrett, J.B. 1975. The protestant ethic scale as a predictor of repetitive work performance. *Journal of Applied Psychology* 60:125-217.

Weber, M. 1930. *The protestant ethic and the spirit of capitalism.* London: Allen and Unwin.

Psychodynamic Therapies

Back, K.W. 1973. Encounter groups and society. *Journal of Applied Bahavioral Science* 9:7-20.

Ellis, A. 1978. What people can do for themselves to cope with stress. In *Stress at work*, C.L. Cooper, and R. Payne, eds. New York: Wiley.

Ellis, A., and Grieger, R. 1977. *A source book of rational-emotive therapy*. New York: Springer Publishing Co.

*Ellis, A., and Harper, R.A. 1975. *A new guide to rational living*. Englewood Cliffs, N.J.: Prentice-Hall.

Eysenck, H.J. 1964. The outcome problem in psychotherapy: A reply. *Psychotherapy* 1:97-100.

Frankl, V.E. 1965. *The doctor and the soul*. New York: Bantam Books.

Freud, S. 1935. *Autobiography*. Trans. J. Strachey. New York: Norton.

Fromm, E. 1955. *The sane society*. New York: Rinehart.

Gibb, J.R. 1971. The effects of human relations training. In *Handbook of psychotherapy and behavior change*, A.E. Bergin, and S.L. Garfield, eds. New York: Wiley.

Golomonbiewski, R.T., and Blumberg, A., eds. 1971. *Sensitivity training and the laboratory method*. Itaska, Ill.: Peacock.

Jung, C.G. 1953. *Collected works. Vol. 7 Two essays in analytical psychology*. New York: Pantheon.

Maslow, A.N. 1954. *Motivation and personality*. New York: Harper & Row.

May, R. 1967. *Psychology and the human dilemma*. Princeton, N.J.: Van Nostrand.

Perls, F.S. 1969. *Gestalt therapy verbatim*. Moab, Utah: Real People Press.

Rogers, C.R. 1968. Interpersonal relationships: Year 2000. *Journal of Applied Behavioral Science* 4:265-80.

_____. 1970. *Carl Rogers on encounter groups*. New York: Harper & Row.

Strupp, H.H. 1973. The experiential group and the psychotherapeutic enterprise. *International Journal of Group Psychotherapy* 23:115-24.

Psychological Factors and Blood Pressure

McGinn, N.F., Harburg, E., Julius, S., and McLeod, J. 1964. Psychological correlates of blood pressure. *Psychological Bulletin* 61:209-19.

Ostfeld, A.M., and Shekelle, R.B. 1967. Psychological variables and blood pressure. In *The epidemiology of hypertension*, J. Stamler, R. Stamler, and T.N. Pullman, eds. New York: Grune.

Scotch, N.A., and Geiger, H.J. 1963. The epidemiology of essential hypertension. II: Psychologic and sociocultural factors in etiology. *Journal of Chronic Disease* 16:1183–1213.

Quality of Life

Andrews, F.M., and Crandell, R. 1976. The validity of measures of self-reported well-being. *Social Indicators Research* 3:1–2.

Andrews, F.M., and Withey, S.B. 1976. *Social indicators of well-being.* New York: Plenum Press.

Campbell, A. 1976. Subjective measures of well-being. *American Psychologist* 31:117–24.

Campbell, A., Converse, P.E., and Rodgers, W.I. 1976. *The quality of American life: Perceptions, evaluations, and satisfactions.* New York: Russell Sage Foundation.

Cantril, H. 1965. *The pattern of human concerns.* New Brunswick, N.J.: Rutgers University Press.

Gerson, E.M. 1976. On "quality of life." *American Sociological Review* 41:793–806.

Robinson, J.P., and Shaver, P.R. 1973. *Measures of social psychological attitudes.* rev. ed. Ann Arbor, Mich.: Institute for Social Research.

Rodgers, W.L., and Converse, P.E. 1975. Perceived quality of life. *Social Indicators Research* 2:127–52.

Shin, D.C., and Johnson, S.M. 1978. Avowed happiness as an overall assessment of the quality of life. *Social Indicators Research* 5:475–92.

Quality of Working Life

*Davis, L., Cherns, A.B., and Associates. 1975. *The quality of working life. Volume 1: Problems, prospects, and the state of the ant.* New York: The Free Press.

Macey, B.A., and Mirvis, P.H. 1976. A methodology for assessment of quality of work life and organizational effectiveness in behavioral-economic terms. *Administrative Science Quarterly* 21: 212–26.

*Sheppard, H.L., and Herrick, N.A. 1972. *Where have all the robots gone?* New York: Free Press.

*Warr, P., and Wall, T. 1975. *Work and well-being.* Baltimore: Penguin.

*Work in America. 1973. Report of a Special Task Force to the Secretary of Health, Education, and Welfare. Cambridge: M.I.T. Press.

Realistic Job Previews

*Wanous, J.P. 1980. *Organizational entry: Recruitment, selection, and social-ization of newcomers.* Reading, Mass.: Addison-Wesley.

Relaxation Techniques

Benson, H. 1975. *The relaxation response.* New York: Morrow.

Jacobson, E. 1964. *Anxiety and tension control.* Philadelphia: Lippincott.

*Kory, R.B. 1976. *The transcendental meditation program for business people.* New York: AMACOM.

Kuna, D.J. 1975. Meditation and work. *Vocational Guidance Quarterly* 23:342–46.

Smith, J.C. 1975. Meditation as psychotherapy: A review of the liter-ature. *Psychological Bulletin* 82:558–64.

Role Conflict and Role Ambiguity

Brief, A.P., and Aldag, R.J. 1976. Correlates of role indices. *Journal of Applied Psychology* 61:468–72.

Caplan, R.D., Cobb, S., French, J.R.R., Van Harrison, R., and Pinneau, S.R. 1975. *Job demands and worker health.* Ann Arbor: In-situte for Social Research, the University of Michigan.

Caplan, R.D., and Jones, K.W. 1975. Effects of workload, role am-biguity and type A personality on anxiety, depression and heart rate. *Journal of Applied Psychology* 60:713–19.

Graen, G. 1976. Role-making processes within complex organiza-tions. In *Handbook of industrial and organizational psychology,* M.D. Dunnette, ed. Chicago: Rand-McNally.

Kahn, R.L., Wolfe, D.M., Quinn, R.P., Snoek, J.D., and Rosenthal, R.A. 1964. *Organizational stress: Studies in role conflict and ambiguity.* New York: Wiley.

Schuler, R.S., Aldag, R.J., and Brief, A.P. 1977. Role conflict and ambiguity: A scale analysis. *Organizational Behavior and Human Per-formance* 20:111–28.

Van Sell, M., Brief, A.P., and Schuler, R.S. In press. Role conflict and role ambiguity: An integration of the literature and direc-tions for future research. *Human Relations.*

Self-Help for Women Managers

*Adams, L., and Lenz, E. 1979. *Effectiveness training for women.* New York: Wyden Books.

*Barnett, R.C., and Baruch, G.K. 1978. *The competent woman: Perspec-tives on development.* New York: Irvington Publishers.

224 *A Topical Bibliography*

*Crain, S., and Drotning, P.T. 1977. *Taking stock: A woman's guide to corporate success.* Chicago: Henry Regnery Company.
*Harrigan, B.L. 1978. *Games mother never taught you: Corporate gamesmanship for women.* New York: Avon Books.
*Hennig, M., and Jardim, A. 1977. *The managerial woman.* Garden City: Anchor Press.
*Jackson, S.L., Merrill, B.E., and Watson, G.F. 1978. *Women advancing in business: The role of management seminars.* Des Moines: Iowa Commission on the Status of Women.
Larwood, L., Wood, M.M., and Inderlied, S. 1978. Training women for management: New problems, new solutions. *Academy of Management Review* 3:584-93.
*Meyers, S., Brody, G., Parness, V., and Sellers, N.S. 1977. *The California study on women in nontraditional occupations.* San Francisco: Advocates for Women.
*Newton, D.A. 1979. *Think like a man. Act like a lady. Work like a dog.* Garden City, New York: Doubleday.
*Trahey, J. 1978. *Jane Trahey on women and power.* New York: Avon.
*Stewart, N. 1978. *The effective woman manager.* New York: Wiley.

Self-Reinforcement

Bandura, A. 1978. The self system in reciprocal determinism. *American Psychologist* 33:344-58.

Sex Differences in Preferences for Job Rewards

Bartol, K.M., and Manhardt, P.J. 1979. Sex differences in job outcome preferences: Trends among newly hired college graduates. *Journal of Applied Psychology* 64:477-82.
Brief, A.P., Rose, G., and Aldag, R.J. 1977. Sex differences in work attitudes revisited. *Journal of Applied Psychology* 62:645-46.
*Kanter, R.M. 1977. *Men and women of the corporation.* New York: Basic Books.
Schuler, R.S. 1975. Sex, organization level, and outcome importance: Where the differences are. *Personnel Psychology* 28:365-76.
Smith, C.B. 1979. Influence of internal opportunity structure and sex of worker on turnover patterns. *Administrative Science Quarterly* 24:362-81.
Taylor, R.N., and Thompson, M. 1976. Work value systems of young workers. *Academy of Management Journal* 19:522-36.

Sex Discrimination

Abramson, J. 1975. *The invisible woman: Discrimination in the academic profession.* San Francisco: Jossey-Bass.

Cook, A.H. 1975. Equal pay: Where is it? *Industrial Relations* 14: 158-77.

Dipboye, R.L., Fromkin, H.L., and Wiback, K. 1975. Relative importance of applicant sex, attractiveness, and scholastic standing in evaluation of job applicant resumes. *Journal of Applied Psychology* 60:39-43.

Ferber, M.A., and Kordick, B. 1978. Sex differentials in the earnings of Ph.D.'s. *Industrial and Labor Relations Review* 31:227-38.

Heilman, M.E., and Saruwatari, L.R. 1979. When beauty is beastly: The effects of appearance and sex on evaluations of job applicants for managerial and nonmanagerial jobs. *Organizational Behavior and Human Performance* 23:360-72.

Taylor, P.A. 1979. Income inequality in the federal civilian government. *American Sociological Review* 44:468-79.

Terborg, J.R. 1977. Women in management: A research review. *Journal of Applied Psychology* 62:647-64.

*Thompson, J. 1976. The women vs. Chase Manhattan: Diary of a discrimination suit. *MBA* February: 19-22.

Sex-Role Stereotypes and Life Stress

*Farrell, W. 1974. *The liberated man: Beyond masculinity.* New York: Random House.

*Fasteau, M.F. 1974. *The male machine.* New York: McGraw-Hill.

Pleck, J.H. 1976. The male sex role: Definitions, problems, and sources of change. *Journal of Social Issues* 32:155-64.

Waldron, I. 1976. Why do women live longer than men? Part I. *Journal of Human Stress* 2:2-14.

Waldron, I., and Johnston, S. 1976. Why do women live longer than men? Part II. *Journal of Human Stress,* 2 no. 2:19-31.

Sex-Role Stereotypes and Work

Almquist, E.M. 1974. Sex stereotypes in occupational choice: The case of college women. *Journal of Vocational Behavior* 5:13-21.

Bardwick, J.M., and Douvan, E. 1971. Ambivalence: The socialization of women. In *Women in sexist society: Studies in power and powerlessness.* V. Gornick, and B.K. Moran, eds. New York: Basic Books.

Bartol, K.M. 1978. The sex structuring of occupations: A search for possible causes. *Academy of Management Review* 3:805-15.

*Chatetz, J.S. 1974. *Masculine/feminine or human? An overview of the sociology of sex roles.* Itasca, Ill.: Peacock.

Fannin, P.M. 1979. The relation between ego-identity status and sex-role attitude, work-role salience, atypicality of major, and self-esteem in college women. *Journal of Vocational Behavior* 14:12-22.

Farmer, H.S. 1976. What inhibits achievement and career motivation in women? *Counseling Psychologist* 6:12-15.

*Friedan, B. 1963. *The feminine mystique.* New York: Dell.

Garland, H., and Price, K.H. 1977. Attitudes toward women in management and attribution for their success and failure in a managerial position. *Journal of Applied Psychology* 62:29-33.

Gordon, F.E., and Hall, D.T. 1974. Self-image and stereotypes of feminity: Their relationship to women's role conflicts and coping. *Journal of Applied Psychology* 59:241-43.

Heilman, M.E., and Guzzo, R.A. 1978. The perceived cause of work success as a mediator of sex discrimination in organizations. *Organizational Behavior and Human Performance* 21:346-57.

O'Leary, V.E. 1974. Some attitudinal barriers to occupational aspirations in women. *Psychological Bulletin* 81:809-26.

Orcutt, M.A., and Walsh, W.B. 1979. Traditionality and congruence of career aspirations for college women. *Journal of Vocational Behavior* 14:1-11.

Quadagno, J. 1976. Occupational sex-typing and internal labor market distributions: An assessment of medical specialties. *Social Problems* 23:442-53.

Rand, L. 1968. Masculinity or feminity? Differentiating career-oriented and homemaking-oriented college freshman women. *Journal of Counseling Psychology* 15: 444-50.

Richardson, M.S. 1975. Self-concepts and role concepts in the career orientation of college women. *Journal of Counseling Psychology* 22: 122-26.

Shinar, E.H. 1975. Sexual stereotypes of occupations. *Journal of Vocational Behavior* 7:99-111.

Tipton, R.M. 1976. Attitudes toward women's roles in society and vocational interests. *Journal of Vocational Behavior* 8:155-66.

*Whitehurst, C.A. 1977. *Women in America: the oppressed majority.* Santa Monica, Calif.: Goodyear.

Williams, G. 1976. Trends in occupational differentiation by sex. *Sociology of Work and Occupations* 3:38-62.

*Williams, J.H. 1977. *Psychology of women: Behavior in a biosocial context.* New York: W.W. Norton & Company.

Yanico, B.J., Hardin, S.I., and McLaughlin, K.B. 1978. Androgyny and traditional versus nontraditional major choice among college freshmen. *Journal of Vocational Behavior* 12:261-69.

Sexual Stereotypes of Managers

Haccoun, D.M., Haccoun, R.R., and Sallay, G. 1978. Sex differences in the appropriateness of supervisory styles: A nonmanagement view. *Journal of Applied Psychology* 63:124-47.
Powell, G.N., and Butterfield, D.A. 1979. The "good manager": Masculine or androgynous. *Academy of Management Journal* 22:395-403.

Sexuality and Work

*Farley, L. 1978. *Sexual shakedown: The sexual harassment of women on the job.* New York: McGraw-Hill.
Hunter, J.E. 1976. Images of women. *Journal of Social Issues* vol. 32 no. 3:7-18.
*Janeway, E. 1971. *Man's world, women's place: A study in social mythology.* New York: Dell.
*Lindsey, K. 1977. Sexual harassment on the job and how to stop it. *Ms* November: 48-51, 76-78.
*MacKinnon, C.A. 1979. *Sexual harassment of working women.* New Haven: Yale University Press.
Quinn, R.E. 1977. Coping with Cupid: The formation, impact, and management of romantic relationships in organizations. *Administrative Science Quarterly* 22:30-45.

Shift Work and Job Stress

Colquhoun, W.P. 1976. Accidents, injuries and shift work. In *Shift work and health,* P.G. Rentos, and R.D. Shepart, eds. Washington, D.C.: New Publication No. (NIOSH) 76-203.
Dunham, R.B. 1977. Shift work: A review and theoretical analysis. *Academy of Management Review* 2:624-34.
Frost, P.J., and Jamal, M. 1979. Shift work, attitudes, and reported behavior: Some associations between individual characteristics and hours of work and leisure. *Journal of Applied Psychology* 64:77-81.
Mott, P.E. 1976. Social and psychological adjustment to shift work. In *Shiftwork and health,* P.G. Rentos, and R.D. Shepart, eds., Washington, D.C.: HEW Publication No. (NIOSH) 76-203.

Taylor, P.J. 1967. Shift and day work: A comparison of sickness, absence, lateness, and other absence behavior at an oil refinery from 1962 to 1965. *British Journal of Industrial Medicine* 24:93–102.

Smoking Behavior and Job Stress

Caplan, R.D., Cobb, S., French, J.R.P. Jr., Harrison, R.D., and Pinneau, S.R., Jr. 1975. *Job demands and worker health: Main effects and occupational differences.* Washington, D.C.: U.S. Government Printing Office.

Glass, D.C. 1977. *Behavior patterns, stress, and coronary disease.* Hillsdale, N.J.: Wiley.

Howard, J., Cunningham, D.A., and Rechnitzer, P.A. 1976. Health patterns associated with Type A behavior: A managerial population. *Journal of Human Stress* 2:25–31.

Jenkins, C.D., Rosenman, R.H., and Zyzanski, S.J. 1968. Cigarette smoking: Its relationship to coronary heart disease and related risk factors in the Western Collaborative Group Study. *Circulation* 38:1140–55.

Russek, H.I. 1965. Stress, tobacco, and coronary disease in North American professional groups. *Journal of the American Medical Association* 192:185–94.

Social Support and Job Stress

Caplan, R.D., Cobb, S., and French, J.R.P., Jr. 1975. Relationship of cessation of smoking with the stress, personality and social support. *Journal of Applied Psychology* 60:211–19.

Caplan, R.D., Cobb, S., and French, J.R.P., Jr., Harrison, R.V., and Pinneau, S.R., Jr., 1975. *Job demands and worker health* Washington, D.C.: HEW Publication No. (NIOSH) 75-160.

Cobb, S. 1976. Social support as a moderator of life stress. *Psychosomatic Medicine* 38:300–14.

LaRocco, J.M., and Jones, A.P. 1978. Co-worker and leader support as moderators of stress-strain relationships in work situations. *Journal of Applied Psychology* 63:629–34.

Mansfield, R. 1972. The initiation of graduates in industry: The resolution of identity-stress as a determinant of job satisfaction in the early months of work. *Human Relations* 25:77–86.

Pridham, K.F. 1977. Toward an adequate theory of stress resolution in work groups. *Human Relations* 9:787–801.

Status Incongruity, Stress, and Health

Bruhn, J.G., Wolf, S., Lynn, T.N., Bird, H.B., and Chander, B. 1968. Social aspects of coronary heart disease in a Pennsylvania German community. *Social Science Medicine* 2:201-2.

Erikson, J., Pugh, W.M., and Gunderson, E.K. 1972. Status congruency as a predictor of job satisfaction and life stress. *Journal of Applied Psychology* 56:523-25.

House, J.S. 1974. Occupational stress and coronary heart disease: A review and theoretical integration. *Journal of Health and Social Behavior* 15:12-27.

Jenkins, C.D. 1976. Recent evidence supporting psychologic and social risk factors for coronary heart disease. *New England Journal of Medicine* 294:987-94, 1033-38.

Lehr, I., Messinger, H.B., and Rosenman, R.H. 1973. A sociobiological approach to the study of coronary heart disease. *Journal of Chronic Disorders* 26:13-30.

Supervisory Responsibilities and Job Stress

Cobb, S. 1974. Role responsibility: The differentiation of a concept. In *Occupational stress,* A. McLean, ed. Springfield, Ill.: Thomas.

Cooper, C.L., and Crump, J. 1978. Prevention and coping with occupational stress. *Journal of Occupational Medicine* 20:420-26.

Rahe, R.H., Gunderson, E.K.E., Pugh, W.M., Rabin, R.T., and Arther, R.J. 1972. Illness prediction studies. *Archives of Environmental Health* 25:192-97.

Wardwell, W.J., Hyman, M.M., and Bahnson, C.B. 1964. Stress and coronary disease in three field studies. *Journal of Chronic Disease* 17:73-84.

Task Design

*Aldag, R.J., and Brief, A.P. 1979. *Task design and employee motivation.* Glenview, Ill.: Scott, Foresman & Co.

Hackman, and J.L. Suttle, eds., pp. 96-162. Santa Monica, Calif.: Goodyear.
Goodyear.

Hackman, J.R., and Lawler, E.E., III. 1971. Employee reactions to job characteristics. *Journal of Applied Psychology Monograph* 55:259-86.

Hackman, J.R., and Oldham, G.R. 1975. Development of the job diagnostic survey. *Journal of Applied Psychology* 60:159-70.

Pierce, J.L., and Dunham, R.B. 1976. Task design: A literature review. *Academy of Management Review* vol.1, no. 4:83-97.

Steers, R.M., and Mowday, R.T. 1977. The motivational properties of tasks. *Academy of Management Review* 2:645-58.

Tolerance for Ambiguity

Katz, D., and Sarnoff, I. 1954. Motivational bases of attitude change. *Journal of Abnormal Social Psychology* 49:115-24.

Maslow, A. 1943. A theory of human motivation. *Psychological Review* 50:370-96.

Murphy, G. 1947. *Personality*. New York: Harper.

Type A

Friedman, M. 1969. *Pathogenesis of coronary artery disease*. New York: McGraw-Hill Book Company.

*Friedman, M., and Rosenman, R.H. 1974. *Type A behavior and your heart*. Greenwich, Conn.: Fawcett Press.

Glass, D.D. 1977. *Behavior patterns, stress, and coronary disease*. Hillsdale, N.J.: Erlbaum.

Jenkins, C.D. 1976. Recent evidence supporting psychologic and social risk factors for coronary disease, Part 2. *The New England Journal of Medicine* 294:1033-38.

Price, K.P., and Clarke, L.K. 1978. Behavioral and psychophysiological correlates of the coronary-prone personality: New data and unanswered questions. *Journal of Psychosomatic Research* 22:409-417.

Rosenman, R.H., and Friedman, M. 1974. Neurogenic factors in pathogenesis of coronary heart disease. *Medical Clinics of North America* 58:269-79.

Rowland, K.F., and Sokol, B. 1977. A review of research examining the coronary-prone behavior pattern. *Journal of Human Stress* 3:26-33.

Waldron, I., Syzanski, S.J., Shekell, R.B., Jenkins, C.D., and Tannenbaum, S. 1977. The coronary-prone behavior pattern in employed men and women. *Journal of Human Stress* 3:2-18.

Women as Managers

Kanter, R.M. 1977. Some effects of proportion on group life: Skewed sex ratios and responses to token women. *American Journal of Sociology* 82:965-90.

*Larwood, L., and Wood, M.M. 1977. *Women in management*. Lexington, Mass.: Lexington Books.

*Orth, C.D., and Jacobs, F. 1971. Women in management: Pattern for change. *Harvard Business Review* July-August:139-47.

Rosen, B., and Jerdee, T.H. 1974. The influence of sex-role stereotypes on evaluations of male and female supervisory behavior. *Journal of Applied Psychology* 59:9-14.

Rosenfeld, R.A. 1979. Women's occupational careers: Individual and structural explanations. *Sociology of Work and Occupations* 6: 283-311.

Terborg, J.R., Peters, L.H., Ilgen, D.R., and Smith, F. 1977. Organizational and personal correlates of attitudes toward women as managers. *Academy of Management Journal* 20:89-100.

*Thompson, J. 1976. Patrons, rabbis, mentors—whatever you call them, women need them, too. *MBA* February:19-22.

*Up the ladder, finally. *Business Week* 24 November 1975. pp. 56-68.

Zellman, G.L. 1976. The role of structural factors in limiting women's institutional participation. *Journal of Social Issues* 32: 33-46.

Women's Career Achievement and Husband's Attitudes

Holahan, C.K., and Gilbert, L.A. 1979. Interrole conflict for women: Careers versus job. *Journal of Applied Psychology* 64:86-90.

Huth, C.M. 1978. Married women's work status: The influence of parents and husbands. *Journal of Vocational Behavior* 13:272-86.

Winter, D.G., Stewart, A.J., and McClelland, D.C. 1977. Husband's motives and wife's career level. *Journal of Personality and Social Psychology* 35:159-66.

Women's Occupations and Status

McLaughlin, S.D. 1978. Sex differences in the determinants of occupational status. *Sociology of Work and Occupations* 5:5-30.

Medvene, A.M., and Collins, A. 1974. Occupational prestige and its relationship to traditional and nontraditional views of women's roles. *Journal of Counseling Psychology* 21:139-41.

Women's Occupations as a Secondary Labor Market

Cooney, R.S. 1978. A comparative study of work opportunities for women. *Industrial Relations* 17:64-74.

Kohen, A.I., Breinich, S.C., and Shields, P.M. 1975, 1977. *Women and the economy.* Columbus, Ohio: Center for Human Resource Research, Ohio State University.

*Kreps, J. 1972. *Sex in the marketplace: American women at work.* Baltimore, Md.: The Johns Hopkins University Press.

Work Environment and Mental Health

Cooper, C.L., and Marshall, J. 1976. Occupational sources of stress: A review of the literature relating to coronary heart disease and mental ill health. *Journal of Occupational Psychology* 49:11-28.

French, J.R.P., Jr. 1974. Person-role fit. In *Occupational stress,* A. McLean, ed. Springfield, Ill.: Thomas.

Indik, B.P. 1963. Some effects of organization size on member attitudes and behavior. *Human Relations* 16:369-84.

Kasl, S.V. 1973. Mental health and the work environment: An examination of the evidence. *Journal of Occupational Medicine* 15:509-18.

Kornhauser, A. 1965. *Mental health of the industrial worker: A Detroit study.* New York: Wiley.

Margolis, B.L., Kroes, W.H., and Quinn, R.R. 1974. Job stress: An unlisted occupational hazard. *Journal of Occupational Medicine* 16:659-61.

McLean, A. 1970. *Mental health and work organizations.* Chicago: Rand.

Work Groups and Job Stress

Klein, S.M. 1971. *Workers under stress.* Lexington: University Press of Kentucky.

Lanzetta, J. 1955. Group behavior under stress. *Human Relations* 8:29-52.

Torrence, E.P. 1954. The behavior of small groups under stress conditions of survival. *American Sociological Review* 19:751-55.

Work Load Dissatisfaction and Mental Health

*French, J.R.P., Jr., and Caplan, R.D. 1973. Organizational stress and individual strain. In *The failure of success,* A.J. Murrow, ed. New York: AMACOM.

Quinn, R.P., Seashore, S., Kahn, R., Margione, T., Campbell, D., Staines, G., and McCullough, M. 1971. *Survey of working conditions.* Document no. 2916-00001. Washington, D.C.: U.S. Government Printing Office.

Work Roles and Job Stress

Frankenhaeuser, M., and Gardell, B. 1976. Underload and overload in working life: Outline of a multidisciplinary approach. *Journal of Human Stress* 2:35-45.

Kahn, R.L., Wolfe, D.M., Quinn, R.P., Snoek, J.D., and Rosenthal, R.A. 1974. *Organizational stress: Studies in role conflict and ambiguity.* New York: Wiley.

Quick, J.C. 1976. Dyadic goal setting and role stress: A field study. *Academy of Management Journal* 22:241-52.

Sales, S.M. 1969. Organizational roles as a risk factor in coronary heart disease. *Administrative Science Quarterly* 14:325-36.

Worker Participation

Case, J. 1973. Workers' control: Toward a North American movement. In *Workers' control,* G. Hunnius, G.D. Garson, and J. Case, eds. New York: Vintage Books.

Forrest, C.R., Cummings, L.L., and Johnson, A.C. 1977. Organizational participation: A critique and model. *Academy of Management Review* 2:586-601.

Locke, E.A., and Schweiger, D.M. 1979. Participation in decision-making: One more look. In *Research in organizational behavior,* B.M. Staw, ed. 1:265-339.

Tornquist, D. 1973. Workers' management: The intrinsic issues. In *Workers' control,* G. Hunnius, G.D. Garson, and J. Case, eds. New York: Vintage Books.

Acknowledgements (continued from page iv)

Pages 47-48: From Cass and Zimmer, *Man and Work in Society* (New York: Van Nostrand Publishers, 1975). Reprinted by permission.   *Figure 3.4:* From L. Levi, *Stress and Distress in Response to Psychosocial Stimuli* (Elmsford, New York: Pergamon Press, Inc., 1972). Reprinted by permission.   *Pages 58-59:* From S.M. Sales, "Some Effects of Role Overload and Role Underload," *Organizational Behavior and Human Performance,* Vol. 5 1970. Reprinted by permission.

Chapter 4

Table 4.2: Adapted from *Organizational Analysis: A Sociological View* by C. Perrow. Copyright © 1970 by Wadsworth, Inc. Reprinted by permission of the publisher, Brooks/Cole Publishing Company, Monterey, California.   *Table 4.6:* From S. Kerr, "Substitutes for Leadership: Some Implications for Organizational Design, " in E. Burrack and A.R. Negandlie (eds.) *Organization Design* (Kent, Ohio: Comparative Administration Research Institute, 1977). Reprinted by permission.   *Table 4.7:* From R.W. Bortner, "A Short Rating Scale: A Potential Measure of Pattern A Behavior," *Journal of Chronic Diseases,* Vol. 22, 1969. Reprinted by permission.

Chapter 6

Pages 113-114: From *A Strategy for Handling Executive Stress* by Ari Kiev, M.D. Copyright © 1974 by Ari Kiev, M.D. Reprinted by permission of Nelson-Hall, Inc., Publishers.   *Page 115:* From C.L. Cooper and J. Marshall, "Occupational Sources of Stress: A Review of the Literature Relating to Coronary Heart Disease and Mental Ill Health," *Journal of Occupational Psychology,* Vol. 49, 1976. Reprinted by permission. *Pages 118-119:* Reprinted, by permission of the publisher, from "Fables for Managers," *Management Review* Oct. 1961, © 1961 by American Management Associations, Inc., pp. 48-50. All rights reserved. *Pages 127-131:* "The Fable of the Farmer's Folly" by Donald D. Ely. Reprinted with permission, *Personnel Journal,* Costa Mesa, Calif., copyright © August 1974.   *Page 140:* From Richard A. Morano, "How to Manage Change to Reduce Stress," *Management Review,* November 1977 (New York: AMACOM, a division of American Management Associations, 1977) p. 21. Reprinted by permission.   *Table 6.1:* From N. Stewart, *The Effective Woman Manager* (New York: John Wiley & Sons, 1978). Reprinted by permission.   *Table 6.2:* From Bonoma and Slevin, *Executive Survival Manual* (Boston: CBI Publishing Company, Inc., 1978). Reprinted by permission. *Page 154:* From Blau, "Understanding Midcareer Stress," *Management Review,* August 1978 (New York: AMACOM, a division of American Management Associations, 1978), pp.57 and 62. Reprinted by permission.   *Tables 6.3 and 6.4:* From James J. Rago, Jr., "Trends in Job Demands Experienced and Personal Reactions to Job Circumstances," 1973. Reprinted by permission.   *Pages 167-170:* R. Leifer, "Mapping of Role Expectations from a Stress Management Program." Reprinted by permission.

Chapter 7

Tables 7.1, 7.8, 7.9, 7.10: From Gallup Opinion Index, "Women in America," Gallup Report No. 128, March 1976. Reprinted by permission.   *Table 7.2:* From J.T. Spence and R.L. Helmreich, "Personal Attributes Questionnaire," *Masculinity and Feminity: Their Psychological Dimensions, Correlates, and Antecedents* (Austin, Texas: University of Texas Press, 1978). Copyright © 1978 by Janet T. Spence and Robert L. Helmreich. All rights reserved. Reprinted by permission.   *Table 7.3:* From I.H.

Frieze et al, *Women and Sex Roles: A Social Psychological Perspective* (New York: W.W. Norton and Company, 1978). Reprinted by permission.   *Table 7.4:* From the Sex Role Inventory in S.L. Bem, "The Measurement of Psychological Androgyny," *Journal of Consulting and Clinical Psychology,* Vol. 42, 1974, pp. 155-162. Copyright 1974 by the American Psychological Association. Reprinted by permission.   *Table 7.7:* From J.E. Gullahorn, "The Woman Professional," in E. Donelson and J.E. Gullahorn, *Women: A Psychological Perspective* (New York: John Wiley & Sons, 1977). Reprinted by permission.   *Figure 7.1:* From G.N.McLean and J.S. Crawford, *Humanity as a Career: A Holistic Approach to Sex Equity* (Rehoboth, Mass.: Twin Oaks Publishing, Inc., 1979). Reprinted by permission.   *Table 7.11:* From J.R. Terborg, L.H. Peters, D.R.Ilgen, and F. Smith, "Women as Managers Scale," from "Organizational and Personal Correlates of Attitudes Toward Women as Managers," *Academy of Management Journal,* Vol. 20, 1977. Reprinted by permission.

Index